read whole book

1) Find state showing how lab[or] incomes etc. have ↑ in the third world, e.g. South Asia, East Asia.

2) Use the paper "To Honor and Obey: ___ " to explain the economic argument behind how technological change". Then Explain the relationship between "economic development, fertility decline, and the emergence of more egalitarian marriages."

3) Show that while (1) & (2) may well be true, this book exposes the "myth of the disposable woman."

4) This leads us to consider questions about the "quality of life" of women (use Nussbaum), questions of "freedom" and "capabilities" (Sen), human dignity in the working place & not just participation or incomes.

5) Conclusion:
   The perpetuation of patriarchy today, which is dangerous in the fact that it is hidden by statistics touting ↑ women's income & labor force participation etc.
   • Third world women benefiting less from global capitalism [than] world women
   • And even then world women facing work/life balance issues etc.

Disposable Women and Other Myths of Global Capitalism

Disposable Women and Other Myths of Global Capitalism

Melissa W. Wright

Routledge
Taylor & Francis Group
New York London

Routledge is an imprint of the
Taylor & Francis Group, an informa business

Parts of chapter 2 appeared in a slightly different version in *Environment and Planning*, 2001, volume 33:2175–2188. ©2001 by Pion Limited, London; 2003. *Geoforum* 34(3):291–301. ©2003 by Reed Elsevier; and *Going Public: Feminism and the Shifting Private Sphere*, edited by Joan Scott and Debra Keates, ©2004 by University of Illinois Press. Used by permission of the publisher.

Chapter 3 appeared in a slightly different version in *Cultural Anthropology*, 16(3):354–373. ©2001 by the American Anthropological Association. Used by permission of the publisher.

Chapter 4 was originally published in *Public Culture*, 11:453–474. ©1999 by Duke University Press. All rights reserved. Used by permission of the publisher.

Parts of chapter 5 appeared in a slightly different version of *Hypatia*, 13(3):114–131. ©1998 by Indiana University Press. All rights reserved. Used by permission of the publisher and *Enviroment and Planning A*, 1999, volume 31:1601–1617. ©1999 by Pion Limited, London.

Chapter 6 was originally published in *Antipode* 1997. ©Blackwell Publishing. Used by permission of the publisher.

Chapter 7 was originally published in *Gender, Place and Culture* 12(3):277–292. ©2005 by Routledge, part of the Taylor & Francis Group. Used by permission. http://www.tandf.co.uk.

Routledge
Taylor & Francis Group
270 Madison Avenue
New York, NY 10016

Routledge
Taylor & Francis Group
2 Park Square
Milton Park, Abingdon
Oxon OX14 4RN

© 2006 by Taylor & Francis Group, LLC
Routledge is an imprint of Taylor & Francis Group, an Informa business

Printed in the United States of America on acid-free paper
10 9 8 7 6 5 4 3 2 1

International Standard Book Number-10: 0-415-95144-5 (Softcover) 0-415-95144-5 (Hardcover)
International Standard Book Number-13: 978-0-415-95145-6 (Softcover) 978-0-415-95144-9 (Hardcover)

Library of Congress Cataloging-in-Publication Data

Wright, Melissa W.
  Disposable women and other myths of global capitalism / Melissa Wright.
    p. cm.
  Includes bibliographical references and index.
  ISBN 0-415-95144-5 (hb) -- ISBN 0-415-95145-3 (pb)
    1. Women--Employment--Mexico--Case studies. 2. Capitalism--Social aspects--Mexico--Case studies. 3. Export processing zones--Social aspects--Mexico--Case studies. 4. Women--Employment--China--Case studies. 5. Capitalism--Social aspects--China--Case studies. 6. Export processing zones--Social aspects--China--Case studies. 7. Feminist criticism. I. Title.

HD6101.W75 2006
331.40972--dc22   2006003253

Visit the Taylor & Francis Web site at
http://www.taylorandfrancis.com

and the Routledge Web site at
http://www.routledge-ny.com

I will tell you something about stories
[he said]
They aren't told just for entertainment.
Don't be fooled.

Leslie Marmon Silko, *Ceremony*

For my mother, Jane C. Anderson Travis,

and

for my father, Ralph D. Wright,

with love and admiration.

Contents

Acknowledgments   xi

1   Introduction: Disposable Women and Other Myths
of Global Capitalism   1

I   Storylines

2   Disposable Daughters and Factory Fathers   23

3   Manufacturing Bodies   45

4   The Dialectics of Still Life: Murder, Women, and
Disposability   71

II   Disruptions

5   Maquiladora Mestizas and a Feminist Border Politics   93

6   Crossing the Factory Frontier   123

7   Paradoxes and Protests   151

Notes   171

Bibliography   177

Index   187

Acknowledgments

I wrote this book in fits and starts over several years, during which time I benefited from the support of numerous people. I want to say from the outset that I dedicate this book to my parents, and I wish I had finished the manuscript in time for my father to see it. My father introduced me to the Mexico–U.S. border at a young age when he took me on his many trips while working for the State of Texas. As we traveled by car and by train into Mexico and along the border, he instilled in me an appreciation for the art of storytelling. My mother, who taught high school in Bastrop, Texas for some 30 years, has always been an inspiration. Her enthusiasm for reaching those students who want to learn and for not letting an underfunded educational bureaucracy lessen her resolve set high standards for me. I am privileged to have her unyielding affection to this day. I am also lucky to have an extended family that has helped me over the years in a variety of ways. And I still seek refuge in the compassionate insights of my paternal grandmother, Mrs. Ima Webb Wright, who died just as I was entering graduate school.

I am indebted to the generosity of the following who have provided comments and advice on all or bits of the manuscript at various stages: Leslie Salzinger, Ted Norton, Marnina Gonick, Sarah Hill, Socorro Tabuenca, Julia Monárrez, Rosalba Robles, Lorraine Dowler, Miranda Joseph, James McCarthy, Joan Landes, Nan Woodruff, Mrinalini Sinha, Irene Silverblatt, Debra Keates, Alfredo Limas, Eduardo Barrera, Felicity Callard, and an anonymous reviewer of the book manuscript. Many of the chapters are revisions of previously published articles, and I am thankful for the many reviewers and editors who helped me with those earlier and often extremely messy drafts. I am also grateful to Rosalba Robles and Estela Madero who have offered invaluable research assistance in northern Mexico over the years. And I have been equally fortunate to work with excellent students, particularly Anu Sabhlok and Kristin Sziarto, who conducted archival research and helped me organize the material.

Arminé Arjona, Esther Chávez Cano, and Guadalupe de Anda have also been superb sounding boards at various points throughout this project. I also want to thank Mariela Paniagua for the amazing cover design and Verónica Leiton for providing the artwork. I am almost at a loss as how to thank my graduate advisors, Erica J. Schoenberger and David Harvey. I started working with them some 15 years ago, and not only would I not have written this book without their initial encouragement and guidance, I most likely would not have embarked on this career. I am indeed grateful. I would like to thank my editor, David McBride, for sticking with me. And I am thankful to Beth Parsons for providing a "home away from home" in El Paso. I also want to add that no one mentioned here is in anyway responsible for the mistakes and oversights within the text.

I have benefited from the support of my colleagues in Geography and Women's Studies at The Pennsylvania State University and also at The University of Georgia. My ongoing relationship with La Universidad Autónoma de Ciudad Juárez continues to afford an important institutional base for my work along the border. The financial support provided by the National Science Foundation, The Pennsylvania State University, and The University of Georgia has been indispensable for making possible the many years of ethnographic research that have gone into this endeavor. Any opinions, findings, and conclusions or recommendations expressed in this book do not necessarily reflect the views of those institutions.

I wish to thank the scores of people in Mexico and in China who must remain unnamed in the book and who tolerated my incessant questions, my relentless presence, and my sense of entitlement to information. I am indebted to them in so many obvious ways, and I am also appreciative of the patience and openness with which I was regularly treated.

And, finally, I want to thank Guadalupe and our daughter, Elena, for everything.

1

Introduction

*Disposable Women and Other
Myths of Global Capitalism*

The most obvious function of myths is the explanation of facts,
whether natural or cultural.

Encyclopedia Britannica Online

Myth is depoliticized speech.

Roland Barthes, *Mythologies* (1972)

Everyday, around the world, women who work in the third world factories of global firms face the idea that they are disposable. In this book,
I examine how this idea proliferates, both within and beyond factory
walls, through the telling of a story that I call "the myth of the disposable third world woman." This international tale is told by people from
all walks of life, including factory managers, corporate executives, and
consumers across the globe who buy their products; it achieves translation across languages, cultures, and historical moments; and it is widely
believed to be a factual account of a woman worker whose disposability
is naturally and culturally scripted. Through several years of ethnographic research, spanning 1991–2003, I made this story the focus of
my investigations within global factories and their surrounding urban
areas in northern Mexico and in southern China. Illustrating what is

at stake in the telling of this myth for these factories, for the people who work in them, and for the constant flow of global capital is my principal objective.

The myth of the disposable third world woman revolves around the trials and tribulations of its central protagonist—a young woman from a third world locale—who, through the passage of time, comes to personify the meaning of human disposability: someone who eventually evolves into a living state of worthlessness. The myth explains that this wasting process occurs within the factories that employ her, as she, within a relatively short period of time and at a young age, loses the physical and mental faculties for which she was initially employed, until she is worth no more than the cost of her dismissal and substitute. In other words, over time, this woman turns into a form of industrial waste, at which point she is discarded and replaced. The myth explains this unlucky fate as a factual outcome of natural and cultural processes that are immune to external tampering. In short, there is nothing, says the myth, that can be done to save its unfortunate protagonist from her sad destiny.

Yet, paradoxically, even as this protagonist turns into a living form of human waste, the myth explains how she simultaneously produces many valuable things with her labor. Indeed, this paradox provides the myth with its organizational structure. For, the myth explains, despite her ineluctable demise, the disposable third world woman possesses certain traits that make her labor particularly valuable to global firms that require dexterous, patient, and attentive workers. And these traits make her so desirable that global firms go out of their way to employ her whenever possible because the things that she makes generate value even as she depreciates in value. So, on the one hand, we hear a story of a woman who is, essentially, wasting away, and then, on the other, we hear that this very woman is creating all kinds of wonderful and popular things that can be bought and sold on the international market. And, as it turns out, the myth explains how this internal contradiction means that this disposable third world woman is, in fact, quite valuable since she, like so many other characters of mythic lore, generates widespread prosperity through her own destruction. This conundrum caught my attention in factories throughout Mexico and China as I sought to understand how someone whose body represents a site of living waste can still create, with that same body, things that are so valuable. How does worth develop from worthlessness?

In making such questions the focus of my investigation and the subsequent analysis, I illustrate how the myth is a discourse with direct consequences for the functioning of global factories, for their

result of global capitalism

employees, and, more broadly, for the spatial circuitry of global capital. As geographer Geraldine Pratt has written, discourses are "sociospatial circuits through which cultural and personal stories are circulated, legitimated, and given meaning" within the production of the material realm that we call "geography" (Pratt 1999, 218).[1] Applied to the concern at hand, I employ this notion of discourses as sociospatial circuits to interrogate how the myth, as a form of discourse, produces specific subjects, their spatiality, and their significance for the relentlessly changing landscapes of global capitalism.[2] This means that I probe the story's internal circuitry to examine how it contributes to the making of a sentient being who is decidedly female, third world, and disposable and yet who embodies a form of labor crucial for the materialization of global capitalism around the world.

I must confess that my motivations for exploring this topic stem from my own political opposition to the myth and from my desire to do something about it. I consider the story, and the material circuitry it supports, to be dangerous for working people, and especially for the women to whom the story is directly applied. I also believe that it implicates not only those who work for global firms but also those who consume their products. I realize that, in admitting these beliefs, I have dashed any claims to objectivity or impartiality with regard to the outcome of this research.

Socially Useful Lies

Not all stories are myths, although I believe it can be said that all myths are stories.[3] Like myths told over the centuries,[4] the myth of the disposable third world woman attempts to provide steadfast lessons about what is accepted as "truth," "factual reality," and deep-seated "human essence" all packaged within a synthetic narrative, laden with symbolism and drama. Myths have muddied the waters between fact and fiction since the time of Plato and the Sophists who transformed the Homeric significance of myth away from "truth" and toward a more complex meaning of, as anthropologist Talal Asad has put it, "a socially useful lie" (Asad 2003, 28). Their usefulness derives largely from their claims to unquestionable authority, which Roland Barthes (1972) captured with his statement that myths are "depoliticized speech." Myths, to use his words, "empty [reality] of history" by cloaking political situations with narratives of human essence and naturalized tautologies. In consequence, myths are vehicles for foreclosing discussions of politics as they use fantastic characters and situations that depict hierarchical relationships broadly believed to have bearing on "real life" without having to explain these relationships.

Common themes across the gamut of myths, including those of interest to me here, include linking chaos to social threats; justifying social hierarchies, such as those between women and men, the wealthy and the poor, and so on; and explaining inequities as resulting from the unstoppable forces of fate. In this way, myths are not told only for entertainment. Rather, such mythic themes course through narrative mediums that have long been used to influence social behavior on the basis that power is naturalized, apolitical, and beyond human intervention. As Asad (2003) writes, "Myth [is] not merely a (mis) representation of the *real*. It [is] material for shaping the possibilities and limits of action. And in general it appears to have done this by feeding the desire to display the actual" (29; my brackets).

Mythic protagonists—such as, gods, goddesses, spirits, and other extraordinary figures—who do not reside in the experiential realm of human existence but who, nevertheless, reflect this experience writ large are key to the function of myth as an explanation or validation of social realities. Often, these figures transcend the specificities of any particular human condition and illustrate abstract qualities that are believed to be part of human existence more generally. For instance, some mythic figures represent the abstract qualities of fertility, love, and power; others represent grief, mischievousness, and greed. These qualities are part of their essence and do not change with superficial transformations in appearance (Littleton 2002). What makes these characters so compelling is that, despite their far-fetched qualities and predestined fortunes, something about them "rings true" with real life. And through their experiences, we are meant to learn something about ourselves and the world in which we live.

The tale of the disposable third world woman shares such properties of the mythic genre. Its protagonist is larger than life in that she exceeds the limits of human experience. No one answers to her name, "disposable third world woman." She has no specific cultural profile other than an undefined one that is found in an amorphous region called "the third world."[5] Her identity as "woman" is likewise too vague to offer any specific insights into her character as, obviously, women do not share some essential sameness.[6] And even though many people around the world encounter the belief that they are disposable, few, if any, identify themselves as the bearers of the abstract condition of disposability (Bales 2004; Chang 2000). The disposable third world woman is, consequently, a composite personality built of different abstractions (third world woman, and disposability, for example), which, while not characterizing anyone in particular, form the pillar of a story intended to explain social circumstances and validate specific practices based on the idea of her in concrete settings. In this fashion, the disposable third world woman functions like other mythic figures, such as the self-obsessed Narcissus and the blindly ambitious Prometheus, who embody intrinsic and indelible flaws that explain not only their own demise but also the demise of *real* people who, in everyday life and in different situations, share their signifying traits. No one may be identical to the disposable third world woman, but through the detailing of this myth, we are meant to learn something about real women who work in real factories and who embody the tangible elements of disposability within their being.

But the story's purpose, as well as the motivation behind its telling, is not only to describe its central character and her disposable fate. It also offers a blueprint for identifying the signature features of female disposability within actual human beings and for handling them accordingly. The story, in other words, serves as a vehicle for establishing the normative characteristics and behaviors of the disposable third world woman. It tells us how a *normal* disposable third world woman should look, act, and be treated. Therefore, it serves as a disciplinary device for patrolling the bounds of that normativity.[7] For instance, a woman who, despite being identified as disposable, refuses to accept the conditions of her disposability appears within the terms of the myth to be *abnormal*. Similarly, practices that treat women deemed to be disposable as if they were not so could also be called *abnormal*. Consequently, I regard the myth as a tool of interpellation, in the sense intended by Louis Althusser (1971), since it establishes the expectations both for identifying disposable third world women within specific populations and for determining how those subjects, so identified, should behave in relation to those who do the identifying[8] (Butler 1997b). In this sense, the myth is an attempt to summon the disposable third world woman into existence as a normalized subject who reaffirms explicit relations of power and hierarchy.

Thus, another and related function of this myth lies in its explanation that the disposable outcome of its protagonist and of those women workers who resemble her is a matter of destiny. According to its logic, the corporate practices that treat such workers as if they were disposable are justifiable and unavoidable, since to treat a disposable worker as if she were not disposable would be silly and irrational. Hence, the obvious violence and suffering that accompany the condition of disposability are not the fault of the companies that employ these women, nor the fault of the people the world over who buy their products. Indeed, not only does the myth detail how this situation is the responsibility of neither global firms nor global consumers, but it also correlates its protagonist's demise with the creation of valuable commodities such that her employment, and the practices organized with her disposability in mind, constitute good business. To achieve this connection, the tale draws upon other staple mythic themes to detail how corporations use science to conquer the hazardous forces intrinsic to the disposable third world woman, such as a chaotic sexuality and a hysterical irrationality. And, at the end of the day, reason, via scientific management and masculinist rationality, harnesses the powerful forces that inevitably destroy the story's protagonist and channel them toward the creation of valuable commodities in some of the most sophisticated manufacturing facilities in the world. As a result, says the myth, the third world woman's path of destruction also leads the way to the capitalist development that heralds modern progress. And, again, in this respect, we see how the tale repeats a popular mythic theme that suffering and sacrifice, particularly on the part of women, are often required to move society in its proper direction (Littleton 2002).

Points of Departure

I began focusing on this myth as an object of study through several years of ethnographic research in nine different corporate facilities located in northern Mexico and southern China. The facilities included electronics, data processing, sewing, a machine shop, plastics, automobile, and textiles operations. Additional material comes from interviews conducted with employees of these and other companies, tours of those companies, and interviews conducted with business consultants, local political officials, workers and their families, activists, civic leaders, and other urban residents.

Throughout the research, I have taken cues from other studies that have exemplified the significance of ethnographic research for understanding the cultural and discursive dimensions of global capitalism. While this literature is too vast to encapsulate here, a few texts stand out as ones that directly influenced my thinking in this book. For instance, Aihwa Ong's (1987) important study of factory workers in Malaysia illustrates how discourses that constitute worker identities are the very processes that configure systems of power and resistance within factory contexts. Ching Kwan Lee's (1998) research in Hong Kong and southern China demonstrates how discourses of cultural identity throughout a firm's international offices also create the work categories within that company's division of labor. María Patricia Fernández-Kelly's (1983) benchmark investigation in Mexican export-processing factories clearly shows how discourses of local cultural identity contribute to the making of an international division of labor across the diverse spaces of global capital. Emily Martin's (1995) and Linda McDowell's (1997) explorations into the embodiment of identity within the workplace confirm the importance of investigating how the body is a constant site of contestation within the rarefied world of corporate capital. Leslie Salzinger's (2003) book on the discursive production of gender within Mexican-based global firms illustrates how managerial discourses of their female workers are not solely descriptive but also productive of these workers' subjectivity. Miranda Joseph's (2002) ethnography of a gay theater group illustrates how the performance of identity simultaneously constitutes the subjects of capitalism without being fully defined by capitalism. And Erica Schoenberger's (1997) study of corporate culture exposes how executive discourses regarding a company's cultural identity guide the material processes that give shape to global capital around the world.

I situate my research in an ongoing dialogue with these and other such studies, all of which demonstrate how there is nothing "merely cultural," as Judith Butler (1997a) has put it, about studies of discursive and symbolic events. These processes are, instead, central to those political and economic practices that we identify as capitalist power, exploitation, and resource distribution. And they are at the heart of the imperatives for political action on the part of people around the world who want to develop alternatives to capitalist exploitation and the many forms of discrimination and misery that accompany it. My research extends this dialogue into an interrogation of the spatial dimensions at play in the discursive-materialist dynamics of global capital. So, consequently, my research into the myth of the disposable third world woman takes me across geographic regions as I follow a discourse that travels not only by word of mouth from factory to factory and continent to continent but also through the materialist circuitry of global capitalist production and consumption.

I began my own research in 1991 in Ciudad Juárez, Chihuahua, Mexico, which, in 1965, was the official "birthplace" of the country's export-processing industries, known as the "maquiladoras" (or "maquilas" for short). Over the next four decades, Ciudad Juárez became an internationally recognized leader in low-cost, high-quality, labor-intensive manufacturing processes. Its adjacency to the United States and the constant inflow of migrants from the Mexican interior contributed to this city's popularity among corporate executives seeking to cut factory costs while maintaining quality standards and easy access to the U.S. market. And I, like several other researchers from inside and outside of Mexico, set my sights on the city's maquiladoras as a window for studying how local social processes contribute to the constant renovation of global capital (Carrillo 1990; Fernández-Kelly 1983; Shaiken 1994; Cravey 1998; Reygadas 2003; Salzinger 2003).

My research required that factory managers grant me entry into their facilities.[9] Some did so quite generously, and provided me office space and as much access as I requested or as much as they could authorize. Others were less generous. While I can guess that the managers who did not participate in my project were reluctant to have a researcher snooping around their facilities, I do not have ready answers for why others permitted me so much latitude, other than to say that each had his (and I use that pronoun advisedly) particular interests in the project. One manager in Mexico, for example, had studied sociology in graduate school for a couple of years before deciding that he wanted to pursue a more lucrative career in business management. But he continued to express interest in sociological issues, such as labor relations, and he expressed a real commitment to supporting academic research. As he told me one day in 1996, "You and I don't see eye to eye on everything. But you can't say that I have gotten in the way of science!" Another manager, in southern China, extended an invitation to me to visit his facilities in Dongguan and in Hong Kong after he had been contacted by one of his colleagues in Mexico. He made numerous arrangements to allow for my research visits into his facilities over a several-month period and over two different occasions. At one point, he explained that he was hosting me as a favor to his colleague, while in a different conversation he said that he wanted me to see how much things were changing in China so that I would not have only "stereotypes" of "Chinese people." Another manager, also in Mexico, was devoted to the study of literature, and on our first meeting, he was walking around the coupon-processing facility he managed while carrying *The Complete Works of William Shakespeare* under his arm. He seemed to enjoy talking with me about my ideas and how I approached the issues I investigated, yet he was also troubled by my critique of the exploitation that was part of his world. He did not, for instance, agree with all of my conclusions, but he also admitted that my focus on the discourse of a third world female disposability was touching on something fundamental to the organization of his facility. I could continue in this vein with personal stories of each of the managers who offered me access, but my point is that I have no standard response to the question of why they let me in other than to say, "Because they wanted to."

When, in 1993, I expanded the project to include research within the Chinese facilities of some of the same corporations I had studied in Mexico, the project expanded from a regional to a transregional or "more global" study. My decision to make this move emerged when I realized near the beginning of the project that a comparative investigation of processes internal to a company's different facilities, located in different parts of the world, would provide the breadth that I needed to understand the larger context in which the myth was told. Multinational firms and their constituent factory units operate within a tightly organized global network that is partly contained within the firm's organizational structure but that also expands into the complex interaction of clients, suppliers, and government officials in different countries simultaneously. And the myth of the disposable third world woman is also a part of this intricate global network. This realization hit me while I was listening to a presentation in the Mexican facility of a diverse multinational electronics corporation. The presenter, a company vice president who was visiting from Belgium, was comparing performance indicators between this Mexican facility and the company's other factories located in China and Brazil. During this comparison, he discussed the ability of managers in each of these facilities to control the turnover rate among the female workers in these different facilities. "You have to know when these workers are not worth keeping anymore," he said. Although at this time I had not yet formulated my argument about the myth of the disposable third world woman, I could appreciate the critical need to move beyond Mexico and investigate the processes he described for "knowing when the workers" were "not worth keeping anymore." Until that point, I had assumed that the discourses I had encountered regarding female disposability were features of a regional "maquiladora" environment. And it was not until I reached southern China that I put together the globality of this story and its significance for the global networks of capitalism.

I made my first trip to the Guangdong Province in southern China and to Hong Kong in 1993, and then returned for an extensive research trip in 1997. By the mid-1990s, managers in most of the Mexican facilities that I studied were competing against the Chinese factories within their same corporate complex for internal resources, and these competitions often hinged upon comparisons between facilities. With the 1979 implementation in China of the "open policy" to allow for foreign direct investment (FDI), southern China, primarily in Guangdong Province, which includes Dongguan municipality and the Shenzhen Economic Zone, erupted with industrial activity. While southern China could not compete with Mexico in terms of proximity to the U.S. market and U.S. infrastructure, it certainly did rival Mexico on its labor costs,[10] nearness to Asian industrial suppliers, and strategic positioning in China, which has the world's potentially largest labor and consumer market. In southern China, I spent most of my time in Dongguan, a city of more than 2 million,[11] which is located in the center of the Shenzhen-Guangdong economic region in the Pearl River Delta.

The decision to take my study into southern China raised some difficulties for me as a researcher that are common to ethnographers who study a multisited field, a domain located in many different places simultaneously (Katz 1996; Sparke 1996). For instance, when I started this research, I was fully prepared to conduct studies in Mexico and along the Mexico–U.S. border. I had studied these regions, had extensive professional and personal contacts in them, and could speak the languages (Spanish and English). I knew my way around. That was not the case for me in southern China. Unlike in Mexico, I was much more dependent upon my managerial hosts, who exercised tight control over my access to corporate facilities, to workers, and to documents. I also did not speak the dominant languages (Mandarin and Cantonese) and relied upon translation provided by my bilingual managerial informants and occasionally by someone whom they appointed to assist me. I was not authorized to bring in my own translator. Therefore, I did not, as in Mexico, have the luxury of private conversations with laborers in China, and since they lived in factory dormitories, I was unable to interview them off premises. While I did interview workers, I was careful to avoid as best I could any topics I thought would compromise my informants or make them uncomfortable in front of their bosses. But basically I was aware that I was not fully aware of all the risks that workers faced when talking with me. I also could not control my own introduction to them. Since I did not understand the spoken languages, I really had no idea of how I was presented, and this made me even more uncomfortable. I was not permitted to move freely throughout the corporate facility, as I did in the Mexican factories, and I could not come and go at will. I had to make arrangements prior to all of my visits, provide a structured research and interview plan, and clear my access with management at all times.[12] My contact with managers and engineers, however, in southern China was extensive and occurred both on and off the work site in Dongguan, Shenzhen Economic Zone, and Hong Kong. And this wide access to management led me to turn my ethnographic focus on managers and engineers.

But, despite this limited access, it was during my research in southern China and Hong Kong that I made a turning point in my work and saw that what I had taken to be a series of regional (Mexico–U.S. border region) discourses about female disposability were, rather, endemic to the organization of production for firms at the global scale. This realization came to me as I was quickly struck by the fact that despite the extremely different circumstances (cultural, economic, political, and so on) that distinguish northern Mexico from southern China, administrators in both regions echoed one another when I asked them to explain why young women cycled in and out of their jobs as if they were constantly being replaced. The repetition of a story about how these young women always turn into disposable waste and how this is to be expected of the women workers who are employed by these factories in third world regions made me realize that this tale, like the factories themselves, travels around the globe and with definite productive effects. In this regard, the myth provided the common ground for my research. And my experiences in southern China changed the way that I approached my studies in Mexico as, once I realized that the myth was significant for the global operations of the companies I studied, I focused my inquiry in Mexico on making the connections between the myth's telling in a particular factory and the international production and consumption networks in which that firm was embedded.

Yet, while the research in Asia allowed me to appreciate the global extent and relevance of the myth, I was able to investigate this discourse more fully only in Mexico. My greater access in Mexico to all levels of corporate personnel permitted me to follow the tale as it wove into the processes for hiring, training, and supervising workers. And I was also able in Mexico to document the many ways that the myth was resisted by workers and activists. That I do not document such events in southern China is in no way meant to indicate that they do not exist or are not significant. In fact, worker protests have increasingly made the international headlines (Douglas et al. 2005; Hutzler 2002; Mufson 1997; Pomfret 2002). And other scholars have demonstrated that workers in China demonstrate myriad ways for subverting the political machinery used to discipline them (see Pun 2005; Lee 1998). During my research, I simply did not have the ethnographic skills to document worker resistance to this tale in China since, as my Mexican research reveals, such acts are often waged through battles that take place in the realms of symbolism and language, which were beyond my reach.

As a result of this imbalance in my methodological experience, I include only one chapter on China in this book. I must confess that I had wanted to present a more regionally balanced text, with an even number of chapters from China and from Mexico. But as I got more into the writing, I came to accept that this was not possible. I simply could not overcome in the analysis some of the distance that kept me from understanding the localized idioms for telling and challenging the myth of the disposable third world woman. Nevertheless, my research in southern China and Hong Kong sets up the other chapters that are based in Mexico and provides the context in which I locate those more ethnographically nuanced accounts. The one chapter I do include on China follows this introduction, and I have placed it in the front of the book in order to draw attention to the significance of this material for the claims I make throughout the book.

3 epistemological approaches:
• Marxism
• post-structuralist feminism
• post-colonial theory

Book Overview

In the subsequent analysis, I have created a theoretical toolkit from three epistemological approaches: Marxism, poststructuralist feminism, and postcolonial theory. Combined, these three fields of thought help me to investigate how a myth about a specifically third world, female, and disposable worker contributes to the generation of capitalist value. They allow me to pursue what happens to this accumulative process when the myth is disrupted or challenged such that this worker's disposability, as well as the value derived from it, fails to materialize. And these theories also push the analysis into a discussion of political strategies for subverting this myth and its productive effects.

Figuring prominently throughout the text is the Marxian critique that *all things of value under capital originate with those energies we call "human labor."*[13] With this insight, I am able to investigate how a story of a worker's devaluation is simultaneously a story of capital's valuation because even as this worker is said to lose value, she continues to generate value as she works. How this worker's own worth as a subject comes to be distinguished from the worth of her labor is one of the themes I follow throughout the analysis. And feminist strands of poststructuralist scholarship enable me to regard the myth as a *productive technology* that actually creates the material embodiment of the disposable third world woman that houses this labor.[14]

KEY

Such an exploration takes me to a common ground between Marxist inquiries into exploitation and feminist analyses of the embodied subject. Marxist geographer David Harvey provides a framework for recognizing such a theoretical alliance in his book *Justice, Nature and the Geography of Difference* (1996), in which he opens up Marx's binary between labor and capital by engaging poststructuralist feminist work on the complexities of embodied subjectivities. Borrowing from Donna Haraway's work on the subjugated body, Harvey refers to the body as a "site of capitalist accumulation," in that its apparent fixity as a culturally specific entity (across the divides of race, sex, ethnicity, wellness, and so on) provides corporeal breadth to the social subjects required under capitalism. In other words, laboring subjects do not present themselves in isolation from the other forms of embodied subjectivities that abound in any social setting, such that someone stands out as merely a laborer or a manager, apart from appearing as a subject located across a spectrum of locally specific cultural identities. It is impossible, for instance, to distinguish the sexed and raced body from the laborer's body or from the boss's body as all combine into the corporeal package that is taken to ground each subject's identity and recognizable set of differences from or affinities with one another. Therefore, determining how the body materializes as a site of multiple identities, where no single identifier establishes the sole definition of the subject's existence (or its "essence"), is vital if we are to understand how the laboring body, under capitalist conditions, emerges as an embodied site of exploitation and accumulation (see Scott 1999).

This combined theoretical approach also extends the feminist analysis into the gendering of work and workers. Much feminist research, from across disciplines, has led the critique into Marxist assumptions regarding the uniformity of the laborer's experience and also regarding the transparency of the laboring body as either a skilled or unskilled entity (Jackson and Pearson 1998; Phillips and Taylor 1980; Cockburn 1983; Elson and Pearson 1981; Lamphere 1987; McGaw 1992). These scholars have challenged numerous assumptions that have been blind to how the subjection of labor proceeds through the many ways that social differences cut across working populations so that no single "worker" emerges as a unified subject with a unified experience. This investigation takes such important insights as a starting point for extending the analysis even further to demonstrate that feminine and masculine subjectivities are wound into a never-ending circuitry of material production, occurring across scales from the most intimate bodily functions to the networks of a global firm. Not only does the feminine stand as the masculine's "other," but also vice versa, in an endless continuum of dialectical processes through which a masculine subject only gains shape as a particular kind of employee through the materialization of the female subject who outlines him by way of her opposition.

Here, I am also drawing directly from the work of Judith Butler (1993), who argues that the human body, as well as the subject associated with it, is always a "matter of production." By this, she means that the material embodiment of the social subject is never fully constructed. It is always materializing, which is why she prefers to use the terminology of "production" over "construction," as a way to keep attention on the incompleteness of the material body.

I agree with this emphasis on the enduring process of production, particularly as it segues well with Marx's insight that capitalism, along with its embodied subjects, likewise is a system whose materialization is never complete.[15] Therefore, by combining Butler's insight into the ongoing production of the embodied subject with Marx's insight into the ongoing production of capitalism, we see how the disposable third world woman's body is a spatial entity that is always being produced along with the commodities that flow through the circuits of capital.[16]

To understand, however, why the mythic protagonist has a particularly third world and female corporeality, I turn to the work of postcolonial scholars, many of them feminist, who provide tools for critiquing the significance of the "third world" for the meaning of a female subject who is seen as embodying a persistent state of underdevelopment (Mohanty 1991; Narayan 1997). These scholars have drawn attention to the problematic usage of the term "third world woman" to refer to a coherent social subject who is typically located in an inferior conceptual position across a host of binary continuums, such as developed/undeveloped, oppressed/liberated, and so forth. While I am unable to evade the pitfalls of linguistic representation since I do rely on references to a "disposable third world woman" to explain the myth, this critique helps me investigate what is significant about the reiterations of "third world" and "female" as they combine within the telling of this myth and its application to specific people.

These critiques have also pushed my own analysis into the political implications of my argument and the implicit call for subversive strategies that runs throughout the text. How to create a politics or coalition that confronts the myth is a question that I cannot fully answer, even though I stress the imperative for doing so. Although I regard the myth as a technology of production and use Marx's analysis to demonstrate the human consequences of this productive device, the analysis does not lend itself to his call for class politics or, even more generally, to an identity politics approach. The myth is organized around an identity that people do not overtly embrace. But more than that, the myth illustrates the difficulties of an identity politics approach for organizing responses to global capital, as working people around the world have rare (when they do have them) opportunities for finding common ground around identity or experience. I therefore throughout the analysis turn to those scholars, feminist in their majority, who discuss strategies for building coalitions that do not assume shared identities or universal perceptions of work experience (and relationships), but that, moreover, explore how an embrace (rather than denial) of social differences can strengthen political coalitions (see Scott 2002; Sandoval 2000; Young 1990; Martin and Mohanty 1986; Haraway 1985). The differences that require addressing are those also of geographic dimensions since workers, even when employed by the same firm, often find themselves in situations in which face-to-face contact is not an option and in which awareness of each other's context is not possible. As feminist geographer Doreen Massey has written, global capitalism exposes the strategic need for creating coalitions with *distant others* across the spectrum of spatialized identities (Massey 2004).

My thinking here obviously reveals the influence of Laclau and Mouffe's (1985) decree that subversive political strategies to hegemonies of power cannot rest upon notions of "we" and "them," which tend to underpin traditional class or identity politics (see also Grewal and Kaplan 1994). Yet to forsake identity politics, including those organized around class, is not to deny the hegemonic force of capitalism and its constituent technologies. If anything, I am certain that the myth of the disposable third world woman exposes the dire need for forming alliances between the consumers and the producers of global capitalist goods. The power of the former has been felt when focused on particular companies and their practices, and many anti-sweatshop, fair trade, and antiglobalization/antineoliberal groups are working with such aims in mind.[17] I would like to see the myth of the disposable third world woman, and the many stories that go into it, emerge as an issue for political activism. Its technical role within the circuits of capitalism provides an opportunity for building coalitions that could have direct impact upon the organization of global capital and the many relations of power supported through it. For, as I argue throughout this book, to sabotage the myth is to strike a blow at the numerous hierarchies that rely upon its constant repetition.

And, finally, before detailing the book outline, I would like to address briefly my presentation of myself as a researcher and author. To begin, I do not in this book attempt to describe how my informants saw me. I find that to be an impossible task for a range of reasons. For one thing, I do not believe that I have either the appropriate knowledge to know fully what "others" think of me or a perspective outside of myself to relate some version of how I appear in the field. Also, my perception of myself surely clouds my ability to decipher how I am understood by informants and how they situate me within the research context. But, I can with confidence say that certain categories were relevant to my positioning in the field: gender, sexuality, race, ethnicity, nationality, age, class, religion, professional status, family, labor politics, and able-bodiness. All of these issues arose in one way or another throughout the course of my study as significant categories for defining who I was and what I was doing in relation to other people. I certainly moved through these categories in various ways. Over the several years of my research, I aged and changed from a student into a professor. My sexuality, age, able-bodiness, gender, race, and so on were variably significant depending upon whom I was interviewing, where I was conducting research, the kinds of topics we broached, and the circumstances in my personal life and in my health. Arguably my race ("white"), my nationality ("U.S.-American"), my gender (female), my class ("professional" or "professionalizing"), and my ethnicity ("Anglo") have not changed, even as the meanings of such categories have modified during my research, and continue to do so.

The Chapters

I have grouped the chapters into two sections, "Storylines" and "Disruptions," which are loosely organized around the myth's telling as a form of power and the myth's interruption as a form of resistance. I do so with the intent of problematizing the binary distinction that separates the concept of power from resistance while still demonstrating why the binary is nevertheless useful as a conceptual device for recognizing prevailing forces that shape social processes and the resourceful approaches for reorienting them and offering alternatives.[18] Each section contains chapters that could be situated in either the Storylines or Disruptions sections since the acts that fall into these categories are unavoidably intertwined. I do not organize the material chronologically or regionally, and since I wrote these chapters at different points in my interrogation of the myth, they do not provide a seamless, linear movement from one to the other. Instead, they demonstrate how the myth of the disposable third world woman, just like any other technology of global capital, is dynamic and changes through space and time. And each chapter reflects my attempt to grapple with this flux at any one point in time.

In the first section, I highlight how the myth facilitates capitalism's constant expansion and its ability to generate wealth from the exploitation of labor around the world. For example, in chapter 2, "Disposable Daughters and Factory Fathers," I examine how the managers and engineers of a motorboat engine factory in Dongguan employ the myth as a means for disciplining their female workers. In this case, the myth justifies their practices for monitoring their reproductive cycles, including invasive procedures for insuring that workers are menstruating, in order to control the turnover rate of their employees. Here we see how factory administrators use the myth to explain that the "chaotic forces of female sexuality" are only temporarily controllable through the scientific practices of factory management. During the period when managers hold these forces in abeyance, a great amount of value can be gained from employing women workers. But, eventually, as in the myth, the factory managers explain how female workers succumb to the chaotic pressures contained within their bodies and how their value as employees begins to wane until they require replacement by fresh workers who enter the same cycle of diminishing returns. While chapter 2 is the only one I present from my research in China, it provides a foundation for seeing how the myth guides specific corporate practices at the ground level aimed at guaranteeing a constant supply of temporary labor constituted primarily of young women workers in third world regions.

Chapter 3, "Manufacturing Bodies," extends this analysis by investigating how the engineers and managers in a television factory located in Ciudad Juárez design ergonomic practices that secure skilled labor from female workers without changing their "unskilled" status in the factory's division of labor. This chapter reveals how the myth operates as a discursive mechanism for producing the embodiment of the disposable third world women through practices that scrutinize and control the corporeal movements of actual women at work. Managers and engineers in this factory carefully monitor the wrists, fingers, backs, eyes, and other body parts of women workers to extract valuable labor from them while determining that these women are worth little of value in and of themselves. And, as I argue, these practices contribute to the manufacture of a laboring body, built of assorted body parts, that does not resemble the common image of a human form but that, nevertheless, is expected to function as the worker's body on the assembly line. In this case, we see how such practices ironically create difficult challenges for the male supervisors of these women workers as they are in charge of ensuring that disposable third world women generate ever more skilled labor.

And in chapter 4, "The Dialectics of Still Life," I explore how the myth's justification of the violence suffered by its disposable protagonist, on the basis of her essentially wasting constitution, parallels other discourses that blame women, more broadly, for the violence they encounter as victims of sexual assault and murder outside of the factory. In this chapter, I juxtapose the myth of the disposable third world woman with other discourses that have been commonly told by political and business elites in Ciudad Juárez to minimize the significance of a crime wave that has claimed several hundred women's lives in that city since 1993. When put together, we see how these discourses echo one another as they repeat a story of how third world women are propelled by cultural and sexual forces toward a condition of waste. Therefore, when women workers are determined to be worthless or when women's corpses are dumped like trash in the desert, these discourses explain how, given these women's "intrinsic worthlessness," such events are both natural and unavoidable. Again, we see how these discourses work into each other to create a powerful mythic figure of a wasting third world woman whose essential properties are said to be found within real women who work in global factories and who experience all sorts of violence, for which they are held accountable.

The chapters grouped in the section, "Disruptions," demonstrate that, while formidable, the myth is far from irrefutable, especially when workers reject this discourse, challenge its factual claims, and/or refuse to be defined by its grim predictions. Each chapter in this section reveals that when such women interrupt the myth's telling or challenge its believability as an explanation of natural and cultural facts, they disrupt also the capitalist accumulation that depends on the story's telling. These chapters further demonstrate, however, that even when women challenge the myth directly, their resistance is not limited to the myth, nor do their acts constitute resistance always and only in segregation from the reaffirmation of certain hierarchies. Such acts reveal the numerous articulations, to borrow from Ernesto Laclau and Chantal Mouffe, that converge in often unpredictable ways as people work with each other to topple social hierarchies of power. They also reveal the complicity of resistance with power, as action against one kind of power relation so often creates or reaffirms another.

For instance, in chapter 5, "Maquiladora Mestizas and a Feminist Border Politics," I engage with Gloria Anzaldúa's provocative theorization of a new mestiza identity as a form of resistance against the racist, sexist, and homophobic practices that have caused a symbolic and political rupture across the Mexican-U.S. borderlands. I use Anzaldúa's concept of the mestiza, who represents a politicized subject emboldened by her own identity as someone who embodies multiple borders, to demonstrate how three women tackle the myth of the disposable third world woman within an electronics and tooling factory (part of the same corporate complex as the Chinese factory in chapter 2) located in Ciudad Juárez. In this chapter, we see how each woman must confront the story as a powerful force that stands as an obstacle for her career and personal goals. Yet, we also see how their efforts to subvert this myth raise some important questions for feminists, including but not limited to Anzaldúa's theorizations of political agency, resistance, and power, since they eschew any efforts at labor solidarity and refuse claims to "feminism," even as each struggles for her rights as a professional woman in a sexist, racist, and exploitative environment.

In chapter 6, "Crossing the Factory Frontier," I illustrate how one woman, unlike those in the previous chapter, does indeed organize a labor stoppage as an effective means for subverting her managers' use of the myth to limit her employment possibilities within a coupon-processing facility in Ciudad Juárez. Her fight against this myth exposes how it operates as a force for cleaving the value of her labor from the value of her person. Yet, even as this woman coordinates with laborers to confront the myth, she does not do so in order to disrupt the accumulation of capital that derives from the exploitation of labor. Instead, she claims that her managers' discourse of her as "worthless" is dangerous both to her and to the firm for which she works and that her disruption of this tale is in the best interest of the company, its shareholders, and its employees. And she bases such claims upon the evidence of her undeniable skill at managing and exploiting labor in the factory.

And finally, chapter 7, "Paradoxes and Protests," demonstrates how a social movement against the violence that has claimed so many women's lives in northern Mexico also represents a potential opportunity for forming alliances against the concept of third world female disposability that is vital for contemporary global capital. This movement also, however, illustrates the many paradoxes of attempting to organize a social movement around identity politics across a diverse international terrain. In this case, the movement has cohered around the political agency of "mothers" and "daughters" as the core activist and victim identities. While this strategy has succeeded to a certain extent in building an international coalition around activist demands of justice for innocent victims, it has also weakened the movement by making it vulnerable to accusations that its participants do not represent "good" mothers and daughters. As the activists respond to these critiques and continue their pressure upon governing elites, they demonstrate the need for forming coalitions with "distant others," who do not share some specific identity, to fight the myth of the disposable third world woman and the devastating consequences that this story wreaks around the globe.

I
Storylines

2

Disposable Daughters
and Factory Fathers

The object before us, to begin with, [is] material production.

Karl Marx, *Grundisse*

That matter is always materialized has, I think, to be thought in relation to the productive and, indeed, materializing effects of material power.

Judith Butler, ***Bodies That Matter: On the Discursive Limits of "Sex"***

China

In this essay, I combine the tools of feminist discourse analysis with a Marxian critique of dialectical materialism to investigate how a group of corporate managers extends their firm's operations into southern China while, at the same time, furthering their own careers on the basis of their skills as modern "Chinese" managers. Fundamental to their endeavors is the myth of the disposable third world woman. The story establishes a standard for measuring the efficiency of their operations and the extent of their own skills as international managers at a time of corporate downsizing when executives are determining which of the overseas operations to sell. As part of their efforts to keep their jobs and facilities in operation, the Chinese managers deploy the myth of

NB = J

" Chinese " managers deploying the myth of the disposable third world woman.

the disposable third world woman to illustrate that they, in contrast to their U.S.-American colleagues based in Mexico, are more adept administrators due, in large part, to their ability to control the disposable cycling of their female labor force. In effect, they rely on the story and on its materialization in everyday practice to demonstrate their own skills and value to the company as they compete for their jobs and careers in a cutthroat global economy.

I conducted this study in the Chinese and Mexican facilities of a U.S.-based corporation I call "On the Water" (OTW). OTW manufactures motors, boats, and other water-sporting equipment and has factories in the United States, Mexico, Brazil, Hong Kong, and mainland China. One facility is a manufacturing operation located in Dongguan, China, on the Pearl River Delta in Guangdong Province. A second facility is located in Hong Kong. It is the administrative complex for the Dongguan factory as well as a manufacturing facility that has been drastically downsized with the transfer of operations into southern China. I refer to both the Dongguan and Hong Kong facilities as "Asia on the Water" (AOTW). Some supplemental material for this study derives from my more extensive research in the Mexican facilities of this firm, which I call "MOTW" for Mexico on the Water. It is situated in Ciudad Juárez, Chihuahua, in northern Mexico.

As I followed the company's production circuit, first into Hong Kong and then into southern China, I relied upon a team of managers and engineers who referred to themselves as "Hong Kong Chinese" or "Chinese" to set themselves apart from the U.S. managers and executives. Three individuals—the general manager, the production manager, and the head engineer—provide the bulk of material for this chapter.[1] These three people all spoke English and presented the corporate environment to me. The general manager, Howard Li, was a second-generation Hong Kong Chinese citizen whose family had originated in southern China. By 1993, he had worked in OTW for fifteen years, where he had started as an engineer and then worked his way up the corporate ladder. He had received his Master's degree in mechanical engineering in Canada and had plans to send his daughter to college in the United States. The production manager, Harry Chen, also was a second-generation Hong Kong Chinese citizen, and he had started his career at AOTW as a line supervisor in 1984. He had received a technical degree from a Hong Kong polytechnic. The head engineer, Stephen Chan, said his family had long lived in Hong Kong. He had started his career at AOTW in 1990 when he moved back from California with his family. He had also worked for corporations in Tokyo.

[handwritten marginalia: the informants themselves agreed that the female workers on the line were "disposable", and some managers & engineers tried to convince the author of this disposability.]

Each of these informants expressed a belief that because I was from the United States, I would be critical of the labor practices in southern China. Yet each also expected that I would see their facility as a reasonable and decent workplace where there was, as Howard Li said, "nothing to hide." While their different jobs and backgrounds informed this study in various ways, these three informants agreed with each other and with their other colleagues whom I also interviewed that the female workers on the line were, for a variety of reasons, disposable. My research in AOTW focused on how and why these managers and engineers tried to convince me of this disposability. I examine the myth of female disposability here as directly linked both to specific AOTW requirements for labor flexibility and labor quality, as well as to the inevitable wear and tear that workers experience after long hours of repetitive work.

In the case of AOTW, as is the case with virtually every multinational firm in the electronics industry, managers hire women to work on the assembly line on the assumption that they are the best electronic assemblers because of their famous "dexterity," "docility," "patience," "attentiveness," and "cheapness" (Elson and Pearson 1989; Salzinger 2003). At the time of my research, the women workers at AOTW—who earned 11 cents per hour—represented one of the world's best bargains. And a manager who dismisses one of these workers before her coveted qualities were fully exploited is inefficient and wasteful. AOTW, again like most electronic manufacturers, assumes a month-long start-up period for their workers and does not expect electronic assemblers to reach full speed until after three months on the job. However, employing a worker beyond her prime opens up the company to the risk of maintaining a labor force whose fingers have stiffened, whose eyes have blurred, and whose minds wander. Contemporary electronic assembly work around the world is typically organized into cycle times during which workers perform the same tasks within a delimited time frame. At AOTW, the cycle time for assembly work is twenty-six seconds, over which time workers perform numerous tasks on as many as five hundred units a day. People in this line of work commonly experience injuries from repetitive stress, such as carpal tunnel syndrome, tendonitis, shoulder and back pains, and eyestrain. Depression due to the lack of future opportunities and advanced training is also considered a prevalent factor in producing less productive labor forces. Moreover, those assembly line workers with more tenure and experience in the industry are more likely to organize grievance committees, subversive tactics, and work stoppages. Consequently, managers face the challenge of devising a strategy for keeping women electronic assembly workers just long enough to extract the value from their dexterity, attentiveness, and docility before the processes of injury, illness, and anger overcome them.

The managers at AOTW confront this challenge by devising a strategy of corporate kinship that binds them to their female labor force via a discourse of Chinese daughters and factory fathers. Over the course of my research, these managers attempted to demonstrate to me how they represented a *new kind of Chinese manager* within the global corporate structure who, unlike their U.S. counterparts, both understands the rigors of the global market while also knowing how to navigate the murky world of a transitioning Chinese capitalism that is still couched in a strange context of Communism, Confucianism, and regional parochialism. To demonstrate their diverse capabilities, these managers claim that the female workers whom they prefer to employ for assembly work are like traditional "Chinese daughters" who, in need of strong patriarchal guidance, regard their managers as "factory fathers." By referring to a common cultural Chinese heritage that connects them to their workers, the Chinese managers claim that their paternal duties justify draconian disciplinary measures for controlling their labor force as well as invasive procedures for monitoring female workers' mobility and sexuality. While this discourse of factory daughters and patriarchal fathers is not unique to industrial history, what is remarkable about its use here is that this factory family converges around the value derived from the wasting of daughters. These are not families that receive something in exchange for their daughters through marriage or other kinship relationships. Instead, this family actually thrives on the disposing of its daughters. The disposability or eventual worthless status of the daughter is the source of this family's tremendous wealth.[2]

My focus here is on the managers: on their verbal explanations of their beliefs, actions, and decisions, and on my observations of them at work. As becomes clear in the following sections, their descriptions of their identity assumed both a difference from me, on the basis of ethnicity, culture, and gender, as well as a sense of common understanding: we were all professionals; we were all "well educated"; we all had traveled internationally; we all spoke English, as either a first or a second language; and we all were familiar with factory systems. This assertion of cultural, gender, and ethnic difference, on the one hand, and sameness based on other qualities, on the other hand, constantly figured into the research and paralleled a similar dynamic that my informants described as pertaining to their relationship with their U.S.-American colleagues. Navigating this tension between difference and sameness was something that the

Chinese managers frequently mentioned as they explained their daily strategies for managing their facilities and their international work relationships.[3] As such, the Chinese managers construct local identities around conceptions of kinship that recreate capitalist relations of production and the disposable labor force so crucial to its operation. And, yet, the story's productive effects do not end with the recreation of this labor force at the intersection of local work sites and global capitalist circuitry. As this case demonstrates, the Chinese managers' own value depends upon the clear materialization of the disposable third world woman since evidence of their worth pivots on their ability to both produce and manage her most valuable labor. And as I accompanied them throughout their days, I constantly focused on how and when the story of female disposability was told, how it developed as a believable description of "reality," and how corporate practices based on this tale appeared rational and justified.

Throughout this research, though, I was not given direct access to the women workers. As a result, my research does not explore the experiences of young women and girls who are described by the discourses I present. And so this analysis is not about workers' work experiences. Nor is my intent to claim that the workers are helpless against the managerial machinations for working them as hard and as long as possible. Several scholars and journalists have found that many Chinese women experience an independence and renovated sense of their own worth as a result of their employment beyond the family purview (Farley 1998; Lee 1998; Gilmartin et al. 1994). And there are many studies of global manufacturing operations that demonstrate how even though women endure humiliating and oppressive managerial policies, they nevertheless use creative and effective forms of subversion (Pun 2005; Ong 1987; Salzinger 2003).

The Capital of Female Disposability

This discourse of factory kinship provides a framework for controlling the rate at which workers come and go, or, as I elaborate further in chapter 4, how they "turn over" throughout the factory complex. In this chapter, I examine how the couching of turnover within this kinship discourse provides a localized idiom for generating a global supply of disposable labor. Toward this end, I break the concept down into two related dimensions, which I define as "corporate turnover" and as "labor turnover." "Corporate turnover" refers to the coming and going of workers into and out of particular jobs, and indicates the percentage of workers who have left particular jobs within a given period of time. The determination of "high" versus "low" turnover depends upon a calculation of whether the turnover rate is inhibiting or fostering the production of capitalist value. According to my interviews in OTW, the optimal turnover rate in both the Mexican and Chinese facilities is an annual 7 percent, which guarantees a certain degree of flexibility within the labor supply.

"Labor turnover," by contrast, measures the amount of time that each individual employee remains with the corporation. The optimal level of "labor turnover," according to my interviews and to other research in multinational manufacturers, for assembly line workers is two years;[4] the optimal rate is much higher for "skilled" employees.[5] In other words, companies prefer to have, on average, a constant turnover rate of 7 percent every year across the spectrum of jobs and a constant labor turnover rate of two years among unskilled assembly workers, such that workers who have more than two years' tenure represent a numerical minority. The desire for a two-year labor turnover rate reveals the belief that unskilled workers operate on a trajectory of diminishing returns. At some point (in this case, within two years), the replacement of these workers is regarded as more valuable to the company than their continued employment. The challenge for managers is to keep these two turnover rates in proper alignment so that the two-year time frame does not disrupt the 7 percent figure. In other words, they do not want their workers leaving en masse, every two years. Such a pattern of turnover would lead to total disruption of the labor process. Instead, they desire a steady rate of attrition, so that the 7 percent of turnover derives from the departure of workers who have entered the period of diminishing returns.

This combined concept of turnover reveals the devastating logic of capitalist value production that captured Marx's attention and led to his proclamation that the more riches workers produce, the poorer they become.[6] He captured this logic within his description of workers as "variable capital," as the kind of capital whose own value varies from the value that they create through their labor. In short, by identifying workers as "variable capital," Marx exposes how the worker is socially produced as a subject whose labor (which is sold as a commodity) is evaluated separately from the laborer's own reproduction, such that there exists a difference in value between the laborer's worth and the worth of the labor produced by this very worker. And this variation in value between the worker's value and the value of this worker's labor is the critical ingredient for the creation of capitalist profit. When the logic of worker as variable capital is extended, we can see that if workers are cheapened while the value of their labor remains constant or increases, then profit grows. The greater the variation between workers' value and the value of their labor, the greater the profit.

Within such logic, we can see clearly the value of disposable workers. Since, under capitalism, profit increases when the difference between the cost for reproducing workers and the marketed cost of their products expands, workers whose labor circulates through the circuitry of production and consumption simultaneous to the depreciation in the cost of their own reproduction represent a most valuable form of labor power. Consequently, the "disposable third world woman worker"—whose social worth is located on a continuum of diminishing returns—is the most valuable kind of worker, so long as her labor contributes to the making of commodities.

The managers at AOTW combine their discourse of factory kinship with the corporate imperative for producing just the right amount and rate of turnover among their assembly workers in order to maximize the variation between workers' depleting value and the appreciating value of the commodities that they manufacture. By putting their workers into the position of daughters who by custom must and do obey their fathers, these managers justify the most invasive sorts of procedures for monitoring their workers' rate of decline in a setting where "disposability" turns on a calculation that measures the worth of discrete bodily functions against each other—but only in the bodies of female workers. While the workers are hired according to the assumption that all women workers in southern China possess the valuable combination of docility, dexterity, and attentiveness (noted above), they are monitored according to the equally widespread assumption that their reproductive cycles and sexual desires will eventually turn their productivity into waste. AOTW managers believe it critical to monitor their workers' reproductive organs, their menstrual cycles, and their sexual behavior on the theory that such monitoring is key both to their role as factory fathers, who are in charge of their daughters' integrity, as well as to their management of commodity production. Ironically, though, the integrity that they endeavor to protect is that of the continuum by which these factory daughters are turned into corporate waste.

In this case, we see how this local discourse of kinship combined with a corporate imperative for disposable labor generates a smokescreen for the attrition caused by illnesses and injuries that plague assembly workers, particularly women, throughout the corporate world. What we see instead is a worker who needs to be turned inside out so that we can evaluate the ratio of her worth, as a laborer, to the value of her labor. Based on this story and on the working subject it produces, the AOTW managers have devised numerous policies that function as a speculum for opening up the private parts of women's bodies to public inspection.

AOTW

In 1993, Asia on the Water opened a factory in the municipality of Dongguan, a metropolitan area along the Pearl River Delta of Guangdong Province. In the 1990s, Dongguan was one of the fastest growing export-processing enclaves in southern China ("The Comeback Kid" 2000) and it confirmed the growing significance of foreign direct investment (FDI) for the post-Mao Chinese economy (see also Gallagher 2005). By 1995, AOTW occupied several, contiguous buildings and had expanded factory production from one to three product lines with a labor force of about seven hundred. Women, between the ages of eighteen and twenty-four, represented 70 percent of the labor force. All hourly waged employees lived and worked in the company's factory complex. AOTW's was one of many new factories in one of the city's industrial estates, and identical buildings, all housing workers' dorms and work spaces under a single roof and owned by dozens of different companies, surrounded it on all sides. AOTW's top managers and engineers commuted weekly from Hong Kong and stayed in managerial quarters within the male workers' dormitories.

At the time of my study in 1993, the AOTW managers were concerned about the company's poor market performance in the previous two years. By 1997, this concern had turned into alarm over the corporate board's decision to "downsize" by selling off either the Mexican or the Asian facilities to a competitor. The AOTW general manager, Howard Li, explained that this decision came on the heels of a protracted internal battle between the AOTW managers and the U.S.-American managers in Mexico (MOTW) over corporate resources and product lines. Howard Li referred to this period as a "civil war" between the Chinese managers in Hong Kong and the U.S.-American (Anglo) managers in Mexico (see Wright 2001). The U.S.-American team had opposed the opening of the Dongguan facility and its subsequent expansion on the basis that the Chinese managers were not qualified—due to cultural limitations—to oversee this operation. When the AOTW operation did expand into Dongguan, the Chinese managers were subject to racial slurs and other forms of hostility by their U.S.-American colleagues. "I was called an 'Asian spy,'" said Howard Li, "and locked out of the office [in U.S. corporate headquarters]." This tension between the American and Chinese managers intensified during the company's financial crisis in the late 1990s. OTW had fallen into dire financial straits: flagging sales of its engines began in the late 1980s and continued into the following decade; there was an erosion of its market across the board against Japanese competition. In addition, internal political upheaval within the firm had shaken investor confidence, and the company's stock lost about 40 percent of its value between 1995 and 1997 without subsequent recovery. In response to this financial crisis, the corporate executive board decided that the company had to scale back production and seek subcontracting relationships with other firms. This decision meant that either the Chinese or the Mexican operations would be sold to a competitor. And this, in turn, meant that a number of long-term American and Chinese employees would be laid off and left to their own devices for securing their jobs with their new employer. As Howard Li said in 1997, "It is between us and Mexico."

The OTW executive board had decided to leave its decision to the outcome of a comparison between the Mexican and Chinese facilities. The Mexican facility had been in business for almost thirty years; it manufactured the components for the gasoline-powered engines that were assembled in Georgia and marketed in the United States and Europe. They produced the company's signature engine, and the retail price of one of those motors generated more profit than the sale of twenty-five of the small electrical motors manufactured in AOTW. By contrast, the Chinese facility was still largely untested in 1997. It was on the edge of the world's potentially largest industrial labor force as well as its biggest retail market, but its labor process, unlike its counterpart in Mexico that had proven adept at manufacturing quality products, was plagued by high defect rates and erratic production scheduling. Chinese managers had to pay ever increasing bribes to local officials. Still, with these problems, there was a sense of urgency about getting into China and being prepared for the opening of the market and the maturation of not only the largest but also one of the least expensive labor markets in the world (see, for instance, Powell et al. 2001; Whelan 2000).

The board informed both managerial teams that they would be compared on the basis of product quality and turnover rate. Product quality was measured in terms of the percentages of defective products for every batch manufactured. Product quality was linked directly to turnover rates in several ways. For instance, high turnover rates—above 7 percent—meant that workers were leaving prematurely, before their "on-the-job training" had been fully utilized. New recruits did not perform as well, on average, as seasoned workers. As the production manager, Harry Chen, explained, "New girls have more problems. They make mistakes." However, product defects could emerge also from turnover rates that were too low if workers were still employed "past their prime." Workers who suffered from illnesses and injuries, for instance, also made mistakes. As Howard Li put it, "This is not work they do for years. . . . You want fresh workers, with fresh eyes and fingers." Quality was considered to derive from the monitoring of the rate of turnover so that fresh workers are constantly cycling into the labor process.

This connection between turnover and product quality meant that the AOTW managerial team was even more keen on demonstrating that they could manage the "right amount of turnover" as they were competing for their jobs against the U.S.-American managers in Mexico. This competition raised many of the old battles that the Chinese managerial and engineering team had fought for years within a company where systematic racism had denied them promotions and access to corporate resources allowed to the U.S.-based employees. While Howard Li admitted that the Asian team had made some gains against racism in the early 1990s, this most recent competition gave rise to further anti-Chinese sentiment as U.S. employees realized that they were at risk of losing their jobs. And Howard Li knew that part of his challenge would be to prove to his overseas bosses and colleagues that the Chinese people were qualified managers, against a racist legacy that gave preference to U.S. and Anglo employees, and that the Chinese factory was well situated to move the company ahead into the next century. He said, "The Americans don't think we can do this here. They think China is backwards. But China is changing very fast. And Chinese people work very hard. . . . If we fail here, then they will say 'I told you so.' And they would say that. I tell you the truth."

At stake in this competition, then, against the U.S.-American managers of MOTW was the ability of the Hong Kong Chinese managers to counter the racism that had been used against them for years within OTW. Toward this end, the AOTW managers relied on a strategy for segregating workers according to sex difference throughout the factory and the division of labor, which enabled them to monitor the most intimate details of their female workers' lives as a fundamental process for controlling the labor process. They paid particular attention to the female workers' reproductive cycles and sexual drives to help them determine how to keep assembly workers for the right amount of time, in order to maximize the value of their dexterity, patience, and docility before the wear and tear of production tipped the balance toward diminishing returns. This managerial strategy was, in essence, a procedure for making use of the rhythm of the workers' reproductive drives to accommodate the company's time frame for extracting value from a disposable labor force.

Managing Feminine Waste

The sexual segregation of the Dongguan facility reveals the central-
ity of sex difference to the organization of production and of labor.
The facility consists of two buildings known as Plants I and II. Plant
I houses the administrative offices and inventory supplies, both male-
dominated areas. On the upper three floors, women assemble motors
through various steps, including wire splicing, electrical assembly,
and final assembly. Across the street in Plant II, male workers paint
and package the motors for final shipping. Like most manufacturing
facilities in the city's industrial estates, both buildings house worker
dormitories. Female workers sleep in Plant I, and male workers and
managers in Plant II.

This mapping of sex difference throughout the facility allowed
for a sexual distinction in the practice of supervision. In the female-
dominated work areas, supervisors are quickly noticed. The workers
are all seated at their stations, where they perform their tasks by
reaching up to overhead bins for the supplies that they use on a table-
top. Talking is strictly forbidden, as is any pause in work, a bathroom
break without permission, or any other disruption to the continual
flow of work. The only voice heard is that of the supervisor, who
occasionally makes comments on the work. The supervisors in Plant
I oversee the work of between twelve and fifteen laborers at any one
time, and their evaluations of workers are publicly posted on each
young woman's station so that her production figures can be easily
seen by other managers and her coworkers.

By contrast, the supervisors in Plant II oversee the work of about
thirty-five employees. The male workers in this facility work in teams
of three to five. Those working in the painting section move around
their area of the plant in order to restock their supplies. The workers
in tooling and packaging also are free to move at will within their
work spaces. The supervisors in Plant II walk through the work areas
but do not stand watch over each individual worker as they do in
Plant I. Worker evaluations are not publicly posted, and since they
are evaluated as teams, their individual performance is not isolated
from the rest.

The dormitories also were supervised differently. The female
workers in the Plant I dormitory were forbidden from leaving the
building at any time and on any day except for Sunday. The male
workers in Plant II, however, walked between the two facilities on
a regular basis. Since the canteen was located in Plant I, they had
to cross the street in order to eat, and those who worked in materials management and in maintenance frequented both buildings. As a
result, the male workers had access to the street and to the activities

there. Street vendors sometimes passed with food, cigarettes, and sometimes clothing. The male workers took breaks outside the doors, where they would smoke cigarettes and talk until a manager walked through, when they would head inside. But the managers did not seem to mind these occasional breaks. Women workers were never seen standing outside the factory doors. As has been documented by other researchers in Chinese facilities, AOTW's rules are not anathema to the export-processing zones (see Woo 1994; Hsing 1998; Chan 1997). Prohibitions on talking or walking, bans on leaving the compound without permission, as well as restrictions against pregnancy, marriage, or engagement are commonplace (see Chan 1997).[7] Indeed, AOTW's restrictions could seem tame when compared to those of some other corporate facilities, where beatings and torture have been documented by journalists (see Chan 2001). In the vast majority of these cases, women workers are singled out for particularly severe policies regarding their behavior, social activities, and sexuality.

In AOTW, the managers explain the stricter surveillance of their female employees by describing their roles as those of a parent with an unpredictable teenage girl who requires a strong patriarchal hand to keep her under control. Howard Li said, "We have naïve girls. Here we are like their parents. They have to obey us. . . . When workers make problems, we find other girls." Stephen Chan said. "Their parents trust us to protect their daughters from the trouble they can find in this city. That is part of my job too." And Harry Chen added that his own knowledge of Chinese culture and his own experience as a father meant that he was particularly suited for his job as production manager over a young female Chinese labor force: "The Chinese raise their daughters to be very obedient," he said. "The family is strict, more strict that in America. . . . The girls, sometimes, do not know what to do when they move away from their family. They can lose their obedience. They are naïve. I have two daughters, and we are very strict with them. I am like that here because Chinese daughters are good daughters, but you have to protect them from dangerous things in the city." When I asked Harry Chen to explain why the workers were not allowed out of the facility after work hours, he said, "It is not right for the girls to go out at night. It is not safe."

This discourse of the "dangerous" city that might tempt the ingénue daughter resonates with depictions in the business and popular press of southern China's rising problem of prostitution that preys on young female workers. For instance, a businessperson is quoted in a *Business China* ("New China, Old Vice" 2000) article as saying, "Shenzhen's [the export-processing] economy is based on sex," and then the article goes on to quote a "charity worker" as saying,

"'Many young women working in factories actually earn substantially less than [US$66 per month].' . . . Many only ear[n] around Rmb 200–300 (US $24–36)—and that's with two or three hours' overtime a day. Many factories simply do not obey the law." That creates incentive for women to move out of the factory dormitory and into another trade. The AOTW managers are careful to guard against such dangers, not by adjusting their salaries but by locking the female workers into the factory/dormitory complex for six or often seven days a week, a practice not uncommon in the export-processing zones of southern China (Chan 1997, 2001; Hsing 1998).

On my initial introduction in 1993 to the AOTW dormitories, Howard Li repeatedly stressed his parental duties to the workers. "In China, the girls are far from home for the first time. We give them a home, a place to sleep and eat and make friends. We are their family here. We tell them, we are their boss and their parents. We are here to take care of them." As we looked into one room that had eight bunks, four to a side and stacked in two tiers, and with just enough space for one person to walk down the middle of the room, he noted that one of the posters on the wall was of the same Chinese singer that his own daughter had on her wall in Hong Kong. "Here they are like our daughters," he said. The belongings of his PRC "daughters" were few. The bunks in each room were topped with a thin pad, and a pillow was the only place the residents had to store their personal belongings. One bunk held a suitcase, a pair of folded slacks, a brush, some hairpins, and a green, metal pencil case. A single blouse hung from the bottom rung of the upper bunk.

Yet, the kinship described in this story of factory fathers and daughters is one of a temporary relationship that daughters move into and out of over a relatively short period of time. Howard Li elaborated, "When it is time for them to go, we ask them to leave. We have new girls everyday." When I asked how the right time for their departure was determined, he said, "It can be many reasons. Someone does not like the work. Or someone wants to have her own family. It is easy to know because when a worker wants to leave, she can cause problems." He did not explain the kind of problems in detail, but through various conversations, I learned that typical "problems" included a range of events, such as a worker's attempt to question a regulation as well as a worker's efforts to see another worker romantically. "You have to watch them, and when it is time for them to go, we know," he said. And, at that time, this worker will be tossed out of this family and replaced by another determined to be just like her. Therefore, linking daughters to problems is a key concept in AOTW, where efforts to decrease problems in production hinged largely on controlling the problems associated with their female workers. And once the problems detected within the female workers outweigh the benefits of keeping them within the family fold, they are dismissed like "disposable daughters" from this corporate family. Therefore, the task of determining how long to keep workers at AOTW was presented in terms of keeping the "good daughters" until they turn into "bad ones."

Daughters and Defects

AOTW managers had a number of regulations that facilitate this balancing of good daughters against bad ones in the management of the turnover rate. Like most facilities in China's export-processing zones, AOTW required a two-year labor contract from workers who, upon signing, paid an initial deposit that would not be returned if the worker left or was justifiably dismissed before its termination (see also Chan 1997). The terms for justifiable dismissal included injury, illness, laziness, pregnancy, or sexual immorality. Dismissing a worker for bad health, such as injuries or illnesses (incurred on or off the work site), was justified on the basis that it was for the worker's own good. Harry Chen explained, "These girls do not know how to take care. . . . We give them medical advice. If they are sick, we make them go home, and their health improves." He then resorted to the in loco parentis concept by saying, "We treat them like our own daughters. If my daughter is sick, I make her stay in bed. Here, one sick girl can make everyone sick, so we make them go home to their families." Likewise, dismissing a worker for moral impurity was justified on the basis that this worker could influence the other female workers and turn them into "bad" daughters. Howard Li also employed in loco parentis to explain why: "Some of the older girls are more disobedient and they try to influence the young ones. It is like an older daughter who disobeys her parents. Then it is time for her to leave the family and marry."

Howard Li's concern with workers' sexual thoughts, in additional to their sexual deeds, resonated with other managerial remarks that diagnosed the problems in production as emerging from the reproductive drives and cycles internal to their workers' bodies.[8] Harry Chen explained, "The problem is you cannot trust these workers. They are like children in the toy store. They tell you they will behave and do their work, but they think about boys and do not do their work." Stephen Chan linked these distracting thoughts to workers' desires for getting married and having children, "These girls are normal. They are young and full of ideas about getting married and having children. They hear that biological clock . . . and we tell them they still have time for a family, but first they can make some money and work here, and then they can have their families." Howard Li corroborated Stephen Chan's view of the biological clock when he said, "These girls are eighteen and nineteen. They are becoming women . . . their bodies are telling them to have children. We want them to concentrate on their work here for two years and then they can go and start a family. If we can keep them concentrating on the work, for just two years, then we can improve our ratings here in the company. I know it." On the issue of pregnancy, the AOTW managers uniformly agreed that pregnant workers should return home to have their babies. "That is everyone's policy here," said Stephen Chan. When I asked why they simply did not write that workers who did not perform up to standard would be dismissed, Howard Li explained that firing someone for not doing her job well would leave the company open to fines but firing a worker for bad health, immorality, or pregnancy was regarded by local authorities as acceptable. In other words, being a "bad daughter"—or a female worker who questions authority, or becomes ill or pregnant—more easily justified dismissal than the mere determination that a worker was not performing work up to standards. This way, the focus of the evaluation was on the integrity of the worker as a subject—as one worth or not worth keeping—rather than on the work itself when questions regarding work rules, cycle times, and ergonomic issues might arise.

When I asked how male workers were evaluated for dismissal, the managers explained that they did not have the same kind of issues as with the female workers and that, as a result, the turnover rate among male workers was substantially lower. "They [the male workers] do not create the same problems. They concentrate more on the work," Harry Chen explained. And for this reason, Chen continued, they did not require as much surveillance as the female workers. "Discipline is not our concern [with the male workers]," he said as he described how only rarely were male workers dismissed. Typically, turnover within that population resulted from personal decisions to leave and seek employment elsewhere. "They find a better job and leave," said Howard Li.

This different emphasis on male and female supervision illustrated a distinct approach between female and male areas of the facility regarding the connection between the production process and workers' bodies and attitudes. Male workers did not undergo the same degree of scrutiny over their attitudes (that is, obedience), sexual habits, or even illness that the female workers did, and their turnover rate was not considered to represent an issue of concern for the managers, who believed that male workers would come and go as other opportunities presented themselves. Their turnover rate was not a reflection of their worth as laborers, simply a reflection of external circumstances. Likewise, if problems arose in the male areas of the production process, managers did not tend to explain them in terms of problems residing intrinsically within the workers. For instance, Stephen Chan told me, "Sometimes we have problems with the paint. That is a very hard operation. So we have higher defects there." Howard Li also corroborated this view that defects in the painting area resulted from the difficulty of the work, rather than from the difficulty of the worker: "We expect problems in painting. We train the workers. New ones make more mistakes, but they learn. It is hard work."

By contrast, defects and problems in the female areas of the facility were regularly explained as emanating from the workers themselves, rather than from the work, and as having a direct correlation to their status as good or bad daughters. For instance, on one morning in 1997, as Howard Li and I walked through Plant I, he explained, "We have problems with quality in Plant I. That is where we have our biggest problems." To emphasize his point, he held up a partially assembled 1.5-horsepower motor, its unattached wires dangling as evidence of its uselessness. He placed it back on the shelf, next to several motors in the same shape. "Many problems. Too many," he said, and then, ensuring that I understood how the problems in the motors had to do with the problems on the line, he directed my attention to a woman who used a pair of pliers to twist two wires together before attaching a plastic cap. "This girl is good here, but there was one before her. She always thought about her boyfriend, always wanted to talk with him, so we told her to leave. We cannot have workers like that and make a good product." Harry Chen backed up this assessment when he said, "We have too many defects in Plant I [the female areas]. The girls do not concentrate. They think of other things. We always have to watch them."

By presenting the issue of defects in Plant I as having origin within the workers while discussing problems in Plant II as emanating from the work, the managers lay out the justification for a differential system of supervision. And since they were under pressure from their corporate headquarters to reduce defect rates in order to win the competition against their U.S. colleagues, this gendering of defects such that those in Plant I were seen as arising from "daughter or female trouble" meant that they turned their attention to ferreting out the sources of this trouble. The male workers, consequently, did not come under the same scrutiny since the problems in their areas were determined to be inevitable consequences of a difficult work process.

For this reason, the AOTW managers justified the most invasive procedures for monitoring the female workers, who were, they
reasoned, always on the verge of turning into bad daughters who
created bad products. Since hormones, reproductive cycles, and dis-
obedience were identified as principal sources of "bad daughter/bad
worker" behavior, these represented the sites for concern. Consequently, periodic pregnancy tests were required of all female workers. Howard Li explained, "All companies do that. . . . We cannot
keep pregnant workers here. That is against the rules." These rules,
as Stephen Chan told me, reflected, again, the managers' responsibili-
ties to protect the moral integrity of their labor force in addition to
keeping them focused on the work, "We have these tests so the girls
will know that if they do get pregnant, we will know. . . . We are like
their parents, we know everything about them, and it is for their own
good." Howard Li further explained, "One pregnant girl will cause
problems for everyone. Other girls will think it is ok, and then we
will have more problems in production. We cannot have them here."
So pregnant workers are summarily dismissed and replaced just like
any disposable worker.

Pregnancy tests, administered on-site, were not the only means
for monitoring the labor force and creating a de facto supply of disposable workers. Howard Li also described a policy (enacted in 1997)
for regulating workers' menstrual cycles by scheduling them for regular physical checkups. He explained this new policy as the company's response to pressure from municipal governments to enforce the
government's policy, as part of the "one-child" policy, for restrict-
ing the number of children to one per family. The one-child policy's
enforcement is based at the county and municipal levels and includes,
among other measures, the monitoring of women's bodies to ensure
against "illegal" pregnancies.[9] Howard Li described the one-child
policy as disruptive because some officials from northern provinces
required that female workers return home once a year for an annual
evaluation. According to Howard Li, the workers had to pay for these
trips out of their earnings and they also lost pay for the time they
were gone. In an effort to reduce the disruption caused by these trips
and to minimize the costs for workers, Howard Li had worked with
some local officials to arrange regular exams in Dongguan so that the
workers would not have to leave the municipality. He described this
situation as beneficial both to the worker and to the company, since
the exams did not significantly interrupt the labor process and were
less expensive for the workers.

However, Howard Li's description of the one-child policy and
of its enforcement did not correspond to the typical government

policy, which was oriented toward married women.[10] Since AOTW would not hire married women and forced married women to leave their employment, the one-child policy enforcement that Howard Li describes and his solution to it were directed also at monitoring the reproductive organs of single women.

Despite the disjuncture between the usual enforcement of the one-child policy and AOTW's interpretation of it, the policy of man-dated physical exams reflects a longheld suspicion intrinsic to various labor codes within China that reproductive organs weaken women. Therefore, their menstrual cycles should be regulated as part of the regulation of the labor process (see White 1994; Furth 2002). Harry Chen made this connection when he said, "We have many girls come here and sometimes they are very poor. They can be sick. And then they cannot do the work. If they are sick, we make them go home." Howard Li explained that female workers are more vulnerable than males for illness due to their reproductive cycles: "Females are more sensitive. They get sick." When I asked if he meant that the women workers were susceptible to illness due to their reproductive organs and cycles, he nodded and then said, "They will not say anything to you, so you have to get the doctor to look at them, make sure they are all right."

Combined, the pregnancy tests, physical exams, and segregation and mobility policies subjected women workers to the utmost disci-pline and surveillance in the name of parental duty and for the benefit of quality control. The information gathered by medical staff during the forced examinations was given directly to the AOTW managerial staff in the event that the worker demonstrated illness, injury, preg-nancy, or another condition that would be seen as adversely affecting her job performance.[11] "Sometimes," said Howard Li, "there is some-thing wrong. We want to know." When I asked what sorts of things, in addition to pregnancy, could be wrong with the workers, Howard Li mentioned that injuries were common among the assembly work-ers. While he did acknowledge that injuries, such as carpal tunnel syndrome, did affect some workers, he did not know to what extent, and he denied that the problem was prevalent in his facility. How-ever, anecdotal evidence indicates high rates of workplace injuries in southern China's export-processing zones (see Chao 2002; Eckholm 2001). Longitudinal studies of repetitive stress disorders have not been published, if even conducted, for these facilities. Still, such stud-ies conducted in electronic assembly operations in other parts of the world have shown that repetitive stress disorders are commonplace, especially in environments like AOTW, where basic safeguards such as worker rotation, regular rests, and wrist supports are not implemented (see Lin 1991).

Meanwhile, at AOTW, managers who receive information from medical personnel regarding the health and fitness of their workers decide if their employees are unfit, whether due to pregnancy or to repetitive stress disorders. If a young woman is deemed unfit for employment as a result of one of these exams, she is easily dismissed and replaced without the company being held accountable. That worker's turnover simply contributes to the continuous flow of female workers through the revolving door of disposability. All the managers have to say, if questioned by local authorities (a rare event, according to AOTW managers), is that they were working in her best interests, just as any good parent would do for their own child. Workers who do pass these inspections of their organs, attitudes, and digits and who perform up to standards are held to the letter of their two-year contract—if they leave before the time limit, they will lose their deposits and face potential fines and difficulty finding work elsewhere. Their disposability is thus inevitably guaranteed by the two-year contract if they manage to maintain their value to the company during that period of time.

All of the AOTW managers in charge of the Chinese facility explained that keeping workers beyond the two-year time frame was not prudent. Their explanations regularly combined concerns over the wear and tear of the work itself with certainties that the reproductive clock of the female laborers could not be kept in check forever. Howard Li put it this way: "Girls line up outside the door everyday. They are young and healthy. This work is hard on the hands and eyes. No one should do it for a long time. Two years is enough. . . . And that is ok with the girls here. They want to start their families. I could not keep them longer if I wanted to." While I have not been able to find long-term studies on repetitive stress disorders in southern China's export-processing zones, the anecdotal evidence supports the findings of studies conducted in facilities located in other regions that repetitive stress disorders are a costly malady that affect a significant percentage of the manufacturing labor force. Harry Chen did not use the words "repetitive stress disorder," but he described its effects when he said, "The girls always slow down after two years. Then it is time for them to go."

The right time for turnover then is when the "girls" slow down. Some take two years, and some less, but whatever the reason for the slowness—the onset of injury, illness, or pregnancy—the AOTW managers have a sure system in place to catch this slowness before it translates into expensive defects, slower production rates, and corporate liability. When a young woman does slow down, there is always another young woman to replace her. With luck, these young women make it for their entire two years; without it, they may find that their health has deteriorated or their bodies pained or even crippled by injuries, at which time they will be declared "unfit" for employment and summarily replaced. Such is the cyclical journey of the labor turnover that the AOTW managers dedicated so much energy and thought to controlling.

Despite his efforts to present the AOTW facility as orderly and his policies as straightforward, Howard Li confessed one day that the pressures to cycle workers into and out of facility, at just the right rate, was difficult at times for him. One day while standing on top of the roof of Plant I in Dongguan, he told me a story of one of his workers, a young woman from a northern province, who had slit her wrists in the dormitory bathroom. She had only worked in the facility for about a year, and, according to Howard Li, she was a very good worker. He thought that she had attempted suicide because she had become pregnant and that the loss of blood had precipitated a miscarriage. Harry Chen, he said, had taken the young woman to the hospital and had called Howard Li, who was in Hong Kong at the time. Harry Chen had assumed that the company would pay for only one night in the hospital and then, per company policy, dismiss the worker and remove itself from liability regarding her well-being. However, in an apparent aberration from protocol, Howard Li told Harry Chen that he would keep her in the hospital as long as she needed to stay and not fire her. He said, "I even paid for her parents to visit her and stay in a hotel. My heart was breaking for them. I did not tell my company bosses. They would not think this was a good idea." After she recovered, the young woman stayed at AOTW for the duration of her two-year contract. Howard Li said that if she had not been such a good worker, he would have dismissed her after her recovery. "I did not have to do that," he said; "there is always someone else I can put in her place."

Modern Chinese Managers

The Chinese managerial strategy for managing the labor turnover in their facility paid off in 1999 when the OTW board decided to sell the Mexican operations and keep the China factory. AOTW's facilities had demonstrated that they could control turnover such that it would occur at a predictable rate, between 5 and 7 percent, over an extended period of time. This turnover rate was far superior to the almost 20 percent experienced by MOTW during the same period of time. Howard Li was very proud of his accomplishment and declared that AOTW was "the company's future" because it had a low-waged labor force that turned over at a constant and manageable rate.

As a result, two product lines, which were formerly in the Mexican facility, were in full operation in the Chinese facility by the end of the year. Howard Li and three of his managers received raises and, as Howard Li put it, "more respect." The AOTW team made corporate history. They had overcome racial and cultural prejudices that had prohibited their vertical ascent into positions of authority over US-American personnel. And the decision represented a shift in the company's strategy for focusing on the Asian market and the smaller fishing motors rather than the larger motors for the U.S. market that favors speedboats.

However, just over a year later, a private investor bought the majority of OTW's stock and removed it from public exchange. The company had hovered on the brink of bankruptcy for over a year; its stock had continued to drop in value, and its market share had also steadily declined. A former vice president and former general manager of the Mexican facility explained that quality defects still plagued the company and contributed to its loss of market share across the board. Still, he admitted that the Hong Kong Chinese managers had proven their mettle in the internal competition for resources. "Those guys knew what they were doing," he said. "They proved a lot of us wrong."

The events at AOTW reveal the complex knots that bind discourses of social difference to the making of corporate strategists and corporate profit. On the one hand, the Hong Kong Chinese managers succeed in breaking the glass ceiling that had prohibited their ascent within a racist and ethnocentric corporate hierarchy that had safeguarded the stronghold of a U.S., Anglo, male managerial class. Howard Li, Stephen Chan, and Harry Chen—all with at least fifteen years of experience in this company—had endured racial stereotyping that segregated them, along with their other Hong Kong Chinese colleagues, into lower paying managerial jobs where they had to answer to U.S.-American bosses who, they believed, were set against their promotions and even against the success of their operations. Their accomplishments in rising through the ranks, while perhaps delimited by the overall corporate financial crisis, represent some progress in the dismantling of racism amongst the corporate elite. And then, on the other hand, these managers accomplish this feat, in large part, by deploying narratives of factory daughters, their filial obligations, and the entitlements of factory fathers. These narratives both justify their invasive managerial techniques as well as function as smokescreens for corporate policies that dismiss workers who become injured, ill, or pregnant during their tenure. These discourses that set the female laborers apart from their managers on the basis of gender while establishing a common ground between them on the basis of the "Chinese family" are effective technologies for producing the materiality of an exploitable laborer: a young woman worker who must be patrolled for her own good. And these new managers emerge, in her contrast, as the good father who can take care of the simultaneously innocent and troublesome young daughter.

Had this study been conducted through a survey questionnaire or other nonethnographic means of inquiry, this investigation into how OTW decided to expand its operations in southern China would probably have yielded different findings. As we see in AOTW, practices designed to boost corporate profits and managerial acumen articulate with practices for distinguishing daughters from fathers, "old" China from the "new" one, "bad" daughters from "good" ones, and "Chinese" from "American" employees. The interviews that gave rise to these conclusions—via descriptions of racism and of the need to monitor female reproductive organs through forced physical exams—do not surface easily in formal interview settings. Rather, they arise in the day-to-day interactions when managers are asked to explain how their stated commitments to workers' well-being seem belied by practices that treat young women like disposable workers. These are questions that require asking in a number of different ways and usually more than once, and the answers often need further explanation. These conversations are not always comfortable for either the researcher or the informant.

Yet only by asking such questions do we truly delve into the complex social relationships that create the domain of the economic. For while Karl Marx's famous words that "the worker becomes all the poorer the more wealth he produces" are as relevant today as when he penned them in 1844, we cannot translate this abstract axiom into specific relevance without exploring the particular idioms by which labor's poverty materializes through capital's wealth. To be sure, we know that workers around the world are indeed facing more pressure to produce more work in return for less remuneration, and we know that women still earn a pittance, as they have for decades, on the assembly lines of multinational firms. But to know these things is not to know how this pattern is constantly recreated across the diverse terrain that is global capitalism.

3

Manufacturing Bodies

No soy yo la que pensáis,	I am not who you think I am
sino es que allá me habéis dado	but, over there, your pens
otro ser en vuestras plumas	have given me a different nature
otro aliento en vuestros labios,	and your lips, another spirit,
y diversa de mi misma	and a stranger to myself
entre vuestras plumas ando,	I roam among your pens,
no como soy, sino como	not as I am, but as
quisisteis imaginarlo.	you would imagine me to be.

Sor Juana Inés de la Cruz[1]

The disposable third world woman's body is not the same as the one that women workers bring into the workplace. Rather, it is a body manufactured during the labor process via discourses that combine bits and pieces of workers' bodies with industrial processes and managerial expectations. As I intend to show here, this discursive production of the materially disposable third world woman's body does not, however, focus exclusively on the manufacturing of solely female bodies. It is a discursive process in which material entities cohere around an array of differences, such as first world/third world, female/male, valuable/disposable, and other traits often paired as binary opposites. In the context of the factory I present here, these oppositional pairs figure centrally, along with another coupled around American/Mexican differences, in the daily operations of a Mexican television factory owned by a highly diversified global firm I call "COSMO." As I attempt to show here, these binary pairs are central to the discursive production of the disposable third world woman's actual corporeality. This productive process begins always with a destructive one that entails a disassembling of workers' bodies into distinctly oppositional parts, such as male/female, third world, first world Mexican, American, and so on, such that COSMO employees represent a supply of an array of body parts, like unattached limbs and free-floating heads, that are then discursively reassembled into the bodies that meet corporate specifications, outlined in engineering and managerial offices. Prominent among these bodies is that of the disposable third world woman.

Yet, as I also attempt to demonstrate, these corporate specifications not only identify the need for variably gendered bodies that bring the disposable woman worker to life. They also reveal the need for culturally circumscribed ethnic ones that reinforce internal corporate hierarchies organized around a belief in the *superiority* of U.S. and European subjects over *intrinsically inferior* employers from the third world. In this way, this chapter focuses on how discourses of sex difference converge with those of ethnic and cultural differences in the making of the odd or, perhaps best put, impossible bodies of global manufacture.

At the time of my research from the mid-1990s to early 2001, COSMO was incorporating more sophisticated production techniques that required skilled labor at all levels of employment, including at the lowest level of electronic assembly operator, a position held almost exclusively by women. The managers of COMSO faced the challenge of having to obtain skilled labor from workers who were considered to be intrinsically and intransigently unskilled. They were, in other words, presented with a version of the conundrum of how to squeeze the blood from a turnip. How do you squeeze skill from a body said to embody the opposite of anything that resembles skill? And what does this requirement mean for the myth of the disposable third world woman and its role in generating value from the labor of working women?

I address these questions by exploring the conduct of supervision—a hierarchical arrangement at COSMO between female operators and male supervisors. At the time of my study, all but one of the one hundred COSMO supervisors were male, while the areas they supervised (the electronic assembly operations) were held almost exclusively by women.[2] Over the course of my research, I began to see the supervisory dynamic between the male supervisor and the female operator as organized around something I call the "prosthetic body of supervision." This body is one specified in engineering blueprints

and managerial expectations for how the supervision of female operators by male supervisors should function in a COSMO factory that
requires skilled labor from disposable women workers. As I explain
throughout this chapter, this prosthetic arrangement of supervision
is an entity built of some pieces of a brainless female laboring body
that functions according to signals sent to it by a bodiless and free-
floating male, supervisory head.

My focus here is on the strategies and policies implemented by
COSMO managers and engineers to guarantee that this prosthetic
body of supervision materializes out of these assorted body parts,
coming from different people, and that the supervisory dynamic functions as needed. I examine, in brief, how even though these bodies do
not walk into the factory, nor do they walk out of it, they do, in fact,
work within it. And I give particular attention to how the space-time
of these bodies emerges in the COSMO production process through
a confluence of managerial and engineering specifications combined
with discourses of sex and cultural traits that help translate the
administrative vision of supervision from corporate blueprints into
the real actions of women and men, everyday, on the factory floor.
By examining how the supervisory dynamic in COSMO represents
a coupling of "his" and "her" body parts around an institutional
arrangement of the supervised-supervisor, we see how it preserves
the integrity of the myth of the disposable third world woman, along
with the value that she produces, even in cases where the real women
who are cited as evidence of this mythic figure are performing skilled
work that requires knowledge and training. It does so by locating
the source of any skilled labor occurring on the assembly line within
a disembodied, male supervisory brain that, through various techniques, transmits skill and training through an unskilled, laboring
female body without actually training or skilling-up that same body.
In this way, the female laborer continues to represent the perpetually
unskilled and untrainable worker whose value diminishes through
time. Thus, the supervisory dynamic within COSMO's version of
flexible production that denies women credit for the skilled labor
they perform is one more effective strategy aimed at ever increasing
the most precious gap separating the value of disposable women from
the value of their labor.

Additionally, this dynamic preserves another hierarchical
arrangement that is pivotal to this corporation's internal division of
labor: that of segregating Mexican employees as "lesser developed,"
from the "more developed" U.S. and European ones, who receive
more benefits and higher salaries in recognition of their superior status. At COSMO, we see how within the prosthetic body of supervi-

sion, the bodiless, Mexican masculine supervisor is always, like the mindless female Mexican operator, incomplete. For without the body of the woman worker on the line, the supervisor does not have a body to demonstrate skill, knowledge, and training—those qualities that substantiate the supervisor's authority over the workers on the line. His skill, training, and authority are made manifest only when she performs her work. Therefore, the supervisor also materializes as an incomplete or not fully developed subject whose partiality reinforces dominant discourses within COSMO, and across the maquiladora industry, of "immature" Mexican men as evidence of the need in Mexico for western development, spearheaded by the U.S. and European firms that set up operations in that country (see Wright 2001). Thus, the prosthetic body of supervision both preserves the disposability of a female labor force, by denying the development of any unique skill within that group, as well as reinforces the discourse of a lesser developed, third world, masculine subject who justifies the notion that "social development" begins in Europe and the United States and extends via capitalist progress to the lesser developed third world (see Chakrabarty 2000).

I conducted the research for this chapter in intervals over a several-year period beginning with six months of research spanning 1993–1994, followed by several weeks in 1996–1997, and then again in 2001. During the initial research period, I also attended six weeks of supervisory training which figures prominently in my analysis. Since my focus is on the efforts to manufacture workers' bodies according to corporate specifications, I keep my attention on the managers and engineers who strategize over inserting certain kinds of bodies, as they imagine them to be, within certain kinds of labor processes, designed to produce quality goods in a timely and inexpensive way. I also prioritize the perspective of supervisors who represent both those being imagined by their managers and engineers as well as those who are charged with overseeing the materialization and integration of disposable female bodies throughout the labor process. Again, as in the other chapters within this section of the book, I do not include the perspectives of those women who are described by the discourses I investigate. Instead, my concern here is with the power that corporate overseers (including managers and engineers) wield and how that power makes itself manifest for transforming their vision of workers (including visions of their bodies) into a reality within the space-time of their factories. By not including the perspectives of the women workers who are the object of so much imagining and of policies designed to bring those fantasies into being, I do not present here those moments when the managers' and engineers' dreams of working bodies fail to materialize as planned. I look at such instances in chapters 5 through 7.

The Body as a Site of Accumulation

My investigation into this process is necessarily dialectical as my concern here is not merely with the construction of the disposable third world woman's body but also with the ongoing processes of production that contribute to the manufacturing of this body and that also derive from it. My focus is therefore on the circuitry through which this body circulates both as something that is produced in the imaginary realm as well as something that is productive within the materialist networks of global capital. I take a cue in this investigation from Elizabeth Grosz, who approaches the materiality of the human body as constantly emerging through the imagining of the social subject that takes shape along with the body associated with it. "The imaginary anatomy," she writes in *Volatile Bodies*, "is an internalized map of the meaning that the body has for the subject, for others in its social world, and for the symbolic order conceived in its generality" (1994, 39). This sort of inquiry does not assume that human anatomy is always observable or prefigured by the material effects of any given body. Rather, an investigation into the ties binding imaginary anatomy to the material attributes of what is recognized as "the body" privileges the unpredictability of the imagination for conceiving of bodies that may not exist as tangible entities in space but that, nevertheless, are believed to function physically as real bodies located in space.

By examining the imaginary anatomy of the supervised and supervisory bodies at COSMO, I believe we have another vantage point for delving into the meaning of the disposable female subject for global capital and the value derived from her wasting. Of course, capitalism does not represent the only framework for examining this process, but it does offer an angle for investigating what is at stake in the ongoing materialization of a body that is valued for its disposability. And furthermore, by approaching this materialization within capitalist circuits, we can see how economic and cultural processes work through each other continually such that cultural entities (including embodied identities) are not epiphenomenal to capitalism but, rather, constitute the discursive stuff of its materialist core.

In the end, this case demonstrates how the application of the two typically opposed theoretical approaches of Marxist and poststructuralist feminist analyses offer insights into the dynamic subjectivities associated with contemporary capitalist spatial and temporal reconfigurations of labor's exploitation. For, while a discourse of capitalism—of profit, commodities, managers, and workers—travels around the globe, the recreation of such capitalist categories is far from a homogeneous process (Gibson-Graham 1996). The very particular cultural identities that people recognize in themselves and in each other are the media through which such capitalist entities take shape and transform along with the ever-changing landscape of global capitalism.

Flexible Disposability

In the early 1990s, COSMO was one of the first maquiladoras to implement a strategy of "flexible" production throughout its manufacturing facility. In the 1980s, "flexibility" had become a buzzword in the corporate world to indicate a shift from Fordist, mass production techniques toward more responsive systems (Reygadas 2003; Carrillo 1990). Essentially this shift indicated a move away from the mass production technologies that pumped out high volume based on standardized production procedures, large inventories, and the presumption of constantly growing demand. Flexibility indicated a move toward batch production of variable product models and labor systems that responded to constant shifts in market demand. This transition toward flexibility also meant that workers were to become more flexible as well and to respond, unlike Karl Marx's notorious "appendages," to changes in production requirements by altering their work patterns. Workers in flexible facilities are not the "fixed-purpose" automatons of mass production, who perform the same tasks over and again; they are thinking and responsive members of a flexible system that constantly conforms to changing market demands. As such, flexible workers must develop the technical and social skills to accommodate more sophisticated operations, learn different tasks, acquire on-the-job skills, and diagnose problems as they occur (Holmes 1989; Piore and Sabel 1984; Schoenberger 1988). A former chairperson of Chrysler, Robert Eaton, summarized this philosophy in a 1996 *New York Times* interview on the meaning of industrial flexibility: "At one point, we were hiring hands and arms and legs, and now we are hiring total people—with minds more important than the other" (Meredith 1996, F8). In brief, if mass production workers were, as Karl Marx diagnosed, treated as unthinking extensions of machine processes—their arms and legs simply moving to the pace of the work—flexible workers are valued for their brains as well as for their brawn.

This transition to flexible production came later to Ciudad Juárez, whose political and corporate elites had invested in the city's reputation as a powerhouse of labor-intensive, mass production facilities with "fixed-purpose" women workers who did one thing very well: assembly (particularly electronic and apparel). But, by the late 1980s, and as I discussed in chapter 2, these same elites began to express worries over competition from China, which was quickly turning into one of the world's most expansive industrial regions, with lower labor costs, located within a quickly expanding and potentially enormous consumer market. The maquiladora industry and the city's political elites began a public relations campaign aimed at convincing corporate investors that Ciudad Juárez could offer what China could not: a flexible production climate, with skilled workers and sophisticated processes, along with the benefits of mass production located near the U.S. consumer market. Spokespeople for the city and for the maquiladora industry stressed how this new manufacturing philosophy would distinguish Mexico from China on the basis of quality and versatility, while continuing to reap advantages of cost in comparison to the United States (Wright 2004). Even if China was less expensive, and the Chinese consumer class growing, it was still, as these spokespeople argued, a relatively untested manufacturing climate that was less responsive, due to logistical constraints, to an evermore fickle U.S. consumer market. Ciudad Juárez, by contrast, had proven its ability to deliver high-quality and low-cost manufacturing within a mass production model and would now dedicate resources and energy to developing a more sophisticated and flexible industrial base, with the labor market and infrastructure to combine versatility with high output. By 1993, COSMO was a showcase facility that political and corporate leaders used to demonstrate the success of this industrial renovation campaign within the maquiladora sector. The factory was a place where other potential corporate investors visited to see if flexible production was really an option in the formerly unskilled, low-tech labor market of Ciudad Juárez (interviews). COSMO administrators were also invested in the successful demonstration of this flexible mass production design as they were also competing for their own jobs, much like the OTW employees in chapter 2, as their employer weighed the advantages of keeping operations in Mexico or transferring them completely to China.[3]

When I began the study in 1993, eight production lines, operating on two shifts, produced three different televisions from start to finish that were shipped "retail ready" to clients in the United States. Each production line was organized in the shape of a "U" that consisted of 150 positions. The first 75 positions, held exclusively by women, were those of circuitry insertion and soldering, the electronic assembly that creates the television's functional innards. At the bottom of the U, a handful of men attached the picture tube to the freshly assembled circuit board, and along the final side of the U, men and women tested the equipment for defects, before a final group of men packaged the unit in retailer-specific packaging, after which the units would be loaded directly onto the shipping dock. The entire system hinged upon workers' ability to change models as clients demanded without slowing down the production system and without increasing the defect rate. Demand for overall production remained relatively constant, around one thousand units per day, split over two shifts, but the variance lay in the models requested. So the work was organized around twenty-two-second cycle times, but the tasks performed during those cycles, particularly in the electronic assembly areas, changed depending upon the model. The female workers in the circuitry and soldering areas performed up to nine separate tasks within their twenty-two seconds, and these tasks changed with each model. The male workers, by contrast, in the picture tube attachment, testing, and packaging areas performed fewer tasks within the same cycle time and experienced relatively little variation among models.

As the ensuing discussion demonstrates, the gendered divisions along the line reflect and support a discursive process through which the female body emerges as an inflexible limit to the kind of flexibility that can be implemented in COSMO. Her anatomical parts are rearranged and assessed in relation to the needs of a factory system that does indeed require skilled work from her but that does not give her the credit for this skill. Her materialization as this sort of working subject occurs dialectically with the reproduction of a masculine Mexican subject who does represent the flexible potential of the entire facility. His parts, like hers, are also rearranged and assessed in terms of their promise for development into a new kind of flexible worker. However, since this flexible Mexican male worker only materializes in tandem with the inflexible female one, his dependence upon her, and consequential incompleteness as an independent subject, is reconfirmed. As such, his partiality reifies other dominant discourses so prevalent throughout the maquiladora industry of Mexican employees (male and female) as indicative of a constant lack of development in Mexico, and throughout the third world, that requires the tireless intervention of those from the more developed first world. In this way, the prosthetic body of supervision in the flexible facility of COSMO reveals the sexualized logic of modern development within its anatomical design and function.

The Prosthetics of Supervision

Training Course for Maquiladora Supervisors, Ciudad Juárez, 1994
The instructor told us to act as if we were approving of someone's

work performance. "Don't use words," she reminded us; "this is to see if you know how to use your bodies. I want to see your body language." Most nodded their heads, lifted their eyebrows, and smiled. A few gestured quiet applause. One did a "thumbs-up." This was one of several exercises that the participants performed in a training session designed to teach maquiladora supervisors some contemporary techniques for monitoring work in a flexible firm. In this class of thirty-odd Mexican employees, all but one a man, we practiced communication skills that fostered team spirit without diminishing our social control over the labor process. "Good communication is more important than ever," she emphasized. "You don't have time to tell people how to do things over and over. You use body language.... They need to do things as if your ideas were already in their heads." In these classes, we were learning about the complex social body of supervision under the conditions of flexible production. These supervisory courses were a pillar in COSMO's effort to upgrade production by enhancing the flexibility of their operations. These classes, however, also reflected an impediment to a full transition to total flexible production in the maquiladoras. The supervisory course emphasized that, unlike in other contexts, such as in Japan or in the United States, where flexible production was already in full swing, only a limited version of flexible production would be possible in Mexico (see also Shaiken 1994; Carrillo 1990). This limit, as both the course instructor and COSMO managers explained, was that presented by the largely untrainable female labor force that still performed the majority of assembly and circuitry work in the maquiladoras and who, as our teacher put it, "will not have the know-how" that the supervisors needed to acquire. "The girls on these assembly lines do not have the education," she told me, to learn the more sophisticated techniques.

She explained this logic more fully in class. "In the old days, you could just tell someone what to do and expect them to do it. But now you can't. Why? Because your workers are doing more things. You can't just tell them one time and expect them to learn it. You have to train them. But the problem is that some of your workers don't even have a high school education. Some of them don't want to learn." The way that supervisors were told to accomplish the seemingly impossible task of training a worker who either did not want to be or could not be trained was to create a corporeal link, such that the worker's body was merely a conduit for the supervisor's knowledge. "You let those workers know you're there. With your body language. You're not there to harass them. You are there because you know how the work needs to be done. They need to feel your knowledge. Know it is there and let it guide them."

Supervisors have several tools, we learned in this class, for accomplishing this feat of inserting one's own knowledge into another person's head. Verbal and physical communication was the focus of our class. We practiced role-playing as both supervisors and operators, in which the former tried various strategies, ranging from constructive suggestions to physical body manipulation, for controlling our body movements and attitudes on the production line. "You know how the work should be done," said the instructor. "The operator does not." The point, we learned, was to replace the worker's own authority over her body with the supervisor's authority so that the work at COSMO would be performed in the proper way.

Limited Flexibility

One question that I sought to answer throughout my research at COSMO was why, given the notion that women workers were incapable of developing skill within a system that requires it, did management still exclusively seek female labor for circuitry and soldering positions that constituted most of the television assembly work? During the process, I heard explanations of the essential natural and cultural qualities of Mexican women that, while limiting the full extent of COSMO's flexibility, still provided the benefits of a labor force that, if properly managed, was the most suited for the repetitive, dead-end jobs of electronic assembly. Consequently, as the managers explained, COSMO had developed a truncated form of flexibility that combined some of the mass production elements associated with the old way of doing things with the exigencies for higher quality and versatility of the new flexible methods. But this limitation was not necessarily a drawback, as Ruben, the general manager, explained: "We are as flexible as you can be in the maquilas.... The truth is that our output is standard, at about five hundred units per line. We have model changes; that is the flexible part. But overall output is the same. It's still large-volume production." Ed, the human resources manager, described how this combination of mass production with flexibility was one of COSMO's selling points to its clients. "We tell them, look, we have all of the benefits of flexible production—higher quality, and all that stuff—but we can give you constant output. High volume and high quality, that is our formula for success." Ed explained, "These girls come here for assembly work. But we can't train them. They don't care about learning anything new. We put them on the line.... Our supervisors make sure they do the work in the right way." Ruben correlated a culture of "machismo" with the female worker's inherent inflexibility: "This is a macho culture. The girls don't want to move up, get into higher positions. We can't train them for those positions. They do assembly. That's the work they want to do. Not the other.... Yes, not the flexible work." Miguel, the morning production manager, echoed this view: "We can't train those girls to do anything else [besides assembly]." And Ed put it in a slightly different way when he said, "The girls here are the same kind of worker that has always worked in the maquilas. They are good with their hands.... We train others [the men] to make the system more flexible." According to such discourses, which construct the Mexican woman as essentially and inflexibly untrainable, she represents in COSMO the stubborn presence of the old, mass production system even as she is integrated into the new, flexible one. And this marking was most evident in the supervision of the cycle times during which each woman completed numerous tasks, supposedly without thinking, within a flexible production system combined with a mass production schedule.

We see this best through an examination of the kind of tasks these women performed during the twenty-two-second cycle time that controlled the rhythm of the COSMO production line and guaranteed a steady output of televisions. The following ergonomic description of position 29 on the line illustrates the extent to which one woman worker had to respond to model changes within the twenty-two-second cycle. For model A, this position is laid out as a series of left- and right-hand motions calculated to insert seven parts within twenty-two seconds:

1. Transport time 3.0 seconds
2. Right hand inserts part A 1.8 seconds
3. Left hand inserts part B 1.9 seconds
4. Right hand inserts part C 1.8 seconds
5. Left hand inserts part D 1.9 seconds
6. Right hand inserts part E 1.8 seconds
7. Left hand inserts part F and check[s] the polarity 2.2 seconds
8. Right hand inserts part G 0.9 seconds
9. Release the pedal (to move circuit board down the line) 2.0 seconds

Note: Do not grab more than five components at the same time.
Rest time: 4.0 seconds
Efficiency rate: 97 percent

For model B, this same position had to insert eleven parts, three of which were different from those in model A, so each motion was pared down to even fewer increments of time. For model C, the worker had to insert seven parts, two of which were not parts used in either model A or model B. In other words, a single worker in position 29 had to remember which parts pertained to which model, how to move her body according to the scripted design, and how to assess the work without slowing down. The calculations behind these movements are based on measurements of the amount of time consumed in the movement of a hand at a particular angle and speed from a state of rest and then back to rest. The engineering of this job relies on time-motion studies, traceable back to Frederick Winslow Taylor, which treat the human form as a series of levers and gears (Rabinbach 1990). One hand grabs a part, inserts it, and then returns to rest. The other does the same. These motions are controlled for their consumption of time by someone who is watching these motions and not by the individual who is actually moving these body parts and returning them to rest. "All possible brain work," wrote Taylor, "should be removed from the shop and centered in the planning or lay-out department" (quoted in Braverman 1974, 113).

This sort of ergonomic design reflects the logic of a system that does not develop skill or valuable experience in a worker since the worker is envisioned as an anonymous assemblage of disconnected parts that move in repetitive motions. Those parts of the body that are not detailed in the design of the work procedure effectively disappear from view as the worker becomes dismantled down to, as the former Chrysler chairman put it, "hands and arms and legs." For worker 29, her back, abdomen, head, and other anatomical features do not figure in the layout of her position. These parts along with the totality of her body vanish from the work design as she is distilled down to two arms and two hands, whose movements are monitored by the supervisor as factors of time. Moreover, as this ergonomic design reveals, the worker's own knowledge of her body is not only useless but also considered to be irrelevant or even dangerous to the work process, since if a worker chooses to move a wrist in such a way as not laid out in the engineering diagram, the entire procedure can be thrown off kilter. The engineering layout for position 29 does not include the possibility of consulting with the worker. It is an instruction outline for telling the worker how to move, regardless of what she feels. Miguel explained this perspective: "Assembly workers move to the clock. Our system depends on it." Such work, therefore, is nothing more than brute repetition as workers repeat the same actions, in the same increments of time, every twenty-two seconds in COSMO, even as they work on different models. The flexibility within the system does not change the repetitive motions that workers in circuitry and soldering endure throughout the day and that, as is well documented, lead to injury, boredom, and depression (Lin 1991; Gopwani 2002; "Repetitive Motion" 1996). The COSMO managers admit as much, even though they shied from answering questions about on-the-job injuries. "This isn't the kind of work you do for a long time," said Ruben. "It gets boring." Ed corroborated this viewpoint: "We want our assembly workers to stay for about two years. After that, they want to leave anyway. This isn't fun work. It's boring." He went on to explain, "That's why we have new recruits all of the time. When the older workers get tired, we replace them with new ones. It's very simple." COSMO had no classes for worker rehabilitation, injury management, or worker rotation into a variety of positions that would use different body parts over time as a way to stave off injury. The managerial attitude was that the women workers on the line would come and go on a regular basis such that the 30–50 percent turnover rate for workers on the female areas of the assembly line would be maintained. "I don't know what to do about turnover [in the female areas of the line]," said Ed; "it's just how it is here." As Ruben said, "None of these girls will be here in three years. That's how it is here." And in this way, the logic of disposability is alive and well even in the flexible facilities of contemporary manufacture, where it represents the rigid trajectory of women workers always losing the initial value for which they were employed.

Yet, the skilled work of flexible production is obviously being performed by these very same workers who are said to be lacking the ability to do so. They, as their managers proudly boast, build up to three different models of five hundred television units each day, every twenty-two seconds. Most are capable of performing the work in at least three different positions on the line. As, Miguel explained, "With the supervisors we have now, we expect the girls to know how to do three different jobs. That way we can move them around if we're short-handed on another line." However, he was clear that while these workers learned three different positions on the line, the work they performed was still repetitive motion work, requiring the use of their hands, arms, and eyes. They therefore contributed to the system's flexibility without experiencing flexible strategies for protecting their bodies from the wear and tear of repetitive work.

These untrainable women also diagnose problems on the line, a process that reflects evaluation and some training, both requiring some brainwork. In 1996, the production managers devised a program called "Mira a Tu Amiga" (Watch Your [female] Friend). The idea behind Mira a Tu Amiga is to catch problems in production before the units traveled all the way to the inspection areas on the line. This program reflects the flexible tenet of a labor force that, through on-the-job training, learns how to diagnose problems, suggest solutions, and self-supervise. So how, given the discourse of a rigid Mexican female untrainability, does this flexible work get done?

COSMO managers and supervisors describe how this apparent contradiction finds resolution in the development of a flexible masculine labor force that provides the pool for internal hires from the male areas of the assembly line into the technical and materials positions that, in turn, constitute the pool for the supervisor, the first level of salaried employment. In the maquilas, this level represents a move into the *gente de confianza*, the company's "in crowd." At COSMO, supervisors earned between US$800 and US$1,200 (depending upon the exchange rate from 1993 to 2001) and had paid vacation time, a pension plan, and other perks not available to the hourly labor force. To obtain this level was a measure of notable success for most of the men who managed to climb up from an entry-level position. Over the course of my research, only one woman had been promoted in COSMO into a supervisory level, a position she held for five years before leaving the company and moving to another employer. No other women were in the pool for internal promotions during the many years of my study.

Critical to this distinction between male and female labor pools is a discourse that produces their bodies as embodied sites of contrasting degrees of modernity. Particularly salient in the interviews is an emphasis on the different kinds of vision that male and female workers develop through their work experiences such that the former acquire an overview of the entire facility while the latter fail "to see" the larger picture. This emphasis on vision illustrates the significance of "vision" as a concept within models of western development that emphasize how the first world can help the third world develop visions for a modern future, based on observable, scientific phenomena (see Escobar 1994, 155). The importance of vision within the overall rubric of human and social development has, as Donna Haraway writes, elevated the status of the eyes as those features of the body "used to signify a perverse capacity—honed to perfection in the history of science tied to militarism, capitalism, colonialism and male supremacy" (1988, 581, quoted in Escobar 1994, 156). As the embodiment of vision, eyes signify the modern instruments through which science and rationality are based, since it is through "seeing" that we establish the factual evidence of reality. Ideas are held in the mind, but modern facts are widely believed to be "available to observation and interpretable as evidence of unseen, abstract laws or tendencies" (in Hannah 2000, 6). We must see to observe, and only through observation of what we take to be the factual basis of reality do we cultivate "vision."

In COSMO, we find this fetishization of vision and eyesight within managerial characterizations of female workers as so fundamentally *myopic* that they are regarded as effectively *blind* to all that goes on around them. In this context, the female body possesses an eyesight suitable only for the tedious tasks set immediately in front of the assembly worker. As I demonstrate in the next section, such discourses reproduce a working subject who is believed to be incapable of literally seeing beyond her limited work station. She cannot, therefore, develop a vision of the entire production process and is effectively cast as ignorant to the reality of the factory process. This same discourse, by contrast, hinges on the recreation of sexually distinct working subjects so that male workers emerge as those with functional eyes that can adjust to distance and, as a result, develop a vision of how they fit within the overall schema of production.

Yet, this discussion of differential embodiments that separate nonmodern (or premodern) women from modern men does not mean that women are excluded from the operation of sophisticated manufacturing operations. In fact, the supervisory dynamic so crucial to COSMO's flexible production rests upon the coupling of atavistic female with progressive male employees who, together, must coordinate their corporeal constitutions into a single, functioning entity. The imaginary anatomy of the supervisor, therefore, materializes in practice through a confluence of his and her parts, both understood as respectively flexibly trained and inflexibly untrainable, that merge into a unified embodiment of COSMO supervision.

Flexible Masculinity

About one quarter of the men who enter the COSMO workforce as operators are eventually promoted as long as they enter a track designated as "masculine" or "men's work," or work that is not the feminine work of circuitry insertion. Ruben explained, "We want good [male] workers from the technical schools. If they do good work in the first two months, then we move them up. Train them.... We have incentives for them." Indeed, the skilling programs at COSMO were continually described as almost a male rite of passage out of the feminized work of assembly. Miguel spelled out the masculinization of training this way: "We have two different kinds of workers here. The ones we can train and the ones we can't. The female workers are the ones we cannot train. So they do assembly. That's the women's work here because they are good with small work."

A new male worker's typical promotional trajectory began with an assembly position, such as the fastening of the picture tube or television case to the chassis. These positions are not located in the feminine area of circuitry insertion but in an area known as "men's work," since they do not involve the minutiae of the electronic assembly (see also Salzinger 2003). "We put men here," said Ernesto, pointing to the packaging area. "The men like to stand. Women don't like to stand." This notion that "standing" was a masculine action was common amongst the supervisors throughout the facility. One supervisor, Andres, explained, "The jobs like this one [he pointed to a man connecting a chassis to the plastic casing of the picture frame] are for men. They stand. They have to move the pieces around. Better for the men." His explanation hinged on the idea that standing signaled masculine positions as opposed to the sedentary feminine ones.

This designation of standing as a masculine trait fed directly into an internal system for tracking male employees into training programs and, eventually, into promotions. Standing was linked with vision, with the ability literally *to see* throughout the facility and, as a consequence, develop an overall understanding of the facility not possible from the position of electronic circuitry, where workers focused only on their particular jobs. "Here," said Ernesto, "they see everything. They see how we coordinate supplies and production. This helps them understand the production, how we put it all together." Five supervisors corroborated this belief that because they stood and could see across the production floor, the men in packaging represented a potential pool of trainable labor. Andres put it this way: "They know what that line over there is doing, and what their line is doing. They can see everything. This is important for our technicians. This is the first step." And, in fact, the majority of internal promotions out of entry-level positions were picked from this part of the assembly line. Although there were no statistics, Ernesto guessed that over half of the inspectors and materials handlers, a first-step promotion up from the assembly line, had initially started as packagers, all men who performed the *masculine* task of standing. From inspection and materials handling, both positions that entailed some light training, they would then be in line for a boost to technician. "The men are better technicians," said Ernesto. "Men understand the technical work [better than women]. It is really the men's work here." And male technicians composed the principal pool that managers used for internally selecting a supervisor, the first level of salaried work, with paid vacation and better benefits than the hourly positions. This entire journey from materials handler to supervisor, which constituted the principal route by which entry-level employees gained training and promotions, began with the designation of standing as a masculine trait that led to vision and then to the further masculine positions up the chain of command. The women in circuitry were, almost without exception, fully barred from entering this path since the feminine work for which they were suited was not, according to COSMO lore, conducive to cultivating the necessary initial skill of vision.

Over the course of four years, only two women at COSMO had joined the technical staff, but neither had been promoted to supervisor. "If you want to see flexibility in action," said Ruben, "just watch those guys on the floor. The technicians, the material handlers are all in training. We've got training seminars every month. The good ones will be our new supervisors." Of the more than one hundred supervisors in the multifactory COSMO complex, one was a woman, and she happened to work in the facility I studied. She had twenty-one years of experience in COSMO by 1997, more than any other employee in the plant, and had worked as a supervisor for five years. However, her vertical mobility from operator to supervisor was not to be seen as proof that Mexican women could also participate in the skilling and promotional programs. Ernesto explained, "I decided to promote her because she knows how to wear the pants [ella lleva los pantalones bién puestos]. She's not like the other girls here. She works like a man," by which he means that she is therefore appropriate for the masculine job of supervision.

I asked Ernesto, "If the women aren't your trained workers, then how do you develop a multiskilled labor force?" He answered, "We look for male workers who will want to learn new things. We need workers who are ambitious and want to improve themselves." And any male worker who failed to enter the masculine trajectory of skill was regarded as unsuitable for employment since men did not belong in the feminized area of unskilled labor. "The guys on the line who don't want to learn, we don't want them here," Pablo, a supervisor, told me. He continued, "They can't do the assembly like the girls. Their hands are too big for the circuits. They are naturally restless. We want them to do what they do best. And the guys like to learn technical work. That's what we need in supervision and in all of our management. We are a technologically driven factory." Ed said, "Most of our, ok, almost all of our supervisors are men. That's the gender breakdown here. Women in assembly and men in supervision. It's how it is in Mexico."

As Miguel put it, the notion that women on the line could not develop the vision necessary for their promotion was central to managerial approaches to training and promotion within the facility. "These girls don't see what's going on here [in the factory as a whole].

They just do their own work. That is it." Only the men develop the eyesight that underscores their ability to have the vision of supervision. But this discourse of vision and the embodiment of seeing that distinguishes male and female COSMO bodies does not create a division within the prosthetics of supervision. In fact, it consolidates the supervisory anatomy around an imaginary pair of masculine eyes, which through the masculine tasks of standing and, therefore, of seeing have channeled vision into a disembodied head that then attaches itself to a sightless, headless, female body. As Ernesto put it, "The supervisors need the girls and the girls need them.... They [the men] have seen the whole factory. They know what happens here. The girls do the work."

Flexible production, therefore, as the logic of supervision reveals, does not emerge at COSMO simply through the identification of masculinity in contrast to an untrainable femininity. It results, instead, from the merging of the inflexible feminine subject with the internally trained and promoted male supervisor so that together they cross the binaries that separate them into more and less flexible, more and less trainable, more and less valuable employees. This merging culminates in the creation of the prosthetic body of supervision, as envisioned at COSMO, through which a male head directs a female body as if a separate corporeal entity existed apart from the individual employees who contribute the constituent parts of this hermaphroditic creation. In this way, we find the prosthetic supervisory in action. It is not a synthetically stable entity where female and male meld into each other, nor are its components fully segregated by a barrier of sex difference. These male/female bits must join together, continually, throughout the working day. The differences are maintained—men do the thinking, and women do the assembling—but they are not autonomous since the thinking cannot be seen without the action that animates it. The flexible supervisor is never to have his identity confused with the women working under him, but he must reveal who he is through what she does. His training as a flexible and skilled supervisor can be seen only if she performs flexible and skilled actions. And her lack of flexibility and lack of skill also depend upon our clear recognition that her body does not respond to her own cerebral signals.

A COSMO Day—1998

6:00 a.m., Tuesday

Supervisors assemble for their daily meeting with their production manager a half hour before the line operators arrive and the first shift begins. They are apprised of problems from the last shift and hear about the defect rates from their line's previous day's performance. Each week, the supervisor whose line had the fewest defects for that week is posted on the public bulletin board, and the supervisor with the fewest defects in a month receives a pay bonus. But everyone's defect rates are announced in the morning meetings, and supervisors with consistently low ratings are publicly admonished and sometimes dismissed. Also at these meetings, supervisors receive a written copy of the day's projected scheduling, including the number of models to be produced and the estimated timeline, even though the production rate of five hundred units per line varies minimally. These projected model numbers are subject to change during the day.

All of the morning supervisors are men, and their de facto uniform consists of a tie and a stopwatch, which most wear on a string around their necks. The stopwatch is a recent addition since the early 1990s, when COSMO organized production with two supervisors per assembly line. But, by 1997, the company had streamlined and cut the supervisory staff by half, so that one supervisor was responsible for the entire line. The stopwatch was then added to the supervisor's toolkit as a way to monitor the twenty-two-second cycle time.

After their meeting, supervisors head to their respective lines on the production floor, where they look over the work left from the previous shift. Partially assembled televisions await their completion at various stages along the line. The supervisors inspect the supply bins to make sure that all material is ready, and they write the model number to be assembled on a board at the head of the assembly line so that workers know immediately which parts to use and how many tasks to perform within each twenty-two-second increment.

When the workers arrive from the buses and take their positions on the line, group leaders (all but a handful of whom are women) gather around the supervisor's desk (located between the circuitry and soldering divisions on the women's side of the line) and receive any special instructions, which they then communicate to the workers in their group. And then the line starts up, with parts and hands and television components moving in carefully choreographed actions.

The supervisors typically stay on the circuitry and soldering side of the line. The most complicated work is performed in this area, which is also where most of the mistakes are made. Since each worker is responsible for, on average, seven different tasks per twenty-two-second cycle, and since those tasks shift with each model, each operator must be able to perform three sets of seven different tasks, every twenty-two seconds, throughout the day. As mentioned above, the other positions on the line do not vary as drastically according to model. The testing and packaging are almost identical for each model, and while the tube attachment does change (different screws are used), this operation involves only two to four tasks. Supervisors, therefore, focus their attention on the high-risk area of the operation, where their own job performance hangs on the balance of defect rates and cycle times.

One supervisor, Ramón, explained, "I stand behind these girls all day. I see them do something wrong. I tell them. I have to watch them very carefully." Supervisors rely on their group leaders and on the Mira a Tu Amiga system to alert them to problems, but even still, they complain of how many mistakes the workers make. Ramón continued, "They make mistakes here. It's hard. They make a mistake, and they [the managers] blame me for it."

Supervisors are not the only ones watching. In fact, they are extremely aware that they are being watched throughout the day. Two floors above them in the managerial wing of the factory is a large window that looks out over the production area. Managers, engineers, visitors, clients, and other company executives are often seen looking down upon the production system. The effect is, as Leslie Salzinger (2003) has noted, to create the feeling of the ubiquitous visibility of a panoptican, where those being watched are keenly aware of their watchers, even when the latter are not present. It is the potential to be watched at all times that generates a certain anxiety of always being monitored, disciplined, and effectively produced as a "subject-to-be watched." Here we see how the panoptic gaze, as used by Michel Foucault (1995) to indicate the power of the one who sees over the one being seen, recreates a corporate hierarchy around the notion that while Mexican men have more vision than Mexican women, it is still a limited vision. The spatial organization of the facility in which managers occupy the second floor above the production personnel and can look down upon them from large windows illustrates the social status and control dominated by the U.S. and European personnel who hold those positions over the Mexican personnel, located on the floor below. The U.S. and European managers exercise in a facility where the Mexican personnel on the production floor are aware that they are always capable of being surveilled by their superiors who stand, unseen, beyond the upper-tier glass windows. The discourses that produce these variably sexed and ethnic bodies around the concept of differential degrees of vision thus reaffirm the significance of this concept as an apparatus of social control within a model of development that privileges those with total vision as more developed over those who cannot see as much or as far. And this privileging reifies a stubborn belief, still prevalent throughout the maquiladora industry, of Mexicans, in general, as less visionary and, consequently, less modern than the U.S. and European administrators of their employers. Ed summed up this sentiment when he said, "Mexicans are immature. The men live with their families until they are twenty-five, thirty, sometimes older. That's just it. They aren't as mature as we are. That's the reality."

The visual monitoring is not the only kind of watching that the supervisors experience as part of the logic that reproduces them as "immature" or not fully "developed." Everything on the line is also monitored by the company's computers that constantly calculate production rate and quality, and that provide the information used by the production managers to evaluate the supervisors' job performance. Most of the supervisors I interviewed mentioned this constant surveillance of them as part of the stress of their job. Carlos, a supervisor, described the tension he feels: "They watch you all the time here. It makes you think about it [being watched] all the time. It makes my job harder because I am thinking about them [the managers] when I should think about the work." Javier, another supervisor, put it this way: "They know everything you do here. That's how they keep the pressure on us. Something goes wrong, and they know before you do."

Indeed, the perception of scrutiny sensed by the supervisors corresponded to the emphasis that the production managers placed on supervisory performance. All of the attention to evaluating supervisors' performance in terms of defect rates and compliance with cycle times reflected the pressure placed on the production managers to guarantee specified production results that would help the company's overall performance indicators. Miguel said, "We get pressure from the top, and we put pressure on the supervisors…. It's all about competition. We mess up here, our jobs go to China." And in 1998, the risk of losing their jobs to Chinese facilities was described as a real possibility by the general manager. "If we don't keep up production, keep defects low, these doors will close and all of this will be in China."

So keeping defects low, without slowing down production, was the supervisor's daily priority, but this job was complicated by the fact that they were to accomplish this feat while working with a labor force that was treated as and expected to be disposable. Ramón explained, "Every year the work gets harder. More things to do, less time. More pressure. But the girls still are the same. No training."

A number of supervisors complained that they had to work with an untrained labor force to accomplish work that required not only basic but also continual training. Pablo well summarized these sentiments when he said, "Everyday, we have new girls to train. But we don't have the time. The schedule stays the same, even if you [have] all new workers. It's very hard for us.... I have new workers every week."

With the turnover rate ranging from 30 to 50 percent for the circuitry and soldering part of the line for much of the year, supervisors often had to integrate two or three new workers every week. Even though these workers were given some assistance by the group leaders to come up to speed and learn their jobs, they received no formal training before they began the assembly process. Some of them had never worked in a factory before and were unaccustomed to the rigors of an ergonomic system that dictated the most intricate motions of their wrists, hands, backs, and other body parts, according to a tight schedule of twenty-two-second increments. "Some girls don't know how to work like this," said Pablo. "There is a lot of pressure."

Besides the obvious difficulty of having to incorporate new workers continually into a production system that does not recognize the need to train this labor force, supervisors are not allowed to perform the work themselves on the line. To do so represents a failure on their part to incorporate their trained knowledge of the system into the untrained bodies of their operators. Javier explained, "If I do something [he pointed to the soldering worker], [like] make that solder, then my manager says, 'He can't do his job.' That's her job. My job is to make sure she does it the right way." Ramón said, "They don't like us to do the work, not even to train them."

This prohibition against the supervisor's actual performance of circuitry insertion or soldering reflects the limited bounds placed on the supervisor's own body, which is further reinforced by a gendering of the division separating the supervisor from the supervised. Pablo made this clear in his explanation of why managers do not like supervisors to do the work: "They say our hands are too big. We make more mistakes than the girls." Miguel elaborated further, "That is girls' work [circuitry and soldering]. We don't pay our supervisors to do that work." Ramón said it well: "My job is technical. It's what the men do here. And this [pointing to a circuit board operator] is for the girls."

Supervisors, therefore, not only encounter a prohibition against using their own bodies to perform work on the line, even as a means for training, on the basis that they are not skilled enough to teach their workers how to do so. They also face a gendered divide that excludes the use of their own bodies on the basis that to do so would violate the segregation of male and female subjectivities and the work associated with them in the factory.

Nevertheless, given the pressure that supervisors feel on a daily basis to make sure that the work is performed up to speed and without defects, they do not always have the option of not using their own hands, wrists, and arms to complete a task or to correct a mistake. But they do so surreptitiously. Ramón explained, "I know when the managers leave for lunch, and then I finish the work when workers are at lunch.... We all do that [sneak around to finish the work without the managers seeing them]." Pablo said he sometimes would pull circuit boards off the line if he knew that a worker was making mistakes. And he would make corrections when the managers were at lunch. They did not want to be caught doing "girls'" work since to do so would compromise not just their skill as supervisors but their standing as men. Pablo expressed this feeling: "It is an embarrassment to be seen doing the girls' work. I am a technician," in a place where that means he is a man.

Since supervisors are by and large hesitant to touch the material, such as circuits and tools—given that to do so indicates their inability to do their own jobs and questions their own masculinity—they instead manipulate workers' bodies, sometimes physically and sometimes with verbal instructions. And their stopwatches help them do so.

For instance, a common sight is to see a supervisor standing behind a worker while timing her every movement in order to keep her in accordance with the cycle time. One day, I watched Javier dedicate half an hour to timing and changing how a new worker moved her arms from the supply bins overhead to the assembly line. "No, like this," he demanded, as he moved her arm in a straight line from bin to table and back again. The whole exercise resembled a physical therapy session, something meant to train her how to move her body in a more acceptable fashion. These interactions often revealed the frustration felt by supervisors who expressed resentment over their vulnerability to workers' job performance for their own evaluations. Ramón explained, "She does this wrong [he pointed to a solderer], and they [his bosses] blame me."

And in such a statement, we encounter the paradox built into the supervisory dynamic that the supervisors, ultimately, must resolve everyday. Their workers, who are regarded as untrainable and, as such, disposable, are not regarded as "worth training" in a production process that requires that their untrainable bodies yield trained work. This training is said to belong to the supervisor. So when the untrained body does not perform skilled work, the supervisor is reprimanded for his lack of skill. The disposable body of the female operator constitutes the site for evaluating his value as a skilled employee, and the basis upon which he competes for his job against his peers.

Thus, the hermaphrodite of supervision that comes together with his and her parts reveals the disassembling and reassembling of the male supervisor and female operator such that neither represents a complete subject in and of themselves. The operators do not have the brains to author the skill that their bodies perform, and the supervisors lack the body to demonstrate their skilled training. Only together do they form a total being in the COSMO division of labor. As such, the disposability of the female labor force remains discursively intact and implemented in the production process as a reflection of fact, as does the discourse, so well articulated by the human resources manager, Ed, of lesser developed Mexicans compared to more fully developed U.S.-Americans and Europeans. The prosthetics of supervision manufactures the bodies of Mexican women and men in a way that protects the value cultivated from the wasting of women workers while also protecting the justification of capitalist expansion as evidence of the need in the third world for more western development.

Circulation

The point of COSMO's strategy, however, is not merely to assemble this supervisory dynamic for its own sake. It is, like all manufactured commodities within the capitalist circuit, a means to many other ends, which are themselves means to further ends, as the intersecting streams of production, consumption, and exchange never cease to flow. COSMO managers are clear about their administrative objectives for their facility. They need to keep costs down while improving quality. And they must do so in order to demonstrate their competitive advantage against facilities in southern China and in the United States, against whom they compete for corporate resources and also for client contracts. The prosthetic supervisor is one strategy for accomplishing this goal in two key areas. It effectively preserves the disposable status of the bulk of the labor force, the young Mexican women, who cycle into and out of their jobs within a limited period of time. In denying these women the credit for the skilled work that they perform, this supervisory dynamic also justifies denying them training, promotional opportunities, and rehabilitation for on-the-job injuries, such as repetitive stress. In this way, the supervisory strategy contributes to the widening of the gap between the value of the women workers, which is always declining over time, and the value of these workers' labor, which, as it reflects enhanced degrees of quality, is constantly increasing over time. The formula for expanding profit, as derived from the expenditure of variable capital, is therefore followed like law.

Moreover, this same supervisory approach expands the variation between a supervisor's worth and the value of that employee's labor by confining the Mexican male supervisor to a partial body that underscores a vision of this employee as an incomplete subject. Since the prosthetic arrangement that limits the Mexican supervisor to a disembodied head justifies assertions that Mexican employees, at all levels, are not as "developed" as their U.S. or European counterparts in the firm, it also justifies paying the Mexican personnel at a lesser rate, for they are lesser people. This prosthetic body of supervision is consequently a tool for widening the gap between the supervisor's worth and the worth of this supervisor's labor in a system that relies so powerfully on the supervisor's ability to preserve female workers' disposability while guaranteeing the exercise of quality labor.

Meanwhile, the televisions that roll off the COSMO line also embody the enhanced value that the firm cultivates by expanding the variation between Mexican employees' worth and the worth of their labor. COSMO televisions incorporate this differential and reflect the flexibility of the system in their different designs; they illustrate the streamlined efficiency of the production process in their retail-ready packaging and manufacturing guarantees; and they indicate, in their mass volume, that even though COSMO is flexible, it is able to keep pace with constant demand in the U.S. market for multiple television sets at affordable prices. The prosthetics of supervision is the nexus where mass production meets flexible production in the labor process and within the odd laboring bodies of contemporary capitalism.

4

The Dialectics of Still Life

Murder, Women, and Disposability

Ambiguity is the pictorial image of dialectics, the law of dialectics seen at a standstill. This standstill is utopia and the dialectical image therefore a dream image. Such an image is presented by the pure commodity: as fetish. Such an image are the arcades, which are both house and stars. Such an image is the prostitute, who is saleswoman and wares in one.

Walter Benjamin, *Reflections*

In 1999, when I first published the essay that constitutes this chapter, a crime wave against women in Ciudad Juárez, Chihuahua, was just gaining international attention. At that time, more than a hundred women and girls had been murdered, many of them tortured and discarded in the city's marginal areas, since 1993. There is evidence, however, that this violence and dumping of female bodies in the desert began years earlier (Monárrez 2005). At the time of this writing in 2006, that number has increased at least twofold, and hundreds of other women and girls are missing. I have chosen to reprint this essay in its original version rather than to revise it to account for events that have occurred in the last several years. I provide a more updated version in chapter 7 of the events surrounding the crimes and the social movement that has grown as a protest to the violence against women in northern Mexico.

In this chapter, however, I keep my focus on the connections linking a discourse of third world female disposability to the forces that treat women as if they were real instances of disposable humanity. Here I make these connections between the internal dynamics of factory production and the urban violence that has, over the last twenty years, transformed Ciudad Juárez into one of the most violent cities, especially for women, in the Western Hemisphere. In doing so, I revisit some of the themes discussed in previous chapters, particularly with regard to the discourses of an essential feminine condition and the high labor turnover that derives from it, and relate them to events occurring beyond the factory walls. My intent is to illustrate how the myth of a disposable third world woman worker travels outside of the global factory system and interacts, often in extremely cruel ways, with other stories that degrade women, especially those who work for low wages around the world. Perhaps, my biggest hope for this chapter is to dispel any doubt regarding the innocence of the myth of the disposable third world woman and to set the scene for the following chapters, in which I discuss how many people expose the tale for what it is and fight against its many dangers.

In this chapter, I shall use Walter Benjamin's notion of a dialectical image to examine the figure of the Mexican woman worker formed within the narrative of her general disposability.[1] The dialectical image is one whose apparent stillness obscures the tensions that actually hold it in suspension. It is a caesura forged by clashing forces. With this dialectical image in mind, I see the Mexican woman depicted in the murder narratives as a life stilled by the discord of value pitted against waste. I focus on the narrative image of her, rather than on the lives of the murder victims, to reveal the intimate connection binding these stilled lives to the reproduction of value in the maquiladoras located in Ciudad Juárez. Through a comparison of a maquiladora narrative of categorical disavowal of responsibility for the violence with another maquila narrative explaining the mundane problem of labor turnover, the Mexican woman freezes as a subject stilled by the tensions linking the two tales.

In the tale of turnover that is told by maquila administrators, the Mexican woman takes shape in the model of variable capital whose worth fluctuates from a status of value to one of waste. "Variable capital" refers to the labor power—what the worker provides in exchange for wages—that produces a value in excess to itself (see Harvey 1982). The excess coalesces into surplus value. Marx says that labor power is a form of variable capital since it is worth less than the value of what it produces. In the turnover story, the value of the Mexican woman's labor power declines over time even as her labor provides value to the firm. Furthermore, this deterioration produces its own kind of value as she furnishes a necessary flow of temporary labor. Her labor power is subsequently worth less than the value of her labor in a number of ways, given that her labor is valuable also for its inevitable absence from the labor process. Where the maquila spokespeople deny any similarity between the women described in the tale of turnover and those described in the stories absolving the maquilas of any responsibility in their murders, I endeavor here to locate the connections.[2]

"Turnover" refers to the coming and going of workers into and out of jobs, and it often comes up during interviews in relation to the problem of worker unreliability. Industry analysts and administrators cite turnover as an impediment to a complete transformation of the maquila sector from a low-skilled and labor-intensive industry to one with more sophisticated procedures staffed by highly skilled workers (see Villalobos, Beruvides, and Hutchinson 1997). Workers who turn over, that is, who do not demonstrate job loyalty, are not good prospects for the training necessary for creating a skilled base. This form of variable capital is therefore the temporary kind. However, the turnover problem has not completely inhibited the development of a higher technological base in the maquilas since some workers are not of the turnover variety. Training programs, combined with an emphasis on inculcating loyalty among workers, have created a two-tiered system within maquila firms for distinguishing between the "untrainable" and "trainable" workers. Gender is a critical marker for differentiating between these worker brands.

Benjamin provides a good point of departure for this feminist interrogation into one of Marx's staple concerns: the dehumanizing process behind forming variable capital, which, he writes, "converts the worker into a crippled monstrosity" (Marx 1977, 481). Through the image of dialectical stillness, Benjamin helps explain how this process involves the creation of not only value at the worker's expense but also a value that is valorized only insofar as it is counterposed to what it is not: waste. The kinship between discourse and materiality is key. In the maquilas, managers depict women as untrainable laborers; Mexican women represent the workers of declining value since their intrinsic value never appreciates into skill but instead dissipates over time. Their value is used up, not enhanced. Consequently, the Mexican woman personifies waste-in-the-making, as the materials of her body gain shape through the discourses that explain how she is untrainable, unskillable, and always a temporary worker.[3]

Meanwhile, her antithesis—the masculine subject—emerges as the emblem of that other kind of variable capital whose value appreciates over time. He is the trainable and potentially skilled employee who will support the high-tech transformation of the maquila sector into the twenty-first century. He maintains his value as he changes and develops in a variety of ways. She, however, is stuck in the endless loop of her decline. Her life is stilled as her departure from the workplace represents the corporate death that results logically from her demise, since at some point the accumulation of the waste within her will offset the value of her labor. And after she leaves one factory, she typically enters another and begins anew the debilitating journey of labor turnover.

The wasting of the Mexican woman, therefore, represents a value in and of itself to capital in at least two respects. First, she establishes the standard for recognizing the production of value in people and in things: value appreciates in what she is not. Second, she incorporates flexibility into the labor supply through her turnover. To use Judith Butler's formulation, this process reveals how discourses of the subject are not confined to the nonmaterial realm or easily shunted off as the "merely cultural" (Butler 1997a). Rather, and as I endeavor to show here, the managerial discourses of noninvolvement in the serial murders of young female employees are indeed linked to the materialization of turnover as a culturally driven and waste-ridden phenomenon attached to Mexican femininity. The link is the value that the wasting of the Mexican woman—through both her literal and her corporate deaths—represents for those invested in the discourse of her as a cultural victim immune to any intervention.

In what follows, I begin by describing some of the stories commonly told to provide explanation for the murders. I then present an analysis of the turnover narratives.

The Murder Stories

Circulating through the media and by word of mouth—as onlookers try to determine if the murder victims were prostitutes, dutiful daughters, dedicated mothers, women leading "double lives," or responsible workers—is the question "Was she a good girl?" The question points to the matter of her value as we wonder if she is really worthy of our concern.

When news of these murders first captured public attention in 1995, Francisco Barrio, then governor of the state of Chihuahua, raised this question when he advised parents to know where their daughters were at all times, especially at night. The implication was that "good girls" do not go out at night, and since most of these victims disappeared in the dark, they probably were not good girls. The local police have regularly posed this issue when bereaved parties seek official assistance in locating their daughters, sisters, mothers, cousins, and family friends. The police frequently explain how common it is for women to lead "double lives" and ask the grieving and frightened family and friends to consider this possibility (Limas Hernández 1998). By day, she might appear the dutiful daughter, wife, mother, sister, and laborer, but by night she reveals her inner prostitute, slut, and barmaid. In other words, she might not be worth the worry.

Related to this story of excessive female heterosexuality is a "foreign serial killer" plot woven by the special prosecutor appointed to the case. In this tale, we hear of how these murders are far too brutal for a Mexican hand and resemble events more common to the country's northern neighbor. The idea here is that a suave foreigner appeals to a young woman's yen for sexual adventure, lures her into his car, and then murders her after having sex. On this theory, an Egyptian with U.S. resident status working in the maquiladora industry was arrested in 1996, but since then another hundred bodies have surfaced.

This version ties into the long-standing Mexican tradition of casting Ciudad Juárez as a city whose cultural values have been contaminated by greedy and liberal forces emanating from the United States (Tabuenca Córdoba 1995–1996). Such was the narrative woven by a Spanish criminologist, José Parra Molina, contracted by Mexican officials in 1998 to examine the crimes. He surmised that Ciudad Juárez was experiencing a "social shock" due to an erosion of its "traditional values" resulting from contact with a "liberal" American society. Consequently, he concluded, you now "see in the maquiladora exits . . . the women workers seeking adventure without paying attention to the danger" (Orquiz 1998, 3C).[4] The logic internal to this narrative explains that exposure to the United States has eroded traditional Mexican values to such a degree that young women are offering themselves, through their impudent behavior, to their murderers. This criminologist, among others, suggested that these women and girls could also be walking into traps set by an international organ-harvesting ring that kills the victims for their organs, which are sold in the U.S. market. The problem here, according to this story, is a cultural one. In such a cultural climate, such murders are bound to happen, and thus, a cultural shift is required to "sanitize" the environment in which women along the border live and work. The cultural decline is found within the girls themselves: as the Spanish criminologist asked in reference to the discovery of a girl's body, "What was a thirteen-year-old girl doing out at night anyway?" The fact that she is commuting does not seem sufficient proof for such experts to conclude that she is out at night due to her economic need in a city full of nighttime commuters. Rather, her presence in the night points toward a cultural decline within which her death, a form of absence, can be logically anticipated. Indeed, her absence ameliorates, to some degree, the cultural decline represented by her presence in the night since it takes her off the street for good. Her death is explained as a cultural corrective against the decimation of traditional values. As the Spanish criminologist said, these girls out at night are "like putting a caramel in the door of an elementary school." When somebody gobbles them up, like children with sweets, at least the source of the tawdry temptation is destroyed.

I characterize this rendition as a "death by culture" narrative, which points to forces internal to a cultural system that are driving the deviant behavior. Death by culture is Uma Narayan's (1997) characterization of the global discourses for explaining women's death in the third world as somehow embedded in tradition, internally driven, and resulting from the distortion of "traditional" cultural values. The above murder narratives recreate the possibility that these women and girls are not only victims of a culture gone out of whack but also emblems of the loss of values. They represent cultural value in decline and in consequence are possibly not valuable enough in death to warrant much concern. When we find girls and women out on the streets at night, seeking adventure, dancing in clubs, and free from parental vigilance, we find evidence of diminished value in their wasted innocence, their wasted loyalty, and their wasted virginity. The logical conclusion is, therefore, not to seek the perpetrators of the crime as much as to restore the cultural values whose erosion these women and girls represent.

A number of *Juarense* activists and local women's groups have countered these murder narratives with a version of the victims as hardworking and poor members of the community who deserve more public attention than they are receiving. Through editorial writing and public appearances, they warn that a "climate of violence against women" pervades the city. They identify male jealousy of wives'/girl-friends' economic independence and sexual and social liberty as motivating factors behind the crimes as well as behind police reluctance to treat the murders seriously. And they have met with the principal maquiladora trade association (Maquiladora Association, or AMAC) in the city to ask for assistance in curbing the violence. During such meetings, the message has been repeated that, even though thousands of workers have to cross unlit, unpatrolled, and remote stretches of desert as they make their way to the buses that stop only on main thoroughfares, and even as many victims disappear while on such commutes, there is nothing that the industry can do to stop the violence (Author interview with activist Esther Chávez in 1998). Rather, the industry's stance is that no degree of funding for security personnel, or outlays for improved streetlighting, or in-house self-defense workshops, or changes to production schedules will help.

This position has not changed noticeably even in light of more obvious connections linking maquiladora industrial activity with the murders. For instance, in March 1999, when the driver of a maquiladora bus raped, beat, and left to die in the desert a thirteen-year-old girl employed in a maquiladora with an American parent company (she miraculously recovered and named her attacker), activists implored the maquiladoras to acknowledge some connection between the murders and the city's industrial activity. One activist, Esther Chávez Cano, who is also the director of the city's new rape crisis center, said, "This case is absolutely horrible. The maquilas should have as much trust in the bus drivers as they have in the managers. This is an example of how terrible things are in this city" (Stack and Valdez 1999). The maquiladoras have yet to respond to this indictment, and their position appears to be much the same as it was when the spokesperson for AMAC was interviewed in January 1999 by ABC.[5] He cited female sexuality and nighttime behavior as the principal issues. In making this point, he queried, "Where were these young ladies where they were seen last? Were they drinking? Were they partying? Were they on a dark street? Or were they in front of their plant when they went home?" The silent corollary to this statement is the understanding that "Men will be men," especially macho men, and if a woman is out drinking or partying or dancing on Juárez Avenida, then she should be prepared for the risks.

The AMAC spokesperson is invoking a death by culture narrative to absolve the maquiladora industry of any implication in the violence. The maquila narrative depicts the murdered women as cultural victims of machismo combined with third world female sexual drives and rural migrant naïveté. It gains purchase with the city's long-standing reputation as a cultural wasteland, where American contamination and loose women have led to moral decay (Sklair 1993; Tabuenca Córdoba 1995–1996). And in such a cultural milieu, the murdering of women cannot be avoided. Their deaths are only symptoms of a wasting process that began before the violent snuffing out of their lives. All of the sorting through of the victims' lives illustrates the deep, cultural roots of waste; for as we scrutinize the victims' sexual habits and sift through the skeletal and clothing remains, we are supposed to wonder all the while, "What *was* she doing there anyway?" "What sort of culture devours its own?"

My interest lies in the similarities linking this death by culture narrative with descriptions of labor turnover. In the story of turnover, the Mexican woman also plays a leading role. She is the culprit of extreme turnover as well as the reason why some measure of turn-over is necessary for profit. She emerges in this story as a dialectic image built of both waste and value. Her odd configuration has roots in the cultural construction of female sexuality, motherhood, and a fleeting work ethic. It also has roots in the physiognomy of the Mexican female form—in her nimble fingers and sharp eyes that eventually, and always eventually, stiffen and lose their focus. The manager of any maquila faces the challenge of having to monitor this wasting process, which, again, according to the turnover narrative, is a culturally driven cycle whose deleterious effects on women's working lives are inevitable. The maquila industry is helpless to divert this culturally driven, corporate death.

Turnover and Corporate Death

To understand how in the maquiladora context the story of turnover produces a female Mexican subject around a continuum of declining value, we must examine it in relation to the value-enhancing process of training. While "turnover" refers to the coming and going of workers, "training" refers to the cultivation of worker longevity and firm loyalty. Both processes unfold through the materialization of their corresponding subjects: a temporary, unskilled labor force and trained, loyal employees, respectively. Trained workers are those whose intrinsic value has matured and developed into a more valuable substance, whereas temporary workers do not develop or transform over time. They simply leave when their value is spent.

Seeing turnover and training in this light adds another dimension to Marx's analysis of variable capital. The value of labor power varies not only because it produces value, as Marx urges us to consider: labor power varies also because it produces waste. The laborer who is worth less than her labor is, in the story of turnover, eventually worthless even as she creates value. The trained subject, by contrast, is one whose intrinsic value increases over time and matures into a more valuable form of labor power, one that is skilled. As one American manager of a U.S. automobile manufacturer in Mexico put it, "Our goal is to take someone who just walked in the door and turn this person into a different kind of worker. Someone whose basic abilities have matured into something special." Skilled labor power does not vary from the value that it produces to the extreme degree that unskilled labor does. Of course, there is some variation; otherwise, profit would not be produced. At issue here is not the precise calculation of the dollar amount of profit that skilled labor creates but instead a sense that the more valuable the labor that goes into the production process, the more valuable the commodities emerging from

it. The German general manager of a hi-fi sound systems manufacturer explained the situation to me this way: "To make quality goods,
you need quality workers. . . . We still need some unskilled workers.
Some of this work is still just assembly. But now we've got products
that require people who are willing to learn something new."

Marx begins his analysis of capital with the commodity precisely
to demonstrate that the things of capital cannot be understood without seeing their intimate relationship to the people who make them.
He, too, was extremely concerned with subjectivity even though he
overdetermined the parameters for considering what sorts of subjects
mattered in his analysis. My view of skill, as a negotiated quality of
value assigned to labor power, takes its cues from feminist analyses
of the valorization of workers and work and the formation of skill
categories. Feminist scholars have demonstrated that we must consider how perceptions of the subject inform perceptions of the value
promised by that subject's labor power and how skill is key for the
differential valorization of the labor force (McDowell 1997; Cockburn 1985; Elson and Pearson 1981). This feminist contribution does
not replace a Marxian analysis but rather, as I hope becomes clear in
the following, reveals how poststructuralist theorizations of subjectivity are not necessarily at odds with a Marxian critique of capital
(see Joseph 1998). Critical for Marx is an exploration of how value
materializes as it does in capital, as we continually make abstract connections linking human energies with inanimate objects. Marx made
this point clearly, but he failed to recognize how the many forms
of labor abstraction that are categorized variably as degrees of skill
complicate the relationship linking the value perceived in laborers to
the value perceived to be embodied in the commodities they make.

Events over the last decade reveal how maquiladora boosters
and managers recognize the tight connection between perceptions
of worker quality and recognition of the sorts of products workers
can make. There are some three thousand maquiladora facilities in
Mexico, with a total employment of more than 1 million workers.
Almost one fourth of these workers are employed in maquiladoras
located in Ciudad Juárez, and approximately 60 percent of these
employees are women. Since the late 1980s, efforts to "skill up" the
maquiladora labor force in the maquila industry have coincided with
a concerted push by city developers and industry spokespeople to
stress the labor market's ability to accommodate the global focus on
product quality over quantity (Carrillo 1990). Industry proponents,
mindful of the heightened competition for foreign direct investment
by Asian countries guaranteeing even lower minimum wage rates for
an immense labor supply, have emphasized that the city offers not

only vast amounts of unskilled labor but also a sizable labor force that is trainable in just-in-time organizational systems, computer technologies, and even research and design capabilities. "Our workers can do anything here with some training, make the best products in the world," the director of a Juárez development firm told me. Rarely is the claim made that this labor force *already* exists in the city. Instead, emphasis rests on the *potential* transformation of the existing labor market into one that will one day be brimming with skilled workers. In 1994, the administrator at one of the largest and most prestigious maquiladora development consultant firms explained the potential this way: "We know that if Juárez is going to prosper into the future, we have to adapt. And we already are. You don't find sweatshops opening here like before. Now we have high-technology companies, and they are looking for workers who can be trained. We are having more of these workers now, and they will help this city grow in the right direction." One highly lauded example of this sort of growth has been the General Motors Delphi Center, which opened its doors in 1995. In "Brain School," a 1997 article in *Twin Plant News*, the principal industry journal, the-then director of Chihuahua's Economic Development Office exclaimed, "The Delphi center will revolutionize industrial production in our area." His view was seconded by a maquila manager who explained, "Without a doubt the most significant change has been the high technology manufacturing. . . . It just proves how the Mexican worker has been able to assimilate the ways of American business" ("Staff Report: Brain School" 1997, 39).

Sorting subjects into trainable and untrainable groups, then, is a first step toward upgrading that minority of the maquila labor force that will eventually assimilate to the demands of a dynamic global economy. Discerning between the trainable and the untrainable—the "quitters" and the "continuers" (Lucker and Alvarez 1985)—requires an evaluation of employees early in their careers in order to put them on the right track, either the unskilled or the skilled one. The Brazilian manager of a factory that manufactures automobile radios explained, "We can tell within one week if the operator is training material. It's obvious from the beginning." The principal marker of the untrainable subject is femininity. As feminist histories of industrialization have noted, the notion of women's untrainability has a genealogy that reaches far beyond the maquila industry (Fernandez-Kelly 1983). The specificities of this untrainable condition vary depending upon how the relations of gender unfold within the matrices of other hierarchical relations found within the workplace: the family, heterosexuality, race, and age, to name but a few. In the maquilas, the discourse of female untrainability plays out through explanations that describe what women do well as "natural" (dexterity, and so forth) and that explain the cultural constitution of Mexican femininity as adverse to training. "Most of the girls aren't interested in training. They aren't ambitious," the same manager of the automobile radio manufacturer told me. "I have tried to get these women interested in training," the American manager of an automobile firm explained, "but they don't want it. They get nervous if they think they will have to be someone else's boss. It's a cultural thing down here. And if they're not ambitious, we can't train them."

This culturally ingrained lack of ambition, nervousness with responsibility, and flagging job loyalty create the profile of an employee whose untrainable position cannot be shifted through training. When I asked the human resources manager of a television manufacturer how he could recognize those workers who were involved in in-house training programs, he said, "Well, most of the workers in the chassis assembly [all are women] aren't taking training. They're not as interested. Most of our trained workers come from the technical and materials handling [completely male-staffed] areas." The gendering of work positions in this particular firm, as in many others, also revealed a gendering of trainability and the skilling-up of the maquila labor force. There are no statistics calculating the percentage of women participating in the multitude of training programs offered throughout the city in addition to in-house training opportunities. However, my interviews with the managers of seven "high-tech" maquilas and with instructors who offer maquila training programs indicated that women represented fewer than 5 percent of those enrolled in any type of skills training. The rate of female promotion into positions defined as skilled in three high-tech firms was less than that.

As a result, Mexican women are said to be principal contributors to turnover because untrainable workers are those who demonstrate the lowest degree of longevity on the job. "If you have a plant full of these girls," the Mexican general manager of a sewing operation explained, "then you're gonna have high turnover. And you can't train workers in that kind of environment." While the trade journal literature rarely mentions gender as a variable in any maquiladora-related phenomena, managers are quick to mention sex difference as a key component of their "turnover problem." The Brazilian plant manager of a television manufacturer elaborated on this connection. "We have about 70 percent females here. That means high turnover. Sometimes 20 percent a month. Now the guys also sometimes leave but if they get into a technical position. . . . They usually stay longer.

Our turnover is high because we have so many girls." The American human resources manager of this same firm said, "You can't train workers if they won't stay around. That's the problem with these girls. You can't train them. They don't understand the meaning of job loyalty." The tautology described in this turnover narrative revolves around the following syllogism: women are not trainable. Trained workers remain with the same firm longer than untrained ones. Therefore, women do not have any corporate loyalty.

Minimized, if not completely missing, from this narrative and from the many articles dedicated to the "turnover problem" in the industry literature (see Beruvides, Villalobos, and Hutchinson 1997; Villalobos, Beruvides, and Hutchinson 1997) is a consideration of how the pigeonholing of women into the lowest waged and dead-end jobs throughout the maquilas contributes to their high turnover rate. Instead, within the maquila narrative of female unreliability we hear how her intrinsically untrainable condition cannot be altered through training. There is no remedy for her situation, at least none that the maquila industry can concoct. Even though trade journal articles abound that make the connection between training and enhancing worker loyalty, these lessons do not apply to her. Meanwhile, Mexican men who are relative newcomers to the industry are the ones climbing the ranks into skilled and higher salaried positions, while Mexican women remain where they have been for over three decades, in the positions of least skill, least pay, and least authority. In fact, as I discuss in the previous chapter, press and academic accounts of the skilling-up of the maquila labor force and renovation of the industry reveal the masculine image of the new maquilas' trained and trainable subject (see also Wright 2001). Things are changing in the maquilas, we know, not because women are changing but because Mexican men are. They have added a masculine and trainable dimension to the formerly only unskilled, feminine labor force. As the American human resources manager of a television manufacturer put it, "The men are more involved in the new technologies here. They are changing the industry." The women, meanwhile, in their status as "untrainable" employees, represent what does not change about the maquilas.

However, it is critical to bear in mind that the untrainable Mexican woman is not completely worthless to the firm, for if she were, she would not continue to be the most sought after employee in the maquiladora industry. Local radio stations frequently air advertisements promising good jobs, the best benefits, and a fun social atmosphere for young women seeking employment. Some maquilas contract agencies to recruit women throughout the city's scattered neighborhoods and migrant squatter settlements. These agencies generally seek female employees and are often expected to recruit one hundred women for a particular firm in a single day. As an employee of one such agency explained in an interview with a local newspaper in July 1998, "The agency offers jobs to both sexes, masculine and feminine, but for the moment, they are looking only for women to work in the second shift" (Guzmán 1998, 5).

Women are so explicitly desired for a number of reasons. Discourses that detail a blend of natural qualities combined with cultural proclivities establish the Mexican woman as one of the most sought after industrial employees in the Western Hemisphere. For one thing, as throughout industrial history, Mexican women are still coveted for what are constructed to be the feminine qualities of dexterity, attention to detail, and patience with tedious work (Elson and Pearson 1989). They are, therefore, perfectly suited for the repetitious tasks of minutiae that still constitute much of contemporary manufacturing and information processing. Adding to the attractiveness of their supposedly natural abilities is the widespread perception of their cultural predisposition to docility and submissiveness to patriarchal figures. These discourses outline a figure who is not only aptly designed for assembly, sewing, and data entry but also, unlike her northern counterparts, seen to be thankful for the work, unlikely to cause trouble, and easily cowed by male figures should thoughts of unionization cross her mind. Discourses of this sort explain, in part, why since the passage of NAFTA maquilas have been setting up operations at an unprecedented pace and have continued to employ more women than men across the industry, even as they emphasize trainability.

Another property underlying her popularity among maquiladora executives is the inevitability of her turnover. Her lack of corporate loyalty is, in the proper proportion, a valuable commodity since her tendency to move into and out of factory complexes reinforces her position as the temporary worker in a corporate climate that responds to a fickle global market. This need is well explained in a 1998 *Wall Street Journal* article about the General Motors Delphi operation: "Delphi says it relies on rapid turnover in border plants to allow it to cut employment in lean times and add workers in boom times" (Simison and White 1998). Part of what is so valuable about the Mexican woman is the promise that she will not stick around for the long haul. Her absence represents for the firm the value that flexibility affords it in a flexible market economy.

Turnover itself is therefore not necessarily a waste but the by-product of a process during which human beings turn into industrial waste. The trick facing maquila managers is to maintain it at the proper levels. Excessive turnover means that women are leaving at too high a rate for the firm to extract the value from their dexterous, attention-oriented, patient, and docile labor. An insufficient degree of turnover, however, represents another form of waste: an excessive productive capacity. For this reason, articles appear regularly in *Twin Plant News* offering advice on how to manage the "very real problem" of *high* turnover (see Beruvides, Villalobos, and Hutchinson 1997; Villalobos, Beruvides, and Hutchinson 1997). Turnover that is too high (as opposed to turnover that is just right) means that unskilled workers are leaving before they have exhausted their value to the firm. The desired rate of turnover most often quoted to me was 7 percent, and that requires that most of the new workers remain at least one year. "If we could get these girls to stay here two years," the human resources manager of the automobile radio factory said, "then I would be happy . . . after that they always move on and try something new." The problem with turnover, therefore, is not that the women leave. Rather, the problem has to do with the timing of their departure in relation to the rate at which their value as workers declines with respect to the value of their turnover.

This task of monitoring the correct turnover rate requires a measurement of the amount of value residing in the labor of the Mexican women who labor in unskilled work. Such measures are necessary in order to balance the value of her productive capacity as an active laborer with the value of her turnover. How does the value of her presence measure against the value of her absence? This is the question that maquila managers constantly pose, and they rely upon a cadre of supervisors and engineering assistants to figure it out. These lower-level managers track the march of repetitious tasks through the bodies of the female laborers who occupy the majority of such jobs through the industry. As I discussed in the previous two chapters, they watch for signs of slower work rates resulting from stiff fingers, repetitive stress disorders, headaches, or boredom. And they note declining work performance in order to justify a dismissal that denies eligibility for severance pay. As the Brazilian manager of a television manufacturer told me, "This is not the kind of work you can do for years at a time. It wears you out. We don't want the girls here after they're tired of the work." In this, as in many other maquilas, an elaborate system of surveillance focuses on the work primarily performed by women workers on the assembly line (Salzinger 1997). Furthermore, according to my informants, any worker who reveals an interest in expressing grievances or organizing worker committees is routinely subject to harassment if not immediate dismissal. The Mexican human resources manager of an outboard motor company said, "We have a policy not to allow workers to organize. It's like that in all the factories. . . . These lawyers [the ones involved in union activities] are lying to the workers and trying to trick them. We try to protect them from this." Workers with feisty attitudes are thus not very valuable to the firm either. So if a Mexican woman loses her docility, one of her values has been spent.

Another method for monitoring the depletion of value in the bodies of women workers involves the surveillance of their reproductive cycles. Women seeking employment in a maquiladora commonly have to undergo pregnancy tests during the initial application process (U.S. Department of Labor 1998; Castañon 1998). However, the scrutiny of their reproductive cycles does not end there. Also common is the continued monitoring of their cycles once they begin work. Reports vary depending upon the age of the employee and the particular factory, but a number of women have described to me and to others how on a monthly basis they are forced to demonstrate that they are menstruating to the company doctor or nurse. In several facilities, women have been pressured to show their soiled sanitary napkins. "They even make the *señoras* do it," one woman explained. "They treat us like trash." This pregnancy test is hardly fail-safe, and a number of women explained how they got around it. One who worked for a television manufacturer said, "I was pregnant, so I sprinkled liver's blood on the napkin. They never knew. But when I started to show, my supervisor got really mean." She was then moved into an area that required that she stand on her feet all day and lift heavy boxes. "I left because I was afraid for the baby." Harassment of pregnant women is common, although illegal, and demonstrates that once a woman displays a pregnancy, she is ripe for turnover. "This is not a place for pregnant women," one supervisor in a machine shop told me. "They take too many restroom breaks, and then they're gone for a month. It slows us down." With the identification of the pregnant woman as a problem for the work process, her value as a worker plummets while her removal—her turnover—appreciates.

These procedures revolve around a dialectical determination of the female subject as one continuously suspended in the ambiguity separating value from waste. She is a subject always in need of sorting because eventually the value of her presence on the production floor will be spent while the value of her absence will have appreciated. The sorting must occur in order to maximize the extraction of her value before declaring her to be overcome with waste. This inevitability, according to the death by culture logic, is driven by a traditional Mexican culture whose intrinsic values are in conflict as women spend more time outside the home. The many characteristics that the managers attribute to Mexican women as a way to explain high turnover, such as a lack of ambition, overactive wombs, and flagging job loyalty, represent cultural traits that are designed to check her independence. She might be subverting some cultural traditions by working outside the home, but her culture will ensure that she not go too far afield by inculcating her with a disposition that makes her impossible to train, to promote, or to encourage as a long-term employee. The maquilas are helpless to divert the forces of a culture that, in effect, devours its own, as women's careers are subsumed to such ineluctable traditional pressures.

Her disposability, then, represents her value to the firm since her labor power eventually, as it is a cultural inevitability, will not be worth even the cost of her own social reproduction, which is the cost of her return to the workplace. And she, the individual who comes to life as this depleting subject, experiences a corporate death when her waste overrides her balance because, as David Harvey puts it, "The laborer receives . . . the value of labour power, and that is that" (1982, 43). Turnover is therefore this turning over of women from those offering value through their labor power to those offering value through the absence of their labor. And as they repeat their experiences on this continuum while occupying jobs for several-month stints in different maquilas, their own lives are stilled as they move from one maquiladora to the next in a career built of minimum wage and dead-end jobs. These women experience a stilling of their corporate lives, their work futures, and their opportunities inside and outside of the workplace that might emerge were they to receive training and promotions into jobs with higher pay and more prestige.

All of the managers cited above agreed that the turnover rate could not be diminished by corporate measures such as higher salaries and benefits. The American human resources manager of the television manufacturer responded, "These girls aren't here for a career. If we raise the wages, that would have a negative effect on the economy and wouldn't produce any results. Turnover comes with the territory down here." The American general manager of the motorboat manufacturer said, "Turnover is a serious issue here, especially in the electronic work that the female operators do. But that's how they are. They're young and looking for experiences. You just have to get used to it down here. . . . I don't think wages would make any difference." The Mexican general manager of the television manufacturer replied, "Wages aren't the answer to everything, you know. Most of these girls are from other places in Mexico. They don't have much experience with American attitudes about work. And that's why we have problems with turnover." The German general manager of the electronic assembly plant explained, "We always try to cut down on turnover, but we don't expect to get rid of it. That wouldn't be realistic. Not in Juárez."

Within such interviews lurks a death by culture narrative, which vindicates the maquila industry of any responsibility in the repeated corporate deaths experienced by most of their female workers. By spinning a tale full of vague referents to the obstinate turnover condition of Mexican women, they are explaining how turnover is part and parcel of a cultural system immune to maquiladora meddling. The specificities of that culture are not the issue. Instead, it is the exculpation of the maquila industry from any responsibility in guiding a turnover process that serves their purposes in some critical ways. Consequently, maquila preventive measures would be fruitless or even a further waste. Competitive wages, training programs for women workers, day care, flexible work schedules, attention to repetitive stress disorders, and a compassionate stance toward maternity would not, according to this narrative, make one whit of difference. These Mexican girls and women are going to turn over, as they always do, because of who they are. Turnover is part of their cultural constitution. And as the women come and go, one after another, day after day, the managers exclaim their impotence against the wasting of women workers. These women, they maintain, are victims of their culture. Their eventual corporate deaths are evidence of death by culture.

Death by Culture

In a March 1999 interview, a research psychiatrist from Texas Tech University who specializes in serial murders commented to the *El Paso Times* that these Juárez murderers "tend to 'discard' their victims once they get what they want from them" (Stack and Valdez 1999). Such a vision of the Mexican woman as inevitably disposable is common to both the murder and the turnover narratives. At the heart of these seemingly disparate story lines is the crafting of the Mexican woman as a figure whose value can be extracted from her, whether it be in the form of her virtue, her organs, or her efficiency on the production floor. And once "they," her murderers or her supervisors, "get what they want from" her, she is discarded.

The vision of her disposability, the likelihood that this condition could exist in a human being, is what is so valuable to those who extract what they want from her. When she casts the shadow of the consummate disposable laborer whose labor power is not even worth the expense of its own social reproduction, she is a utopian image. In this particular manifestation, the Mexican woman is the utopian image of a culturally victimized variation of labor who guarantees her replacement—after being worn down by repetitive stress syndrome, migraines, or harassment over pregnancies—with fresh recruits who are, perhaps, leaving another place of employment for one of the same reasons. That the same women are turning over as they move from one place to another does not disrupt the utopian image of their constant decline as part of their progression toward disposability. Quite to the contrary, their value circulates through their continual flow from one factory to the next, since as a woman leaves one place of work, perhaps having been dismissed for missing a menstrual period, and then enters another once her menstrual flow resumes, she again represents value. Her fluctuation between value and waste is part of her appeal for her employer.

This image of her as the subject formed in the flux between waste and value provides her contours as a variation of capital. With such a constitution, she can be nothing other than a temporary worker, one whose intrinsic value does not mature, grow, and increase over time. And therefore, as a group, Mexican women represent the permanent labor force of the temporarily employed. The individual instances of this subject come and go as women deemed wasteful to a firm's project are replaced by new recruits. Her cultural constitution is internally driven and immune to any diversionary attempts by the industry to put Mexican women on a different path. Instead, she will repeat the pattern like women before her and perpetuate the problem of turnover so valuable to the maquilas.

Such a utopian image of the Mexican woman as a figure permanently and ineluctably headed toward decline, always promising that her labor power will be worth less than the cost of her own social reproduction, evokes Benjamin's elaboration of the fetish. Benjamin renovated Marx's analogy of the fetish as phantasmagoria to refer not only to the social relations of the market embedded in the commodity but also to the social relations of representation that were sustained in the commodity. According to Susan Buck-Morss (1989, 82), Benjamin's concern with "urban phantasmagoria was not so much the commodity-in-the-market as the commodity-on-display." Benjamin's point is that the mechanics of representation are as critical to the creation of value as the actual exchange of use values in the marketplace.

The fetish of the Mexican woman as waste-in-the-making offers evidence for Benjamin's view of the fetish as an entity "on display." As a figure of waste, she represents the possibility of a human existence that is perhaps really worthless, and this representation is valuable in and of itself. If we really can see and believe in her wasted condition, then she opens up a number of valuable possibilities for numerous people. For the managers of the maquiladora industry, her worthlessness means they can count on the temporary labor force that they need in order to remain competitive in a global system of flexible production. The image of the murder victims—many of them former maquila employees abducted on their commutes between home and work—also represents value for the industry as cultural victims. Through the descriptions of Mexican cultural violence, jealous machismo, and female sexuality, maquiladora exculpation finds its backing. No degree of investment in public infrastructure to improve transportation routes, finance lighting on streets, boost public security, or hold seminars in the workplace will make any difference. Others can also benefit from the widespread and believable representation of the Mexican woman as waste-in-the-making. The perpetrators of serial murders, domestic violence, and random violence against women can count on a lack of public outrage and on official insouciance with regard to their capture. And the city and state officials in Chihuahua who are concerned about their political careers under the public scrutiny of their effectiveness in curbing crime can defer responsibility.

The stories of this wasting and wasted figure must always be told since, to adapt Butler's calculation to my purposes, the naming of her as waste is also "the repeated inculcation of the norm" (Butler 1993, 8). The repetitive telling of the wasting woman in the turnover and murder stories is requisite because of her ambiguity: the waste is never stable or complete. The possibility of her value—of fingers still flexible or of a murdered young woman who was cherished by many—lurks in the background, and so the sorting continues as we search for evidence of the wasted value. Her dialectic constitution is suspended through the pitting of the two antithetical conditions that she invariably embodies. We find this dialectic condition through the questions that ask, Is she worthy of our concern? Are her fingers nimble or stiff, her attitude pliant or angry, her habits chaste or wild? Through the posing of such questions, her ambiguity is sorted as if it were always present for the sorting. Meanwhile, she hangs in the balance.

II

Disruptions

No need to use
this part → Use
only Part I of book

5

Maquiladora Mestizas and a Feminist Border Politics

The U.S.–Mexican border es una herida abierta (is an open wound) where the Third World grates against the first and bleeds.

Gloria Anzaldúa, *Borderlands/La Frontera*[1]

I would now rouse women's essence, spirit, to rise as birds in flight over fields, leaving swiftly earth's dust, that they may speedily cross the frontier into the great world of light and brilliance.

Qiu Jin (1875–1907), Chinese revolutionary and advocate of women's rights[2]

To disrupt the myth of the disposable third world woman is to disrupt the capitalist systems that require that the story constantly be told. So when people take on this myth with the intent of subverting it or somehow disabling its force, they also are confronting the capitalist processes that depend upon it. In this and in the following two chapters, I shift focus from the power of the myth to the power of those who resist its telling and who deny its validity. The case presented in this chapter is of three women who work in MOTW, the Mexican branches of the global firm (OTW) studied in chapter 2. I refer to them as "maquiladora mestizas" as a way to illustrate their local roots as well as their significance for considering the political and global implications of their actions. By juxtaposing their entanglements with the myth of the disposable third world woman, I hope to illustrate how any disruption of the local practices that identify certain women as disposable laborers has implications far beyond the confines of the factories where those actions take place.

Imagining the Border

Along stretches of the Mexico-U.S. border, a new mestiza is emerging. Her language is Spanish, English, and "Spanglish," and her job is in the maquiladoras. Sometimes she has a college degree, but often she has simply worked her way through the corporate ranks, moving up from hourly wage positions and into jobs with prestige, power, and significantly more pay. She comes from both sides of the political border. Her nationality is Mexican or American, but she calls herself "mexicana," among the other place-based identifiers, such as Mexican–American, *fronteriza*, *norteña*, American, and Chicana. A number of these *mexicanas* hold prestigious posts in community and business associations on both sides of the border. They have defied expectations limiting their role to the low-wage and unskilled positions (see Frobel 1980). In so doing, they expose the limits and failures of the disposability myth to control their fates. And they raise some sticky issues for a feminist approach to the politics of race, gender, class, ethnicity, and nationality along a border where such identifiers compromise the distance between the politics of Left and Right.

I refer to these *mexicanas* as "mestizas" in order to engage with Gloria Anzaldúa's discussion of a "new mestiza" (Anzaldúa 1987). The mestizas I discuss are new political subjects in the Mexico-U.S. borderlands who, by reinforcing the symbol of the border as a permanent division cutting across the social terrain, have made gains as self-identified *mexicanas* in the maquiladoras. They raise challenges for Anzaldúa's argument, which contends that only through resistance to the discourse of a border as a dividing line can *mexicanas* gain political ground in the cultural borderlands. And they challenge feminist theory, more generally, to contemplate the dynamic linking negotiations of space to those of identity as part of a politics for framing coalitions with distant others (see Massey 2004).

Anzaldúa's image of the new mestiza is as a cultural subject who forges political unity by dissolving the international divide from both the social imagination and the political practice. "The U.S.-Mexican border *es una herida abierta* [is an open wound]," she writes, "where the Third World grates against the first and bleeds." Along this border flows "the lifeblood of two worlds merging to form a third—a border culture" (Anzaldúa 1987, 3). She argues that in the divided border geography of the postcolonial period, the *mexicana* is devalued and her cultural integrity defiled. Writing as a new mestiza, Anzaldúa calls for "an exoneration, a seeing through the fictions of white supremacy, a seeing of ourselves in our true guises and not as the false racial personality that has been given us and that we have given ourselves. I seek our woman's face, our true features" (1987, 87). Her prophetic vision is a battle cry for *mexicanas* to seek unity where the state, along with heterosexist, misogynist, imperialist, and racist ideologies, has segregated *mexicana* from *mexicana* throughout the borderlands. At the heart of this journey for cultural reunification is a political subversion of the meaning of the border in both discourse and practice. Through reimagining the border not as the place of division but as the unified seam, where different manifestations of an essentially unified culture meet, she foresees an emerging geography that will ground a reinvigorated cultural and feminist politics.

Anzaldúa offers an imaginative elixir for a practical problem that plagues *mexicanas* who are involved in political community groups that attempt to organize cross-border events. Today on the U.S. side, a dramatic militarization (Dunn 1996), a rekindled enthusiasm for walls that physically delineate the political line (see Fox 1995–1996), and widespread condemnation of Mexican immigrants as parasites in "American" society have strained social networks and antagonized historical tensions on both sides (see also Anaya and Lomelí 1989). Imagining a unified border subject is no easier on the Mexican side, where the divisions between Mexicans and Americans, of Mexican descent or otherwise, are steadfastly reinforced by nationalist ideologies that separate "real" Mexicans from emigrants and their descendants in the United States (see Tabuenca Córdoba 1995–1996).

While these stubborn assertions of geographic division stand at odds with Anzaldúa's vision of geopolitical unity, they do not necessarily represent insurmountable obstacles for the conceptualization of a cross-border politics. Instead, they illustrate the need for understanding how discourses of geographic difference work into the materialization of political subjects and their communities.

Against the background of Anzaldúa's work, I present some of my ethnographic research on how *mexicanas* navigate the shifting social terrain of the Mexico–U.S. borderlands in their attempts to scale the corporate ladder in the multinational maquiladoras, where they confront a powerful belief that they, as "mexicanas," are the local representatives of a global condition of female disposability. These *mexicanas* represent a new mestiza in the sense that they have subverted historical discourses of who they are as women of Mexican descent and where they consequently belong in the multinational firm. I call them "maquiladora mestizas" because they express a cultural identity based on their deft navigation of the multinational maquiladora workplace and the politics of difference that characterize the Mexico–U.S. borderlands. And they confront the myth of their disposability and, in the process, expose what is at stake for the recognition of value and power within their workplaces when the myth is challenged.

Through a focus on the maquiladora mestiza, I hope to demonstrate that a feminist politics should consider how expressions of difference actually contribute to effective political strategies (Young 1990; Sandoval 2000; Mouffe 1992). Crucial to such an endeavor is a critical inquiry into the relationship between the border as a metaphor for myriad social divisions and the border as a material space that is policed, enforced, and physically crossed (see Katz and Smith 1993). In seeking to understand how metaphoric spaces materialize into places characterized by particular sorts of residents, I draw from Judith Butler's (1993) work on the interplay of discourse with matter in the formation of intelligible social subjects. Butler argues that discourse performs on matter such that the discursive markers of identity, as in race, sex, ethnicity, and so on, come into view as the materials that constitute the real corporeality of the body. Consequently, what is perceived to be materially grounded is actually discursively constituted, and is therefore in flux, despite its location in seemingly immutable matter. With this argument, Butler carves out a political space between discourse and matter, in which she demonstrates that political action can include efforts to disturb the codes for constructing subjects from the materials identified to be located in their bodies (see also Butler 1997b). She refers to such disturbances as "resignifications," or "radical rearticulation(s) ... of the symbolic horizon in which bodies come to matter at all" (Butler 1993, 23).

This notion of resignification is important for my own interpretation of the maquiladora mestiza as a new subject who has subverted the historical meanings of her language, body, sexuality, opinions, and labor in the maquiladora corporate community. This concept allows me to engage with Anzaldúa's concept of a "new mestizaje" in order to consider the complexities of resistance as a conceptual and political category. As Anzaldúa imagines, we find in this case that challenges to systems of power occur across the social spectrum, where individual assertions of identity intersect with myriad social structures, such as race, class, nationality, and gender, such that no single identity wins out as more significant than the others. For this reason, resistance does not emerge as an oppositional "twin" to structures of power; it does not, in other words, develop as a process of action that is defined by the terms of any single system of power. Nor is it an all-out escape from systems of power. It is, rather, as Michel Foucault (1995) urges us to consider, a constant navigation of the meaning of subjectivity across the spatial contexts of its construction. In thinking through the meaning of a "maquiladora mestiza," I examine her move up the corporate ladder and her recent prominence in probusiness cultural groups such as the League of United Latin American Citizens (LULAC) and the Maquiladora Association (AMAC) as a challenge to representations of *mexicanas* as the unskilled and docile labor force of international renown. Yet, this move also simultaneously reinforces practices for exploiting *mexicana* labor, at extremely low wages, and for excluding the majority of *mexicanas* from the benefits of the international mobility that multinational capital and its managers enjoy. The maquiladora mestiza demonstrates that her social strength rests on an interpretation of a bifurcated border geography and of a differentiated *mexicana* subject. Therefore, with the concept of resignification, I hope to show how a class politics is inextricable both from the politics of place (see Harvey 1996) and from politics of identities located in particular places (see McDowell 1999; Pile and Thrift 1995). And I wish to demonstrate that a feminist politics of the Mexico-U.S. border, one that takes into account how women on both sides conceptualize their communities and alliances, must understand that class neither forms a discrete category nor is isolated from the social politics of identity in the cultural borderlands.

Mexico on the Water

The material for my argument originates with an eighteen-month ethnographic project I conducted in 1993 and 1994 in a maquiladora which I shall refer to as "Mexico on the Water" (MOTW), the Mexican branch of the same corporation discussed in chapter 2. MOTW manufactures the carburetors, electrical components, and dashboard gauges for the company's larger motorboats.

MOTW set up shop in Ciudad Juárez in the early years of maquiladora development. It was the first maquila actively to seek male employees at least a decade before it was deemed necessary to compensate for a shortage of female workers in the local labor market. In an interview conducted in 1992, Bob, the first general manager of MOTW (who had left before I began my ethnography in 1993), had explained that he intentionally excluded women from the labor force: "This is not a tool shop, and the girls out here are not the right kind of worker for what we do. Our products are men's products, and I think the men, here or anywhere, understand the work better," he said. In the early 1990s, however, MOTW expanded its operations to include electronic assembly and gauge production and, as a result, began hiring women, who were deemed more suitable for this kind of work. This transition raised some harrowing challenges for the MOTW managers.

At MOTW, I studied how managers faced the challenge of producing quality goods with labor which they understood to be lacking in quality. This challenge takes on a particularly gendered and national dimension. These managers need to produce goods for a market which places a premium on American masculinity, a marker of quality in MOTW, and they evaluate their goods in terms of whether they reflect this desired condition. Yet, the MOTW managers attempt to accomplish their goal with laborers who, in their view, represent the opposite of this valuable masculine, American condition: disposable Mexican women. In an apparently contradictory move, they have hired Mexican women for the electronic and gauge production areas because these employees continue to be broadly construed as "dexterous," "patient," and "docile" enough to perform the necessary tasks. Moreover, as women increase their presence in the engineering labor market, the company hired its first female engineer and, simultaneously, needed to hire a Mexican woman to handle the complexities of a quickly expanding labor force. The hiring of women at all levels of the corporate hierarchy signifies a shift at MOTW from a company with a purposely male labor force and management to one with a notable presence of women. And this transition plays havoc with the company's well-worn customs for recognizing value in MOTW products, peoples, and spaces of production, where disposable women are seen to represent a threat to such value.

In this chapter, I focus on the experiences of three women in particular who challenge the company's traditional schema for recognizing the markers of disposability as a condition of female Mexican subjectivity. In my inquiry into what is at stake in these women's challenges, I rely on a Marxist critique of the social construction of value in a capitalist setting. Capital, says Marx, is not concerned with producing just any kinds of value, but particular things that embody value. This value can only be seen, recognized, and, in effect, valorized under the particular circumstances for evaluating different people as embodiments of a similar kind of value calculated as a condition of their labor.

Marxist scholars have elaborated on Marx's critique of the capitalist labor theory of value to emphasize the importance of understanding that the issue is not only about the construction of value in things, but also about its construction in the people who make those things. As David Harvey has put it, "The paradox to be understood is how the freedom and transitoriness ... of living labor as a process is objectified in a fixity of both things and exchange ratios between things" (1982, 23).

With this statement, Harvey pushes us to ask how the numerous energies that people express in their activities and in their thoughts can be understood as the conditions of a similar kind of value, which lends itself to quantification and qualification of a trait found in inanimate things. Thus, this is a process for viewing people as well as objects. Feminist scholar Diane Elson emphasizes how this sort of question involves "seeking an understanding of why labour takes the form it does, and [asking] what are the political consequences" (1979, 23; my brackets). These Marxian concerns are germane to my analysis, as the question that interests me here is not why Mexican women, as a group, are paid so little for their labor but, instead, why does disposable labor assume a female Mexican form and what happens when it fails to do so?

Yet even though I formulate this question with these Marxian critiques in mind, I cannot approach it from a strictly Marxist viewpoint. Feminist scholars have shown that any evaluation of labor as something of value, or waste, courses through an evaluation of the different kinds of people who embody different properties of labor (Elson 1979; Scott 1999). These feminist interventions have forced us to address how the historical constitution of women and racial minorities as laborers of inferior degrees of value has underscored the longheld industrial traditions of paying them less and of not recognizing the skill in what they do.

Taking these feminist interventions as a point of departure, I use Butler's theorization of resignification to examine how the three women I showcase here defy the traditional methods in MOTW for identifying value in people and in the things they make when they refuse to be defined by a myth that links them to a global resource of disposable labor. Their resignification is not an escape from capitalist exploitation. Quite to the contrary, as each rests her claims to her own skill and worth upon her ability to exploit valuable labor from the workforce. But, nevertheless, their efforts to resignify their own meaning as "mexicanas" shake up the production of value in the firm and its performance in the global market of commodity exchange. In order to illustrate the implications of their endeavors, I begin with the significance of gender and nationality for the spatial organization of MOTW production.

Making American

Even though MOTW is a Mexican subsidiary of its parent corporation, the corporate literature reinforces the idea that not only is MOTW an American business, but also all OTW products are American, no matter where they are produced. The authors of one of the official biographies of the company chronicle "the progress of this American institution" from the patriotic application of OTW technology, motors, and boats in U.S. war efforts, to OTW's commitment to supporting the U.S. sportsman tradition, and to fighting Japanese "incursions" into the global market. The current general manager of MOTW operations, Steve, explained, "This is an American company to the core." MOTW managers are careful to display the Americanness of their Mexican-located facility: "We are an American factory, and we want everyone to know that," Roger, the production manager of Plant II, told me. To visualize the Americanness of this Mexican subsidiary, I will begin with the spatial layout of the facility. Within the spatial relations of production, we find determined efforts to buttress the functioning of an American system and the production of unmistakably American things by Mexican laborers.

MOTW consists of two facilities: Plants I and II, each with its own production manager, engineering, and American-led supervisory teams who oversee forty-two product lines and almost eight hundred Mexican employees. A human resources manager, materials manager, and engineering manager are responsible for the operations of both facilities and answer to the general manager, who is the primary liaison with clients and other corporate offices. The MOTW administrative area is separated from the production area by a solid wooden door, which is guarded by a security officer who prevents unauthorized individuals from passing into the administrative interior. Inside this protected space, English is the dominant language. Mexican administrative assistants speak English to the managers, colorful posters of speedboats with muscular men and bikini-clad women boldly broadcast the charms of OTW products in English, the phone are answered in English, and meetings are conducted in English. As Roger said to me, "This is an American company, so you've got to expect the administration to be English speaking." The production area, by contrast, is a world of Spanish, where the bulk of MOTW's employees, who are monolingual Spanish speakers, work.

However, managers explain that, even though the vast majority of MOTW's production employees are Mexican, the factory is American by virtue of American control over the labor process. "This is the brains of the operation," Bob told me when describing the administrative area. "We control everything from here." The people in charge are to be American at all times, as is reflected in the corporation's policy which does not allow for any Mexican to hold a position of authority over an American: "You would expect the top people to be American employees here," said Burt, the manager of Plant I. "We make American products and we need people who understand that."

Corporate policy mandates that all those in management positions at MOTW either be U.S. citizens or possess a U.S. Green Card and reside in U.S. territory. Therefore, any nonnative U.S. citizen must apply for residency and a green card and pay taxes to the U.S. government in order to qualify for a promotion into management. As a result, any Mexican national promoted into management is, for all intents and purposes, an American employee. Under these rules, it is thus impossible for a Mexican employee to wield corporate authority over an American one. And in those cases where an American and a Mexican employee share the same title, such as at the rank of production supervisor, the American employee receives (at a minimum) one third more in wages and also supervises the Mexican supervisor. Understanding the national border within the corporation's division of labor is key for individual career strategies, in a place where to "Americanize" is to climb and to "Mexicanize" is to descend the social ladder of power and prestige.

When I asked Steve if he thought the company would ever have Mexican managers—that is, managers who were classified as Mexican personnel—he replied, "If we ever try to get into the Mexican market, sure. But as long as we're selling these boats in America, I don't see it happening." Within the logic internal to MOTW, there was a connection linking the national identities of MOTW employees with the marketability of MOTW goods. Even though all labor is technically absorbed in the product, and thereby made invisible according to Marx, the identity of this labor is brought to the surface through marketing strategies that emphasize national content, such as "Made in America." MOTW products, in the end, bear the mark "Made in America"; the boat and engines undergo final assembly for the U.S. market in the United States. Steve and the other MOTW managers, however, felt a need to guarantee that the internal operations of the factory did not disrupt the identification of MOTW products as American made. The labor itself might be invisible, but its social identity is part and parcel of the process for manufacturing value. For this reason, any identifiable traces of female Mexican labor within MOTW goods was especially dangerous according to MOTW managers, who were in charge of manufacturing products geared toward a male American market.

The Invisible MOTW Women

Whereas the "Americanization" of the product is assured by the "American brains" behind its manufacture, the masculinity of the product is protected by the masculinization of the labor process. On my first tour of MOTW in 1992, Bob guided me through the carburetor-assembly area, which he called "the heart" of the operation, which dominates the one large room in Plant I, and then through the "computer numerical control" area that dominates the space in the other part of the building. We observed engineers at their computers and desks, and we walked through the painting section that was soon to be transferred out of the facility. With the exception of the secretarial staff, all of the employees I saw were men. And it was not until the following year, when I began my ethnographic study, that I discovered the women, who then composed about 35 percent of the production labor force and worked behind the male labor processes. Off in the corners and against the back walls, they assembled ignition switches, horns, drive shafts, and fuel systems. They cut and spliced wires, and manufactured gauges for dashboards. When I asked Burt in 1994, why the former general manager had not shown me those female work areas, he said, "Bob was proud of our carburetor and tooling operations. We were the first maquila to have those type of operations and to be successful.... We have the girls in electronic assembly but that's not what we're known for."

The spatial arrangement of male and female work spaces successfully squirreled the women out of view and away from the "heart" of MOTW production. This spatial practice both revealed and embraced a managerial discourse of MOTW as a "man's shop," while the women worked invisibly behind dust-proof doors and against rear walls to fashion the "incidentals" of motorboat production. Steve explained, "We think of ourselves as a tool shop. And across the industry the belief is that men are better at this work than females. It's a macho place. No doubt about it."

This depiction of MOTW as a "macho tool shop" made sense against the backdrop of what was to be understood by Mexican femininity and women's work in the maquilas. In my earliest interviews, several MOTW managers contrasted their facility to the maquila archetype of electronic assembly and sewing. Burt explained, "We're not like the electronic maquilas down here. We're building the basics of an expensive product. It's very different, and we're a different kind of place." Roger said, "We're not building televisions here. So you won't see as many females in our plants." The stereotype of the female electronic assembly line, I was to understand, did not characterize MOTW, either in kind or in quality. This was not women's work. "The work we do here is what men usually do. We get guys who have worked on their cars or have some kind of experience with tools," Burt said. "It's a different quality of work."

Such explanations contributed to a representation pervasive through the maquilas of the Mexican woman as (1) especially suited for unskilled electronic assembly of low-end goods, and (2) particularly unsuited for engineering work, skilled jobs, or any tasks deemed "physical" (Salzinger 1997; Fernández-Kelly 1983). Burt said, "We haven't worked with women much. We have a different kind of operations. We need more skilled labor." As Steve put it: "We sell our boats to men. It's not a television."

Still, in 1993, women were already putting together many of MOTW's products, and by 1997 about half of the eight hundred production workers were women—a shift having to do with the other pervasive construction of Mexican women as dexterous and innately deft with tedious, hairsplitting tasks. Roger said, in 1994, "Things are definitely changing here. Plant II is mainly electronic work, and we've just got that going over the last three years. That means we're hiring more female workers because they're good at this work." Steve said, "I think when we decided to put the electronics operations down here it was because we knew that women in Mexico had experience with electrical assembly. And it made more sense to do it here for a lot less money than we were doing it in Europe or in the U.S."

The hiring of women to work in electrical assembly raised a paradox for the managers of MOTW. Although their labor process had shifted, since the late 1980s, from a purely "mans' tool shop" to one including "women's electrical assembly work," the product, a decidedly "man's product," had not changed. When I asked Steve if he thought OTW customers knew that Mexican women were assembling some of their products, he said, "No, and it's my job to make sure they don't find out." The social construction of Mexican women as naturally suited for electronic assembly did not shift their construction of them as not suited for making MOTW products. If anything, it intensified the managerial conviction that their control over the labor process was even more critical. Now they would not only have to concern themselves with the Americanization of the product, but they would also have to supervise its masculinization.

This challenge can be seen in light of the twofold problem raised by the social constructions of MOTW products and of Mexican women as entities of contrasting values. First, the process of social construction is never complete. In order for MOTW products to be seen as "American" and "masculine," they had continually to be seen as the opposite of "Mexican" and "feminine." This process gained backing from managerial efforts to explain that the value in MOTW products was other than the typical value found in electronic feminized maquila production. As the managers reiterated how their products were of a superior caliber compared with an assembly-line television, they repeatedly emphasized how those products associated with female Mexican labor were of inferior quality and value, as opposed to the masculine ones emerging from MOTW. And, as we shall see shortly, in order to preserve the representation of Mexican women as the cheap opposition who outline the limits of masculine value, they did not train their new female employees sufficiently for their jobs. To do so would belie their faith in this labor pool's intrinsic disposability.

Second, and related to the first problem, the construction of the Mexican woman as incapable of producing American masculine value also exercises a productive effect. As Judith Butler (1993) argues, there is no reference to a body that is not, at the same time, a further production of that body. It can then be said, in the case of labor, that there is no reference to someone's labor power (that is, what is exchanged for wages) without further producing a quality of his or her labor. As a result, to view the Mexican woman as cheap and disposable because she has no skills and is not trainable is at once a construction of her as an embodiment of waste, even as her body provides the source of much value through her labor. The trick is to take advantage of her disposable labor without jeopardizing the value of the product (or the value of the company). At MOTW, this challenge means guaranteeing that no evidence of Mexican women, or "mexicanas," is found in the things that they make. The value of their labor power resides both in its disposability and in its disappearance both from MOTW's products and from its visible work spaces.

The complexities underlying this task become clear in the following elaboration of three women's experiences in the company. In these cases, we shall see how managerial concerns over the inner workings and outer markings of the Mexican woman's body lead to fears that Mexican women are infiltrating the male spaces of MOTW production and contaminating them and the company's products with a cheapening disposability. These three women, Rosalía, Cynthia, and Mary, worked simultaneously at MOTW, and their stories overlap in numerous ways. Each of these women described herself to me as "mexicana," and each faced the challenge of having to navigate the discourse of the *mexicana* in order to legitimate her claim to residency in the American domain of administration, where she could earn a higher salary and exercise more authority. In these three cases, being an American or a Mexican, masculine or feminine, Anglo or *mexicana* hinges on a performance of the subject position as it is understood in the symbolic realm of representation. We shall see how Rosalía, a woman who was born and raised in Mexico, transforms herself into an American; how Cynthia, a woman born and raised in the United States, slides down the corporate scale as she is seen to embody the *mexicana* image; and how Mary, another Mexican–American woman, unleashes a contagion of female Mexican presence in the masculine spaces of the firm. And each struggles to resignify herself within the dominant discourse of who *mexicanas* are and what they mean for distinguishing between people of value and of waste inside and outside of the MOTW walls. I do not present these women's stories in chronological order since they intersect with each other's at different points in time.

Rosalía

When I met Rosalía, she was the personnel director for Mexican employees. She had been working in the maquilas for twelve years, having started out as an operator, then having moved from clerk to secretary, and finally to the assistant personnel director position at her previous maquila employer. She was raising her two children single-handedly and had just received her college degree in business administration after years of night school. She was the only career woman in her immediate family, and she expressed pride in her accomplishments. "A lot of people say that women can't have a career. You hear that about Mexican women especially, but it's not true. You have to want it, but you can do it," she told me when I asked her to describe her career history.

At the time of that conversation, Rosalía's office was in one of the cubicles designated for Mexican administrative staff in the production area. In the history of MOTW, no Mexican woman had ever moved above that position; however, within two months of my research, Rosalía not only would make a bid for a promotion but also would be the first *mexicana* to occupy an office in the American administrative area, and she would hold authority over American employees. A month after this promotion, I asked Rosalía to describe the events surrounding her move. "It was obvious that Steve needed some help with the American personnel. I was already doing the insurance work.... I told him I could do the job. I showed him my books on the U.S. labor code.... He knows that I'm professional. I'm not just any *mexicana*."

Steve explained his decision to me this way: "I knew it was a big deal to move Rosalía into this office, but I also knew that she was the best for the job. They look at her and see just another Mexican woman, but I know Rosalía. And I know she's tough as nails and ambitious. She'll end up showing us all that she's not just some Mexican woman who's in over her head. She'll fit in with the Americans."

Still, when he announced Rosalía's promotion, four of the five managers stormed out of the meeting in protest.

"This is an invasion of my privacy," Roger growled as he marched out of the office. "What's wrong?" I asked Burt as he exited the staff meeting room. "Roger is pissed about Rosalía. I am, too. I don't see why she should have an office here. She was fine where she was," he replied as he walked toward his office, located across the hall from hers. Outside I asked Roger what irritated him so much about Rosalía's promotion; he said, "I don't want to sound like a bigot, 'cause I don't have anything against Mexican people. But she's very Mexican and a woman in that culture doesn't know what it's really like to play hardball."

"What does this have to do with privacy?" I continued.

"Look, she's just not qualified to oversee our affairs. For Christ's sake, she's just a secretary. They're probably having a goddamned affair," Roger barked. Burt jumped in, "She's supposed to handle our insurance claims or worker's comp?" He added sarcastically, "She doesn't even know what that means."

Inside, the grumblings from other American employees were more subtle but still audible. I approached Cynthia, one of the quality engineers, who said, "What does a Mexican woman know about sexual harassment? She's *mexicana mexicana*." "*Mexicana mexicana*," as I was assumed to understand, meant that Rosalía was a particularly Mexican *mexicana*, who would then fit within the lower ranks of MOTW's political and economic hierarchy.

On this issue, Cynthia was quite vocal: "Do you realize that she is now my boss? And she makes more money than I do. That's an insult." Part of the protest was directed at Steve, who had disrupted the social code by allowing Rosalía to move physically into American social space. They feared a sullying of the American sphere by the presence of a *mexicana*. Burt and Roger summed up this sentiment when each complained, "What do you think our bosses in Illinois are going to think when they come into our offices and see her?" Cynthia was also concerned about the image: "Rosalía won't know how to act around corporate people. She looks out of place, and that's no accident."

Rosalía knew of these misgivings. She immediately enrolled in an intensive English course, bought some new suits at a department store in El Paso, and filled out the paperwork for a green card. She would be moving to El Paso. Within one month, she had checked out the El Paso schools for her children and chosen the neighborhood where she would like to live. I asked her why she was making the move, and she responded, "Well, the job is an American job. That means I have to get a green card."

In order to qualify for the human resources position as it was structured in the corporation, Rosalía had to become an American resident with a green card. The human resources manager's position was a structurally "American" one. It was paid in U.S. dollars, it forfeited taxes to the U.S. government, and it fell under the U.S. labor code. No less significantly, it was ranked above several American positions in terms of pay, status, and corporate power. Rosalía was demonstrating that this human resources manager was not going to be a Mexican but rather an American employee.

She put it this way: "In the maquilas, you have to understand the difference between being Mexican and being American. They say right to my face that a *mexicana* can't do this job. That I don't understand sexual harassment or can't stop a strike. You watch. I am *mexicana* but I have American business sense, and that means I know both sides." In showing that she could reside in the United States, Rosalía played off the metaphor of the international border outside the firm in order to renegotiate her position vis-à-vis the border inside it. She was leaving her *mexicanismo* behind. She was Americanizing and, no less significant, she was proving that unlike the overwhelming majority of *mexicanas*, she was not culturally bound to sexual chaos.

Steve told me one day over lunch, "She really surprised a lot of people when she announced that. I think they thought she wouldn't be able to leave Mexico. But you know, I think she's got her sights set on an international posting. She's serious. She wants to be treated like an American and have a real career…. I think she can do it."

However, Rosalía's own description of this movement reveals that she considers herself to be a new kind of *mexicana*, one who understands how the border as a metaphor interacts with the material organization of power, capital, and prestige in the political borderlands. When I asked her if she would miss living in Ciudad Juárez, she said, "I will always be *mexicana*, but I also need to understand American issues. Here I am American. I represent American employees to the corporation. I translate policy. So I need to know what it means to cross the bridge every day, to have your kids in an American school and try to keep up with what they want. I am *mexicana* but I'm not the traditional version." She is not, in other words, the "disposable" type. "This company recognizes what I have to offer," she later elaborated.

And she did transform herself in front of everyone's eyes into what was broadly construed as the prototype of an American manager. Her dress suits changed to darker hues; her hems grew longer, and her heels shorter. Within a few weeks of her language class, she rarely spoke Spanish. She also handled a delicate insurance problem regarding offshore American employees and impressed her skeptical colleagues with her acumen in a U.S. corporate bureaucracy. I asked Steve how he found her job performance. "You know, she really has changed. I think they don't even know she's Mexican up in headquarters."

Rosalía's apparent abilities to dispel labor disruptions further impressed the other managers. In February 1995, following a 70 percent peso devaluation (against the U.S. dollar), thousands of workers walked off their jobs in the maquiladoras. Rumors spread that someone was trying to organize unions throughout the industry as factory managers came under pressure to raise wages both to compensate for the immediate cheapening of their labor force (in dollar terms) and to stem the decline of the workers' buying power. Two of the factories neighboring MOTW were paralyzed by a walkout, and the almost five thousand striking workers at the nearby RCA television manufacturer forced a shutdown in the firm's Illinois operation (see Kern and Dunn 1995). Yet at MOTW, work continued as usual. Steve was bursting with praise for Rosalía when I asked him how MOTW stayed in operation. "She really knew what to do. She had informants spread out all over the place.... In the doctor's office. Everyone talks to their doctor, and on the lines. She's tough, tougher than anyone thought she could be. She's shown that she's not your average Mexican woman. In fact, I think she's as American now as I am."

Rosalía was also making her presence known beyond the MOTW walls. One year after her promotion, she was appointed to a prominent position in the maquiladora trade association in Ciudad Juárez, and she expressed the hope of opening the door for other *mexicana* managers to participate in the group. As Rosalía crossed some Mexico-U.S. divides, she resignified herself in MOTW. She became a professionally savvy *mexicana* by rearticulating what it meant to have her knowledge as a *mexicana*, her language, and her own political vision. She manipulated the border as a metaphor for division in order to carve her place as a particular type of *mexicana* with mobility across the international divide. And she assumed a politics of geographic difference. Her movement into American space meant putting some distance between herself and the majority of *mexicanas* employed at the firm. She was skilled, worth keeping, and definitely neither cheap nor disposable. Yet she still identified herself as a *mexicana*, one with the ability to make links across the border, to forge political connections, and to strengthen her position through her own awareness of herself as a political agent. She is not the kind of new mestiza who Anzaldúa envisions, but she is the type that is becoming more prominent in the contemporary place that is the Mexico-U.S. borderland.

Alongside Rosalía's efforts for promotion, there was another attempt by one of her American colleagues, Cynthia, to gain ground in management. Rosalía was the corporation's point person for managing this affair, and her handling of it reveals her view that the failure to recognize the politics of geographic difference in the maquiladoras is disastrous for a *mexicana* who aspires to improve her own material standing.

Cynthia

When I first met Cynthia in September 1993, she worked as a quality engineer overseeing the production of the fuel systems. The job description for this position involves more managing than engineering, and her role was as the managerial liaison to the manufacturing engineers, all Mexican men, on the shop floor. With a college degree in engineering and chemistry, Cynthia had the most years of education in her family, and she was taking night classes at the University of Texas at El Paso to complete the requirements for a master's degree in industrial engineering. Although her parents were first-generation immigrants from Mexico, she said she learned to speak Spanish well in high school. She had started working at MOTW two years earlier when she decided that even though she was from Ohio, her roots were along the border. "You know," she told me, "my family was all migrant workers. Picking tomatoes. My mom told my dad one day that she just couldn't stand the sight of another tomato, and they went to Ohio and opened up a panaderia [Mexican bread store]. That's where I worked as a kid."

Cynthia described herself as ambitious. She spoke of her participation in the probusiness group LULAC and in El Paso political circles. She told me of her aspirations to move into management from our first interview. "I'm a good manager and I'm the best writer they've got around here. I write all of the reports even for the other guys. I'm working on something for Steve right now." Steve agreed, "Cynthia writes well. She's talented, but she's always in some controversy. I can't tell you how much time we spend trying to figure out the 'Cynthia problem.'"

This was evident after just a few days at MOTW. During one of the weekly managers' meetings, soon after Rosalía's promotion,

Cynthia's name came up when Roger stated, in a commanding tone, "Somebody has got to talk with Cynthia."

The next morning, Cynthia came into my office and closed the door. "Do you know what they said to me? Those fuckers.... My bows. They say I can't wear my hair bow!" She took a sparkling purple bow from her hair and showed it to me. "My mom gave these to me for my birthday.... And it's Rosalía telling me this.... First it was my hair: 'tone it down.' Steve calls me in his office and says he wants me to look more like an American engineer. He said I had gone too Mexican. Who the hell does he think he's talking to?"

Over a series of conversations, Steve explained to me that Cynthia simply did not look professional, given her position. "I don't know if she's here to discover her roots or what. I don't care. I just want my engineers to act like engineers. I can't have my boss coming down here and bumping into glitz and bows when he wants to talk about the fuel system.... This might sound bad, but that's just how it is in this world. If she wants to be a manager, she had better tone down the Mexican stuff."

Cynthia was not bending to the pressure. One day she came in wearing a violet blue dress suit with rhinestone buttons and a bow to match. "I dare them to say anything," she told me in the hallway. When I asked Cynthia if she was tempted to yield in an effort to mitigate tensions, she expressed anger and said, "Look, I'm not a white girl like you. And I'm not ashamed of who I am. I show it. I'm a woman, I show it. I'm *mexicana*, I show it. Outside, I wear blue jeans but here I'm professional and that's what I show. If they don't like it, fuck 'em."

Meanwhile, she had received written memos not detailing the nature of her clothing but stating in vague terms that she was not fulfilling her professional duties. One of the evaluations gave her low marks on professional conduct, and Cynthia understood this to be in preparation for her legal dismissal. Rosalía explained the conflict in these terms: "Here you have to be one thing or the other. You are either Mexican or American. There is no place for a Mexican–American here."

Paradoxically, while hours of staff time were dedicated to the controversy over Cynthia's appearance, her performance as a quality engineer, measured in terms of product defects and reliability, won the highest award in the company, worldwide. The corporation flew her and her parents to Miami so that she could attend the award ceremony. However, this award did not prevent her forced resignation a short while later.

In the days just preceding her resignation, Steve made an announcement that he had promoted a Mexican man into the engineering manager job that Cynthia had coveted. "I don't think the maquilas are ready for a Cynthia yet," he told me in explanation of this decision. "This guy acts like an engineer. I know where he's coming from." By this I understood that he was impressed with a strictly masculine presentation, the wearing of ties, and an unambivalent understanding of the difference between the Mexican and the U.S. domains in MOTW.[3]

I asked Rosalía to explain why Cynthia's self-presentation was such a problem and worth so much attention when her work was clearly helping the company. She justified the concern over Cynthia's appearance by discussing how the international border operates. "Well, it might seem irrelevant, but how people look and act is really important for keeping everything running. It's like the border, you have to show your papers. It doesn't matter who you are. If you don't act right, then they won't let you in. They have their rules. So do we. Cynthia doesn't want to accept them. She doesn't seem professional and it bothers everyone. She really doesn't know who she is here. That's her biggest problem."

What Cynthia presented was an incongruous image at MOTW. She asserted herself as a "Mexican American" woman, a particular version of *mexicana*, in a context where a clear-cut division was the norm. By refusing to acknowledge the border as a metaphor for division, she threatened a social order built around an international segregation within the division of labor. And she directly challenged the predominant discourse of the *mexicana* as unprofessional. This was an effort at resignification not simply of her individual self, but also of the symbolic interpretation of the *mexicana* in general. Unlike Rosalía, she was not adjusting her own presentation to fit the dominant symbolic framework of space and subjects. Instead, she tackled the representation and perceived place of the *mexicana* and met forceful opposition. In some ways, she, like Anzaldúa, imagined a possible unification of the Mexican with the American side. She attempted to negotiate a social ambiguity, inserting the Mexican with the American, and the feminine with authority, in a context where such discursive and material alignments were cast as impossibilities.

However, Cynthia's expressions of social unity across a rejoined geography did not challenge the class divides inherent in the division of labor that separates professional *mexicanas* from day-laboring *mexicanas* across a nationalized border. "These girls," she explained in reference to the female operators under her charge, "are lucky to have this job and they don't even know it. Mexican culture really doesn't teach them how to respect their jobs. My family is Mexican but when it comes to work, we've got the American work ethic." Cynthia may have threatened a social order crafted around the exclusion of a particular manifestation of *mexicanas* in American administration, but she expressed steadfast dedication to the nationalized and sexualized bordering of class divisions that preserved the capitalist integrity of the operation. For example, when she heard that I had attended a labor meeting in Ciudad Juárez, she called me at home. "Are you one of those bleedingheart labor people?" she asked. When I replied that I did not know what she meant, she informed me that she could not take any risks and would not talk to me again. I then received a call from Steve, who asked if I was a "labor spy."

Despite her problems at MOTW, Cynthia did not leave in a weak position. She sought support and advice from an extensive legal community both in El Paso and in Ciudad Juárez. Fearing a lawsuit, Steve authorized a bonus and provided strong recommendations to another company, where she began working. Shortly afterwards, she was named in a widely circulated industry trade magazine as one of the top women employees and as a highly regarded engineer in the maquiladora industry. She attributed much of her success to her experience as a woman knowledgeable of both the American and the Mexican cultures located in the border environment.

As she said to me before her resignation, "You know, I think these white guys are in for a big surprise.... There's a lot of us, and we know what we're doing. This is one of the few places where a *mexicana* can really do something in industry and be recognized. We know both sides down here, and that scares them."

Mary

The events surrounding the short-lived employment of Mary, a Mexican–American supervisor, reveal the contradictions inherent to manufacturing products of high quality with people deemed to be disposable, due to their intrinsic low quality. In 1994, MOTW hired Mary to work with unskilled female workers in the company's new gauge operations. Gauge production is a critical operation, with ramifications for client safety and the overall aesthetic appeal of the boat. "Customers always look at the dashboard. If they don't like the way it looks, how the dials read, then they may not buy the boat," said Roger. Burt said, "Gauges are important on a boat. Can't have someone taking off for the ocean with bad gauges."

This critical area had been sent to Mexico from one of the U.S. facilities after Steve won what he called a "bloody turf battle" with his counterpart in OTW's China facility. "We all compete with each

other for the operations," he explained. "A manager is only as important as the quality and quantity of the people under him." Questions
had been raised over whether the Mexico facility could handle the
task. Steve convinced them that, under his watch, gauges would be
up to standard. "My neck is on the line," he told me. And Mary was
brought in to supervise the operation. Like the other American supervisors, Mary was Mexican–American and bilingual, and had previous experience in manufacturing, but unlike the others, she referred
to herself as *mexicana*. When she accepted this position, she came
out of her retirement after a twenty-year career as a supervisor in a
clothing maquila. "I always like a challenge," Mary told me as she
described why she came out of her brief stint as a "full-time grandmother" helping her daughter with child care. "My family is a working family. Migrant farmers ... sitting around makes us nervous."
In the summer of 1993, Mary returned to the maquila labor force
and resumed her El Paso–Ciudad Juárez commute. "They told me I
would be in a sensitive area. That our quality would have to be very
good. I knew I was working with young kids.... You always do in
the maquilas."

Her job was to supervise thirty-five employees, mostly women in
their late teens and early twenties, in the start-up of the gauge production line. The making of gauges entails a painstaking inspection
process. Almost half of the workers were inspectors of some sort.
They tested product functions, inspected for paint consistency, or ran
durability tests. The production line began when an automatic winder
wrapped fine copper wire tightly around a bobbin; this would then
be tested for current flow and placed in a housing, after which more
wires could be attached, more tests run, and then the painted dial
face connected. Only two operators had the delicate task of stamping
on the dial face—a process requiring a steady hand and unwavering
attention to detail. Two more inspection steps preceded the sealing
of the gauge, which was followed by a final test before they would be
packaged and shipped to the final assembly plant in Georgia.

Isolated behind the dust-proof doors and in a windowless room,
the laborers in gauge production did their work beyond the notice of
the rest of the facility. "I guess you could walk around this plant,"
said Roger, "and never know those girls are back there." And Mary
had explicit instructions not to allow the workers to leave their area
without permission, and to stagger restroom breaks so that no more
than one worker left the area at a time. All of the gauge workers wore
gender-distinguished uniforms, and all the women had to cover their
hair completely with hairnets—a policy which was only sporadically
enforced for the few men in the area. Men wore the nets like caps,

over the top of their heads, whereas the women pulled the nets completely down to their necks. Mary explained this preoccupation over women's hair: "Well, they're all supposed to wear the nets. But we let the guys just sort of stick them on top 'cause it bothers them more.... They don't want the girls' long hair getting in the paint or in the wires. It's the girls we worry about the most."

This heightened attention to evidence of femininity, such as long hair and miniskirts, extended to other body parts as well. Mary described the policies regarding female appearance: "The girls can't wear fingernail polish ... and we don't want pregnant girls in here. The fumes aren't good for them." Indeed, as in many maquilas, a policy both for refusing to hire pregnant women and for encouraging those who become pregnant to leave their job was tacitly enforced, although such practices violate federal legislation prohibiting discrimination on the basis of pregnancy. "We all know we're not supposed to hire pregnant girls. It's that way in all the maquilas," said Mary.

Consequently, the young women who worked in MOTW gauge production and who were subject to the practices concentrating on control of their hair, their nails, their clothing choice, and their wombs as they manufactured gauges in the back room of Plant II also reinforced the traditional gendered pattern for delineating the social hierarchy of the MOTW division of labor. According to the payrolls of MOTW, the women in electronic assembly and gauge production received the lowest wage rates and, over time, had the highest turnover rate. "These workers don't come here with commitment," Rosalía explained. "So we don't expect it. I wish we could." Ramón, a supervisor in carburetors, said, "The girls in electronic assembly are important but individually not as important as the guys out here. We need to work with them [male employees] and try to keep them. The girls ... leave when they want a family." And the company expectation, according to Steve, for their longevity was two years at the most, just as it was in the company's Chinese operations (see chapter 2). The females were, in short, regarded as individually disposable after a two-year window of time, and training and other incentives designed to improve their longevity were regarded as a waste of time. "Why would we train workers in that area?" Steve asked in response to one of my questions.

Mary had to work with this assumption that training women in electronic assembly was not warranted. "They put me in with a roomful of girls who didn't have any experience and expected us to do it right the first time," she said. "That's the problem. They want American quality, without the time." Steve explained, "I expected a slower system, but the quality needs to be up to standard. This is an American operation ... and it's Mary's responsibility to make it work."

From the beginning, however, Mary, her managers, and her workers confronted the contradiction of hiring workers who are not "worth the training" to make something conforming to strict quality guidelines. Gauge manufacturing got off to a very shaky start and had not settled into a routine two months into production, when it was supposed to be operating at almost full capacity. Even though this problem seemed to be one involving a simple miscalculation of how much time would be needed to bring gauge production up to standard, the MOTW managers cast the matter as a national and gender crisis. As I show in the next section, they framed the problem as one in which Mexican women were making gauges that had their stamp of *mexicana* femininity all over them. Mary challenged their belief that such stamping devalued the product by asserting that she, as a skilled *mexicana* supervisor, knew how to turn unskilled *mexicana* laborers into a valuable labor force.

Female Contamination

After three months of production, about two thirds of the gauges were defective. A problem which caused a great deal of anxiety was the rate at which faulty bobbins came out of the wrapping machine at the beginning of the production process. Erratic paint quality further diminished the number of acceptable units, and, making matters worse, demand for gauges was at a high as the company readied for the holiday season. Steve was receiving calls on an almost daily basis from his client—the final production assembly plant in Georgia—to discuss the gauges and predictions for a resolution of the problems. He, in turn, called meetings with Mary and her immediate boss, Roger. "We're shipping out Mexican product," he said in one such meeting. "And that's got to change."

Mary explained that the problem lay in technological systems and in the lack of training. "It's too much to learn and get good at in two months," she exclaimed in one meeting. In order to "make an American operation out of this," to use Roger's words, they agreed to take the following measures. Roger would tell maintenance that gauges were top priority, and Mary would work overtime until things were back on track.

Within ten days, however, Steve was informed that not only was MOTW still shipping what he would call "Mexican" quality, but also the lack of acceptable gauges had idled almost one hundred workers in the Georgia facility. "I won't be shutting down Georgia!" he announced. By this time, Mary and the operators in her area were putting in fifty to sixty hours in a six-day, and occasionally seven-day, workweek. After a month of overtime in an anxious climate, the operators started to quit. In one week alone, Mary lost more than half of her employees and was spending more time on teaching new hires than anything else. One operator, an eighteen-year-old woman who had worked at MOTW for about six weeks, said, "We're killing ourselves in here.... They're always yelling at us and telling us that we're not doing it right. But they don't even give us time to learn how to do it."

Mary asked Steve for some more time to bring the workers up to speed and to lessen the pressure on everyone: "I've got more new workers than old ones," she said. "And it's hard to teach them what to do and get everything out." Steve explained the impossibility of more time. "At this point," he said, "we don't have any time." He and the other managers repeatedly stressed the reasonableness of their expectation that Mexican women ought to be able to pick up this work with virtually no training as this was the kind of work that comes "naturally" to women. As Burt said, "These girls do electrical assembly all the time."

Mary, exasperated with her bosses' refusal to allow her more training time, decided to take matters into her own hands. She made some *de facto* amendments to the work rules in the gauge area as a way of introducing some flexibility into the labor process while still expecting overtime from the workers. "I had to do something, or everyone would have left," she told me.

Without her managers' approval, she immediately relaxed the uniform requirements. Everybody still had to wear the smocks, although she did not object to the women wearing male smocks, which some found more comfortable, and she allowed workers to remove their hairnets as long as their hair was pulled back. "Those things itch," she said, "and after a few hours you're ready to tear them off!" She promised coffee and donuts for everyone on Saturdays and announced that anybody working on weekends could work a half day during the week without losing their production or attendance bonuses. They simply had to arrange with her in advance which day they should take. She also took measures to relax the working environment by allowing them to bring in music and by loosening rules governing restroom and water breaks.

Over the next couple of weeks, the turnover rate stabilized and the defect rate improved. Mary was optimistic: "You can't ask these kids to put in six- or seven-day weeks without a break.... Things got better right away."

Although they were not completely out of the woods, the crisis had seemed to pause. The Georgia operation was back in business, and calls had slowed as more gauges were passing the inspection tests of their clients. Mary was not being summoned for daily emergency meetings. And Steve told her, "Whatever you're doing is working." However, he would soon change his mind even though, by Georgia's standards, products were continually improving. Mary's new measures caused a panic over her apparent subversion of longheld company policies regarding the threat posed by "mexicanas" and the rules regarding the control over their bodies and the spaces they occupied.

One morning, in a private meeting, Rosalía alerted Steve to the fact that things were "getting out of control" in the gauge area. She was concerned that Mary's tampering with the attendance schedules would disrupt the attendance and punctuality policies of the company, introducing Mexican chaos into their professional system. "This is not a Mexican sweatshop," she said. "She can't just change it around when it's convenient."

Steve decided that he would talk with Mary about the attendance policy on the following Saturday, when she came in for an overtime shift. "I agreed with Rosalía, we have to stick with policy. We need to follow the rules like any American company, but I didn't think it was an emergency." What he encountered, however, when he went to speak with Mary in the gauge area on Saturday morning shocked him: "I thought I'd walked into a Mexican fiesta," he said. "The only thing missing was the piñata."

According to Steve, after he pushed through the set of dust-proof doors separating the gauge area from the rest of the plant, he saw women talking loudly and walking around the work area with no apparent regard for their work stations. Music, he said, was blaring from a jam box next to the empty donut box located atop a work table. Mary, he said, "looked just like a Mexican grandmother." His American supervisor was beginning to look like a "mexicana" in his eyes, a woman who did not deserve a position with authority at MOTW. Steve described his alarm at the next Tuesday morning staff meeting: "I don't know what she's doing in there, but there are girls running around everywhere. And they want to bring their children.... There's no telling how many babies those girls have."

Mary described the scene this way: "Steve came in ready to jump all over me for not telling Rosalía about our scheduling changes and then he has a heart attack because I told him that one of the girls had asked to bring her baby on Saturdays." She had not let her.

During the staff meeting, concerns over the gauge area shifted from the quality of the product, as it was measured by performance tests, to apparent loss of control by American managers over Mexican females. They agreed that the product was sure to suffer. Burt said that they could not "tolerate" a "Mexican occupation" of the gauge room. Roger raised the issue of fingernail polish. "Some of those girls wear fingernail polish," he said. "Just what we need is a call [from corporate headquarters] asking how purple fingernail polish gets into the gauges." They discussed the dangers of not enforcing the hairnet policy. Roger was sure that hair would slip into the paint and said, "We should just stamp 'Made in Mexico' across the speedometer." They talked about the significance of allowing female operators to wear male uniforms. They voiced doubt over the prudence of allowing the workers to roam the main areas without supervision. And they agreed that, given how things were going, it was only a matter of time before Mary would let someone bring her baby to work. "That's a liability issue," said Steve. "We're not in the day care business." Burt summed up the meeting by saying, "The thing that bothers me is that we don't know what type of product they're putting together in there. Now that's the problem."

Throughout this meeting, no one mentioned that, as far as their client was concerned, the product was approaching corporate standard. The managers, however, were alarmed over the quality of their gauges, not because of the performance of the gauges in inspection tests, but because they feared that the telltale traces of Mexican women could be identified in them. They made the connection between seeing women roaming the work spaces and relaxing their uniform standards with a loss of managerial control over the labor process. Their lack of control, in turn, meant that the product would not emerge as planned, but instead as a product of disposable *mexicana* labor. Steve implied this connection when he said, "What I don't want is for someone ... to walk in this plant and find a bunch of Mexican girls running around.... I'll hear that we're going Mexican on them and our product going to hell."

The root of the problem, they decided, was that Mary was not "American" enough to "Americanize" the labor process, and was not disciplined enough to keep the feminine influence within its proper bounds. Roger was assigned the task of speaking firmly to Mary about the situation and of advising her that she was being placed on probation. According to Roger, he was trying to be as diplomatic as he could when he told Mary that she needed to "represent the corporation out there" and perform her job to the standards of "American professional behavior." He said, "I told her that we were worried about the product."

Mary was furious. She said, "I told him [Roger], 'I am as American as you are,'" by which she meant that her identity as a "mexicana" did not disrupt the skills associated with an "American" identity at MOTW.

Soon thereafter, the managers decided to demote Mary for being, as Roger recorded on her evaluation form, "unprofessional," "failing in the performance of duties," and not producing quality product. In addition, they demanded that she attend three hours of supervisory-training classes offered by the University of Texas at El Paso every week on top of the overtime she was continuing to perform. He also denied her a routine salary inflation compensation. Mary's demotion put her on equal footing with the other Mexican supervisors, at a level below the American supervisors.

Mary begrudgingly attended the supervisor classes. "It's an insult," she said. "They're putting me in there to humiliate me. As far as I can see, they're the ones who aren't being very American. You know they want top-quality work without paying for it or even giving enough time for training. And then they turn around and say it's because Mexican females don't do good work. If you don't put in the training time, you can't expect anyone to do it!"

On the heels of her demotion and salary cut, and with mounting evidence that Mary would not mend her attitudes, the managers decided to fire her. When I asked Roger why the managers focused so much on Mary's supervisory style rather than on the obvious improvements, according to performance tests, she made in production, he said, "We want a good product. That's what this is about really. It's a long-term issue.... We're an American operation. We've got an American product.... Mary doesn't understand."

Shortly after Mary's departure, the gauge production line was returned to a U.S. facility. The politics over Mary's supervisory methods; the uniforms, fingernail polish, and hairnets; and whether or not MOTW would turn into a day care facility had taken its toll on the organization and its budget. The women who could not be placed in other electronic-assembly positions were encouraged to leave. Eventually, the line was outsourced to an external producer. "This makes us look bad," Burt said; "losing a line means something's gone seriously wrong."

Steve explained that, despite all of the turmoil, he had no regrets over his actions: "I'd rather lose a line than ship out inferior products," he said.

Mary sued the company in court and received some back pay. "He didn't expect me to fight," she later said of Steve. "He thought that because I'm Mexican, I'd just let him walk all over me. He was wrong."

Feminist Politics and the Maquiladora Mestiza

Speaking of the new mestiza and *mestizaje* almost ten years after the publication of *Borderlands/La Frontera*, Anzaldúa says, "The new mestiza is sensitive to and aware of her ethnic and cultural *mestizaje*. She is politically aware of what goes on in these different communities and worlds and therefore brings a different perspective to what is going on. She is no longer just a Chicana. That is not all that she is. She is the feminist in the academy, the dyke in the queer community, and the person working in straight America" (Anzaldúa and Hernández 1995–1996, 9). And at MOTW, she is the *mexicana* working in American administration. To borrow (and thereby distort) Anzaldúa's image, she is the maquiladora *mexicana* resignified to be the new maquiladora mestiza.

Clearly, one of the key issues for the MOTW operation is how the production of value in the factory works out through the processes for identifying nationality and gender as markers for more and less valuable people and the things that embody their labor. And this calculation revolves around the continual efforts of MOTW managers to resolve the perplexing paradox described, to some degree, by Harvey (1982): how will they turn the vibrant energies of Mexican women into a feature of male, American goods? Another way of putting this question is, how will they manage people, whom they regard to be disposable, in the manufacture of quality goods?

As maquiladora mestizas, Rosalía, Cynthia, and Mary bring the above paradoxes to the fore as they navigate the myth of the disposable third world woman found in the local discourse of *mexicana*. In confronting this myth, each woman resignifies its meaning for her, but as they do so they also raise questions for Butler's (1993) version of resignification. Can we think of resignification as a partial subversion or, more to the point, even as a radical rearticulation with status quo conditions and subjections? The maquiladora mestiza is resignified to the extent that she was never predicted to emerge and is still a surprise when she does. But her resignification as a new border subject is simultaneous with the reinforcement of the corporate script for crafting employee identities around the markers of sex, nationality, and culture into the spaces and positions of the corporate workplace. While each woman expresses a cultural hybridity that resonates with Anzaldúa's vision for *mestizaje*, each actively works toward maintaining the border of a class division on which the maquiladora industry thrives. As Rosalía Americanizes, as Cynthia makes a name for herself throughout the industry, and as Mary subverts corporate policy to improve the labor process, the majority of *mexicanas* in the maquiladoras continue to work for poverty wages. Many live in economically strained conditions, and fewer than a fraction will ever rise in the corporate ranks. Their success begs the question: Is a political articulation possible between Anzaldúa's version of a radical mestiza and the probusiness, maquiladora mestiza in a feminist border politics?

Rosalía, Cynthia, and Mary disrupt some codes for interpreting their subject positions while holding steadfast to others. Their new *mestizaje* is evident in their hybridity and in their proclamation of themselves as women who know both sides of the border and the subjects who inhabit those places. Yet excluded from their *mestizaje* is a mixing with nonprofessional *mexicanas*, and even with each other in a social sense, except that each of them supports maquiladora trade associations and is active in politically conservative business groups. Moreover, each brings diversity to the firm and provides corporate managers with evidence of the firm's commitment to moving women and minorities through the ranks. In seeking how they might articulate with Anzaldúa's vision of a new mestiza, I have attempted to illustrate what is at stake in the formation of border subjects around a geography of difference and what, therefore, must be challenged by a feminist politics that seeks to forge coalitions across a spectrum of "distant others."

6

Crossing the Factory Frontier

[Two women have just passed through a U.S. immigration checkpoint between Ciudad Juárez and El Paso]

.... "Ya la hicimos, compita! ¡híjole! y con el de la migra de veras pusiste cara decente: 'American, sir, American.' ¿Y a poco eres americana?"

"No, pero ya sé pronunciar *American*."

...."We did it, girlfriend! Wow! You sure do put on a good show for the *migra*. 'American, sir, American.' Are you really American?"

"No, but I know how to pronounce *American*."

From the short story, "American, Sir ...," by Arminé Arjona, *Delincuentos* (2005)

In this chapter, as in the previous one, I detail a woman's journey across the internal corporate divides of gender and nationality that have historically worked to circumscribe Mexican women within the spaces of marginality and inevitable disposability. In this case, however, the woman I call "Gloria" wields the power of a labor strike over her American bosses. Her deft navigation of the social spaces of her factory complex demonstrates how her fight against being labeled as a local instance of disposable third world labor is also a fight for the company's well-being, as she and many of her Mexican peers understand it. For, as she demonstrates, her managers' efforts to label and thereby treat her as disposable, via the insistence that she is not trainable and has no skills, are evidence of their clear mismanagement of the company. This battle takes place across the stage of Gloria's body, which is the site of much scrutiny on the part of her managers. Her style of dress, her gestures, her language, her hair, her figure, and so on emerge as factors in her managers' evaluations of her intrinsic value. Yet while they deride her for being "too much of a Mexican woman," she turns this derision on its head and affirms a Mexican female identity that represents anything but disposability. This locally subversive act has repercussions beyond the factory walls and lasting implications for this global firm's internal structure and competitive position.

Gloria's struggle exposes how a question raised by contemporary feminist theorists is pressing also within the quotidian spaces of global factories: how can we conceptualize and recognize the intricate relationship between "real women" (women as social agents) and "woman" (an ideological representation of a female subject) (Fraser and Nicholson 1990; Scott 1999; Poovey 1990)? In addressing this issue, feminist scholars have shown how women often face the tricky situation of having to disavow the ideological identification of "woman" in order to become the kind of women they want to be. This certainly is the case when women come up against the global machinery that identifies them as disposable. And in such cases, we encounter a question related to the one above: can we theorize how women participate in their own representation of themselves as "real women" while simultaneously rejecting the representation of themselves as exemplars of "woman" or, more specifically, of "disposable third world woman?"

In this chapter, I will open up this discussion by way of an exploration of Gloria's journey through the ideological representation of her as a "typical Mexican woman," in which that identity is understood as the local representative of a global resource of disposable factory labor. Gloria has the goal of being recognized for her skills and managerial acumen within the Ciudad Juárez facilities of a U.S.-based firm that is initiating efforts to upgrade its Mexican labor force as part of a larger strategy for making the transition to more competitive flexible production. Through Gloria's endeavors, we see how the discourse of a "typical Mexican woman" is of a "docile," "submissive," and tradition-bound worker who is inherently expendable due to an intrinsic nontrainability (see also Salzinger 2003). Gloria has worked in this firm for over twenty years in an officially unskilled capacity. To gain skill and be promoted, she subverts the dominant representation of the "typical Mexican woman" as the local subject of a larger disposable condition, and she forces her managers to realize that they have misidentified her. She demonstrates that whereas she is indeed a Mexican woman, she is anything but someone bound to traditions and biological processes that render her worthless.

Gloria launches this struggle in a maquiladora that I call "Tres Reyes," the Mexican facilities of the firm Three Kings. When I arrived in Tres Reyes in 1993, its managers had initiated a shift toward a more flexible facility, in terms of both its client networks and its labor process, as a way to enhance overall performance (Wilson 1990; Gereffi 1991; Shaiken 1994). In August 1993, the signature elements of just-in-time production were being implemented (see Piore and Sabel 1984; Holmes 1989) and, most significantly for this study, a new initiative of "skilling up" the labor force was just underway. The managers hoped that by upgrading more of the Mexican labor force, it would improve its quality performance and its competitive edge. And, as in other maquiladoras, Mexican women were, by and large, excluded from this managerial vision of the skilling process. In Tres Reyes, as in so many other facilities, the skilling of the labor force is associated with the integration of men into the training programs rather than the training of women despite the latter's domination of the employment rolls.

My interviews with managers in Tres Reyes reflect how the discourse of the "typical Mexican woman" as untrainable—due to docility, lack of ambition, rampant hormones, and so forth—recreates the image of the disposable third world woman worker at the local level. A noted difference at Tres Reyes, however, is that despite this discourse, many of the company's employees (female and male) have worked there for numerous years. The company's technological system actually functions more smoothly when workers with experience are employed. The discourse of disposability does not, as in other firms, connect directly to a systematic process for ensuring a constant turnover rate (within two years) of the employed labor force. Instead, the discourse operates as a mechanism for denying workers with many years of experience the recognition and pay increases that are customary within the maquiladora industry as incentives for maintaining workers in a volatile labor market. Yet, even without these incentives, and for reasons that I explore in the following analysis, many workers do remain at Tres Reyes. Gloria confronts these numerous contradictions when her managers claim that despite her many years of service to the firm, she is neither a valuable employee nor trainable material. In her bid for a promotion from an officially "unskilled woman's job" as supervisor (a position defined within Tres Reyes as unskilled, in contrast to other firms) into a skilled managerial slot, she encounters the power of the discourse of the disposable plant woman worker, identified at Tres Reyes as a "typical

Mexican woman." Her efforts to gain skill in the eyes of her bosses are therefore attempts to present herself as a person of value, capability, and growth—as a woman with a future despite the discourse of her intrinsic disposability.

It should be said that at the time of my study, three of the four managers at Tres Reyes were women and all of the managers identify themselves as "Mexican–American."[1] The discourse of the typical Mexican woman cuts across gender and nationality. And we see through Gloria's efforts how the distinction between skilled and unskilled labor is a matter of deploying representations of both a national divide between Mexico and the United States and a sex difference among employees, such that Mexican men, unlike Mexican women, are seen by their managers as capable of acquiring solid "American business" skills. In the interpretation of Mexican men as capable of "Americanizing," in contrast to typical Mexican women, lies the reification of female disposability as a localized version of a global condition.

Consequently, when Gloria eventually moves into a managerial post, she scrambles the material codes for reading the difference between skilled and unskilled employees and, in so doing, subverts the ideological representation of the disposable third world woman. In her new position, she represents an impossibility: a skilled and valuable Mexican woman. The old guard of Tres Reyes managers claims that she is confusing the boundaries between skilled and unskilled employees, and they not only oppose her promotion but also quit in protest when she gains it. At issue in this struggle is a disagreement over who is working for the company's best interests: Gloria and her supporters, who believe that the managers are mismanaging the firm, or the managers, who believe that the company falls into unstable hands upon her promotion.

Among other things, this story illustrates that the capitalist continuum of uneven development (Harvey 1989) works through the negotiations of local identities specific to a particular place in time. The working out of social identities at the local level is not epiphenomenal to the functioning of the global firm. Instead, as we see here, the crafting of a local schema for recognizing the abstract categories of the division of labor, of which the disposable third world woman is one, within the local working population is of paramount importance to the generation of capital.

This analysis grows out of ethnographic research that I conducted over a year's period (1993–1994) in Tres Reyes and in subsequent interviews through 1998. This facility is located in Ciudad Juárez, Chihuahua, across the national divide from El Paso, Texas. Unlike in other chapters, I present the ethnography through specific conversations in order to recreate my interpretation of the events surrounding Gloria's changing identity and the implications for the company's functioning.

In tracking Gloria's journey from an unskilled employee to a skilled and powerful manager, I faced my own dilemmas in representing her efforts as a form of resistance. As geographer Cindi Katz writes, "In the crossroads of improbable possibilities and the performances of deception are some of the dilemmas of doing fieldwork" (1996, 171). My dilemma emerges when I see Gloria's actions as simultaneously resistance and compliance to the social relations of capitalism within Tres Reyes. I locate her resistance to the subversion of the practices monitoring the discourse of the "typical Mexican woman" and its linkages to disposability. Yet, she does so as she consolidates her authority over the labor process and the extraction of value from the poorly paid laboring energies of a vulnerable workforce. Within this dilemma, I encounter the added difficulty of theorizing the relationship between a woman as a social agent and the ideology of female disposability that she wants to escape. When Gloria forces the firm to recognize her skills, she is, in many ways, the author of a new story that defies the myth of the disposable third world woman, and she does so as she carefully preserves the notion that someone, somehow, has to be recognized as the most expendable worker within the capitalist division of labor.

A Manager's Tour of Tres Reyes

Tres Reyes is the wholly owned Mexican subsidiary of Three Kings, a coupon-processing firm based in Memphis, Tennessee. My study was based in Tres Reyes Plant I, a facility consisting of two buildings, administration and production, where about five hundred operators, five supervisors, and some forty-five section leaders (supervisor's assistants) worked along with Gloria and all but one of the four Tres Reyes managers. I entered the production facility with an invitation from management. For the first two weeks at Tres Reyes I interviewed managers, watched them work, and recorded their versions on how the firm operated. I attended meetings and had a work space within the general manager's office. After the initial two weeks, I then moved my research into production when Gloria, a supervisor and the interim superintendent, agreed to participate in my project. For the next several months, I followed Gloria on her days, worked in her office, and often met her at her house on the weekends. I interviewed all of the supervisors and most of the section leaders at Tres Reyes, as well as about forty operators, over that period.

My first understanding of Tres Reyes history came out of the initial conversations I held with managers. Their oral history of Tres Reyes was of a firm that had peaked in the mid-1980s and was currently reorganizing to pull out of a desperate financial crisis. They described how in the early 1970s, the corporate officers decided to take advantage of the young maquiladora program opening up in northern Mexico and expand operations by relocating all labor-intensive processing to Ciudad Juárez. The Mexican facility employed about one thousand production workers by 1978, working under a Mexican and male management team. In the early 1980s, corporate streamlining replaced all of the Mexican nationals with the Mexican–American staff. The former general manager, Tommy, recalled, "When I took over in 1982, the company was really struggling for the first time. We needed to make some changes. So one day, I went to the store and when I saw those scanners at the checkout, I thought, 'Hey, we can do the same thing at Tres Reyes.' ... We put in the computer system and suddenly we have the information right at our fingertips ... that means we don't need the same quality of workers we had back then. Scanning is automatic. You don't have to read or even concentrate. The computer does it all." After dismissing the Mexican production managers, the El Paso–based administrators, all U.S. citizens, moved into the offices in Ciudad Juárez. Additionally, claiming that supervisors were no longer needed to perform technical tasks, Tommy cut the supervisory pay in half, dismissed the male supervisory staff, and promoted a number of Mexican women to replace them. He described this move as a "deskilling" of the work rather than an "upgrading" of the workers.

> *Tommy*: We put in the computers, the scanning ... and we just didn't need as much from the supervisors. Once I put in that system, we could really streamline and focus on production. All the information was stored on a disk, and we just needed a couple of people to handle that end of things. After that, the supervisors were just there to make sure that people got to their places on time and that sort of thing. They didn't have any technical skills.... The old supervisors did. They had to know how to handle all of that information. Coupons are like banks. You've got to keep all the figures straight. Now the computers do all that hard work.

Tommy's version of deskilling was corroborated by other managers who spoke of the lack of skills among the Mexican women supervisors in contrast to the formerly more skilled Mexican male supervisors.

Melissa Wright (hereafter, MW): Are your supervisors skilled employees?

Carmen (human resources manager): What do you mean by skill?

MW: I mean, have they developed valuable knowledge and techniques? Are they different from the operators?

Carmen: They have some people skills, but I wouldn't really call them skills. Probably most of the operators could do what they do. They just don't have a chance.... It wasn't always like that. The supervisors used to be skilled before we put in the computers.

MW: Why do you even have supervisors?

Carmen: We need someone to make sure the workers do what they're supposed to do.... But they don't have anything I would call technical skills.

Martin (the general manager): I've been thinking about your questions about skills, and I think speaking for the managers, we see the Mexican side different from how we used to see it. Before the computers, we really had to work together because they controlled the actual information. Supervisors then really had to know the business. But now they don't so much, or at least that's how we see it. And I'm sure that when Tommy hired Gloria and then the other women supervisors that he thought he was hiring an unskilled labor force.

In a separate interview, Tommy seconded Martin's suspicion when he explained why he had chosen to promote Gloria out of the possible candidates for the supervisor promotion. "She was hungrier than the rest," he told me.

Georgina (customs manager): It's Mexico. It's a very authoritative culture. They need someone standing over them all the time.... Does she [Gloria] have skills? I wouldn't say so.

Gloria's skills, or lack thereof, became a corporate issue when local managers and corporate executive officers decided that they would hire a Mexican national as part of a corporate strategy to make the facility more "flexible." Their first step toward "flattening" the work hierarchy was to integrate the Mexican production staff into decision-making roles and diminish the social division segregating "Mexican" from "American" positions. Their hope was to facilitate communication between the two national domains of production and administration.

In a joint interview, Martin and Tommy both explained that they encouraged the promotion of Mexican nationals as part of Tres Reyes's more "flexible" strategy.

> *Tommy (the formal general manager)*: The automation took care of our problems in the 1980s, but now Tres Reyes has got to become more flexible ... and be responsive to clients and have better communication with the production workers.

> *Martin (the current general manager)*: "We want to improve communication between administration and production. That means training more Mexican nationals and giving them more responsibility.

One of the proposed actions for meeting this goal was to hire a Mexican national for the formerly American position of production manager. Like many multinational maquiladoras, Tres Reyes had a traditional split between "American" and "Mexican" jobs. Traditionally, the American jobs were those in management and engineering located above the Mexican production positions, such as supervisors, technicians, and operators. At Tres Reyes, as in most of the other maquilas I studied, all of the Mexican positions were subordinate to American ones. The American jobs fall under U.S. labor codes, pay U.S. taxes, and conform to a pay scale that is commonly one third (or more) higher than the wages for the same position when it is designated as a Mexican job.[2] Although both Tommy and Martin agreed that the company would save money by hiring a Mexican national into a former American position, both stressed that the decision was designed to enhance flexibility rather than to cut salary costs.

The American–Mexican split in the division of labor also found an expression in the spatial layout of Tres Reyes. Makers of national difference segregated the Tres Reyes complex into the Mexican production and American administrative domains. I found the designation of the Mexican area as the "Spanish" site and of the American area as the "English" site. Language was a marker of professionalism in a place where to be Mexican was to represent a position subordinate to any American position within the division of labor. For example, in Tres Reyes administration, the ambient background music originated from an El Paso country-and-western station. I asked Carmen why they chose this station over a Ciudad Juárez station even though most of the clerks were Mexican nationals, and she replied, "This is the American part of Tres Reyes, so we have an El Paso station." By contrast, a Ciudad Juárez station filled the production area with the sounds of *cumbias, corridas*, and Mexican pop. The effective marking of language areas was one mechanism for stamping the national code built into the division of labor into the spaces of Tres Reyes. To paraphrase from Pierre Bourdieu (1984) in an understanding of the symbolic capital of linguistic and cultural markers, Spanish was a stylistic impossibility within Tres Reyes administration, because Spanish itself was a marker of Mexicanness, and Mexicans worked in the lesser skilled jobs in production.

> *Martin*: I think there has always been this feeling that the Mexicans just don't have good business sense and that they can't be trusted to make decisions. I think you could say that there's been an "us and them" mentally. Something like, we're the professionals and they're the hired labor.... Speaking English, *I think, has been more symbolic than practical* [my emphasis].
>
> *Georgina*: We have a different work ethic over here. The American work ethic is very different from the Mexican way of doing things.... I am Mexican–American, my parents came from Mexico, but I could never tell you that I understand their [the "Mexican"] way of doing things.... They don't have "American" business sense.

Indeed, even though the managers had decided to hire a Mexican national into a formerly American position, they sought someone who would fit in with the "American" schema in administration. The requisites for the position included an ability to speak English, even though all of the managers agreed that English was not necessary to perform the job while Spanish was.

> *Martin*: It was a big move to hire a Mexican and I think everyone wanted to find the most Americanized Mexican they could.

The significance of the national distinction within this context of finding the most "Americanized Mexican" was articulated to me as an issue of skills. Seeming more American than Mexican was an indication of professionalism. To reflect "Americanness," therefore, was to reflect an acquisition of the skill required to hold an American job. All of these jobs were described as skilled, and certainly more skilled than any of the Mexican positions.

> *Martin*: I think there was a lot of uncertainty about how to fill the position. Most of the managers thought that the Mexicans really couldn't do it.... I think the idea was that if we

could find someone who seemed more American, then that would be the right kind of person.

Once the managers decided to fill the production manager position with a Mexican national, only two candidates were under consideration. One was Gloria, suggested by Martin, and the other was Mauricio, a male supervisor. In a heated debate over who had the most qualifications for the job, the discourse around the typical Mexican woman was preeminent among those arguing that Gloria did not have the proper qualifications. Unlike Mauricio, she could not develop the professional skills for that position because as a Mexican woman she was bound within a cultural tradition and could never Americanize. At Tres Reyes, such a fate meant that she would never acquire managerial skills.

> *Martin*: And there was this feeling that none of the Mexican women could ever become the type of American manager we wanted. She just wouldn't reflect the right corporate image.
>
> *Georgina*: We needed more degreed Mexicans ... we want someone who can work with us, on our side ... someone who understands American business. The Mexican culture, unfortunately and I hate to say this, just doesn't allow its women to really get ahead. And they don't want to. I think we have to look to the men.
>
> *Martin*: We definitely were looking for someone who could fit in with us, with an American group. And I just don't think anyone thought that Gloria could ever fit in. I mean, Gloria didn't want to fit in with the Americans. She made that clear, and that bothered everyone.

The discourse for understanding Mauricio as skilled emerged through a discussion of how he was different from a Mexican woman. He therefore could escape the "unprofessional" Mexican culture by demonstrating more American national traits indicative of a business culture.

> *Carmen*: I think that of all the employees that Mauricio will probably have a career. He's ambitious. He's got an education. He's smart. And I think he's got a good head for business.
>
> *MW*: How about any of the women supervisors?
>
> *Carmen*: I think that they're about as high up as they're going.
>
> *Georgina*: The Mexican women can't get ahead. It's a culture.

Before describing how Gloria proved them all wrong, I will describe her version of the social geography of Tres Reyes. From her perspective, we see not a history of deskilling but of the flexible skills required of a supervisory team working with a predominantly young, migrant labor force during years of technological change. In her discourse, she and the other Mexican women supervisors are professionals who skillfully oversee the social complexities of the production domain.

Gloria's Tres Reyes

Gloria was one of the first ten Tres Reyes employees. She was seventeen and desperate for a job after her family moved from Parral, a town near Chihuahua City, in 1972. Her father found work in El Paso as a trash hauler, and her mother started cleaning private homes. As the oldest daughter, Gloria was expected not only to find a job but also to take care of her eight younger siblings since her parents were out of Ciudad Juárez for most of the week. She thought of working for RCA, the TV manufacturer which had just opened its doors, but decided on Tres Reyes because she preferred the relatively quiet atmosphere of coupon processing.

She characterized contemporary Tres Reyes as a complex social milieu that reflected the urban changes within Ciudad Juárez. Tommy promoted her to supervisor after she had worked at Tres Reyes for thirteen years, during which time she had trained hundreds of operators and had worked as a supervisorial assistant. In contrast to the managerial version of the simplification of supervisory work over time, she said her job had become more difficult over the years due to changes in the social landscape of Ciudad Juárez.

MW: Is the supervisory work easy?

Gloria: Absolutely not.

MW: Why? Hasn't the computer system made it easier?

Gloria: In some ways, but the city is more complicated. The people are more complicated.

A few days after I arrived, Gloria gave me a tour of the production floor. Her version of Tres Reyes resonated with managers' insofar as she saw production to be a "Mexican" production domain apart from the "American" administrative area. For her, however, Tres Reyes production was a microcosm of Ciudad Juárez, and instead of a production area of homogeneously unskilled workers, she described an organization of people possessing a wide variety of characteristics that affected their job performance.

We started in Receiving and followed the coupon's path through the floor.

> *Gloria*: The coupons come here from El Paso in those packages and boxes. We don't need many people in this area, just a handful, but it's important to get the numbers right. If you mess up here, the whole thing is wrong. So I put trustworthy people in this area, some of the women who have worked here for a while. The ones with children.
>
> *MW*: Why the ones with children?
>
> *Gloria*: They're here to work, nothing else.

Then we moved to the *prepa* area, where the packages were opened and coupons dumped in heaps of crumpled and often torn pieces of paper.

> *Gloria*: The *viejos* [older people] work here.
>
> *MW*: Why?
>
> *Gloria*: They have to straighten out the coupons, stack them. Make them neat. Young people get frustrated. It's boring work to them. They want to work with computers and be in the center of things....
>
> There's really not any work for older people in the maquilas ... the maquilas won't hire anyone over twenty-five.

As we stood on the fringes of this work area, one of the materials handlers wheeled a cart full of packages from the receiving area. Suddenly, the thirteen quiet workers leapt from their seats and dashed over to the cart. Two of the women reached the cart before the others, rifled through the packages, and grabbed a couple. One of them tossed a package to another woman standing off to the side.

> *Gloria*: The *viejos* are hard to work with, very cranky. They go through the packages to pick the cleanest ones, and those two [women] are in charge. Marsela is bossy and you have to watch her, but she keeps everyone in line and she's [a] very

good worker. She's almost seventy. The problem with her is that she picks on the young women for what they wear.

On an afternoon a few months later, I watched Marsela reduce one operator to tears because she was offended by the younger woman's style of clothing and had called her a whore. A supervisor moved the younger operator out of earshot of the older one.

From *prepa*, we moved into sorting, the manual sorting area. Here about ten workers categorized coupons into stacks of manufacturer brands or grocery client.

> *Gloria*: This is the difficult area because they have to read and memorize the codes.... But these workers make the least money. It's harder to keep up with production bonuses.
>
> *MW*: How do you keep people here?
>
> *Gloria*: I asked Martin and Carmen to change the system so that these workers make more money. But they don't ... understand that this is harder work. They think it's just not as productive. So I help these workers out. We have a flexible agreement.... I help out their production figures.... And I don't put migrants here.
>
> *MW*: What do you mean?
>
> *Gloria*: I only put *juarenses* [people born and raised in Juárez] in here.

She then explained how the recent migrants from other parts of Mexico were not as trustworthy. Those from Torreón and Durango, she said, were too timid; those from Mexico City [*chilangos*] were confrontational; whereas the employees from Chihuahua City were militantly independent.

Most of the 350 employees worked in the computer-scanning section located in the middle of the production floor. Once the coupons are flattened and stacked into neat piles by the *prepa* workers, and the minority of coupons without bar codes sent to the manual sorting area, the bulk of coupon orders are processed by workers who scan the bar codes with an electronic eye.

"We put the new workers here," said Gloria, "but we have to spread *cholos* [gangs] apart. We can't put *cholos* together, but this is where the *jovenes* [youth] are the best workers ... they like to work with computers, new technology."

Then we walked over to the materials handler's station, where young men carried trays of coupons, loaded others onto dollies, and wheeled them around between work areas in the facility. "These guys are all rancheros [or *los ranchos*], from the country. They have better manners than the *cholos* or the *roquers* [those who listened to contemporary hard rock].... They get along with everybody."

She identified the rancheros by their cowboy boots and western wear and by their taste in music. Anyone seen to be a ranchero was considered to be perfect for the materials handler position. Like her managers, Gloria also read the division of labor on the sleeve of the labor force.

Additionally, Gloria, like most other supervisors I met, was not comfortable asking a woman to move a box or pick up a tray. She preferred to ask men to do those things and explained her preference in terms of a female dislike for moving objects and lifting anything.

> *MW*: Why are there no women here [in the materials handling area]?
>
> *Gloria*: They carry things and get dirty ... it's tiring. The boys like it, but not the girls.

From the materials section, we moved to invoicing and shipping, where I learned that more of the unmarried young women and the *roquers* worked because the supervisor there, Emi, was "good with the young women" and would "run off a troublemaker within a week." The *roquers* were, in Gloria's estimation, always potential troublemakers, and they seemed to blur some with the *cholos* on the Tres Reyes plant floor.

What emerged after this tour was a mapping of the Tres Reyes production area into sections of older and younger, female and male, married and unmarried, single mothers and wed mothers, rockers, rappers, gang members, urban and rural, and migrant and local employees who performed a variety of tasks. Gloria clearly did not see the Tres Reyes production domain in the same way as her managers. And her vision of how women became supervisors was also at odds with the managerial account of their promotion. She describes how incompetent male supervisors were replaced with women who were adept at reading the complex networks within the city's labor force.

> *Gloria*: A good supervisor has to know people and the work. Mainly it's the women who care enough to ask questions and

get to know people personally. That's why my supervisors are so good.

Tres Reyes had more women supervisors than any other maquila I had studied. Whereas the managers described the movement of women into supervision to be an outcome of deskilling, Gloria said quite the opposite. She described how Tommy, the former general manager, had dismissed the previous male Mexican supervisors because they were not good at their jobs.

> *Gloria*: We started to have problems and they couldn't bring things under control.
>
> *MW*: What sort of problems?
>
> *Gloria*: Workers not doing their jobs and there was a walkout.... I told Tommy that I could get things under control.
>
> *MW*: How did you do that?
>
> *Gloria*: I've worked here longer than anybody and I know the city. And I work with some very good supervisors. We work together, like [a] team. That's why I picked them.
>
> *MW*: You picked the supervisors?
>
> *Gloria*: Well, we decided who would apply for supervisors' jobs. We knew who could do it.

Unlike her managers, she did not see the company as run by the computer system. Instead, she said that the workers actually exercised a great deal of control over their own work because they controlled the pace. The challenge for supervisors was to make sure that workers performed their jobs up to speed and within the proper quality ranges. To accomplish this task in such a way as to seem automatic, Gloria organized an elaborate social system that her managers did not know even existed. Moreover, given their descriptions for her, they thought her to be incapable of such organizational skills.

Gloria's Division of Labor

Gloria enforced the corporation's division of labor but not in the manner described by her managers. She had developed over the years an elaborate social network of insiders and outsiders to a patronage system encircling her. Her social network extended through the supervisors to the section leaders and down to the operators in a dynamic system of give and take, which she manipulated to oust rivals to her authority at all levels.

She described her social strength as one built around *confianza*, a word usually translated to mean some combination of intimacy, trust, confidence, and loyalty. Gloria intended for all of those senses to be understood when she said she had *confianza* with someone or that *confianza* did or did not exist with others.[3]

She explained that her networks of *confianza* were critical for identifying who belonged where within the division of labor and for controlling them in their jobs. She relied upon her networks of *confianza* to identify the employees—as *cholos*, single, rappers, mothers, and so forth—and to keep these various sorts of people in line. Her interpretation of social identity was an interpretation of someone's position in the division of labor in much the same way that her manager's interpretation of her as a typical Mexican women was simultaneously an interpretation of her as unskilled. However, her *confianza* networks eventually forced her managers to realize that they had misinterpreted who she was and therefore where she belonged within the Tres Reyes division of labor.

When I met Gloria, she received only a supervisor's salary. Still, she and the other supervisors clearly saw her as the boss in production, where there were five supervisors working under her, another fifty or so section leaders under them, and then the almost five hundred operators.

Everyone had a set wage structure, time schedule, and production standard. The operators had to process so many coupons within a given period of time, then they received bonuses above that amount. Section leaders had to ensure that the people in their areas met their collective minimum and only received bonuses when their workers produced more than the minimum degree of work. Supervisors received a salary but were immediately chastised if their area did not meet production projections. Every operator or section leader who committed an infraction, such as not meeting production quality standards, suffered a loss in pay. Every supervisor feared reprisal over an unexplained deficit in their production numbers.

"You can't expect people to do something for you if they're always afraid of losing their job," Gloria explained. Her response to this rigid and punitive social arrangement was to trade flexibility for loyalty. Several operators talked of how Gloria would help them out, give them advances and personal loans, provide pointers, and even turn a blind eye to an occasional absence as long as they were loyal to her. Loyalty meant advising a supervisor of a *rebelde* (someone who thought of organizing workers for any reason) or *lider* (someone who challenged authority and resisted being managed), or notifying a supervisor if someone was cheating and stashing coupons in the bathroom trash to pad their numbers.

In exchange for loyalty, the operators were treated with leniency and respect. One operator, Miriam, explained that she had worked at Tres Reyes for over a decade because "when you find a supervisor who will talk to you and find out why you missed a day or why you weren't feeling well, then you stay. In other maquilas, they don't care.... Of course, you have to give something in return."

The return to Gloria was an internal policing system. Information passed up and down the floor, favors were handed out, and loyalty promised such that Gloria knew most of the five hundred operators by name. She also knew whom she could not trust if the employee had not responded to supervisory efforts to cultivate *confianza* with them.

Emi, another supervisor, explained how *confianza* worked: "I tell my section leaders that their job is to get to know everyone. Know why they work here. About their families. If they go out to the bars or go back home. If they have kids. If they're *cholos*. You have to know all of this...."

MW: Do you have *confianza* with your workers?

Emi: Yes, if I don't, I run them off [*los corro*]. You know, this isn't like the Phillips factory where everything moves on time. We've got to keep them motivated and working. You can't have a *rebelde*.... I can spot a *rebelde* in a week.... Then run him off.

MW: How can you tell you have a *rebelde*?

Emi: From experience, and then the others tell me. They say, "He won't do what you say," or, "He's making comments." That kind of thing.

The *confianza* that Emi has with her workers forms part of Gloria's network of *confianza* because they have *confianza* with each other.

Emi: I'll do anything for Gloria. She knows that because she'll do anything for me.

MW: What do you have to do for each other?

Emi: Just back each other up, no matter what.... She watches out for us on this side. They [the U.S. managers] don't know anything. *She runs this place and they don't even know it* [my emphasis].

Gloria spoke of her *confianza* with the supervisors as the critical link in her network since she needed them to organize workers in their areas. She was also in a position to mete out favors to them in exchange for their loyalty and trust. For example, when a supervisor, Lulu, had a miscarriage and then fell into a noticeable depression, Gloria gave her a month of paid leave without notifying the managers. She said that Lulu needed time and was a good supervisor with high performance ratings, even if the rules did not allow for such a break. Martin told me later that he realized that he had not seen Lulu for a while but her work was being done, her check was getting cashed, and no one mentioned anything at all.

> *Martin*: Whenever I made the rounds, they would say that she had just stepped out.

Again in contrast to the managers' version of events, Gloria saw her move into the interim superintendent spot as a temporary pause en route to being production manager. For this reason, she knew that she had to make a good showing in the job because her performance would be evaluated when she applied for the manager's job. Part of this strategy was to make sure that quality was up, that there were no labor disputes, and that *rebeldes* were run off. She said her goal was to make production *seem to operate as if by computer*. Her first test occurred immediately upon assuming the position in the midst of a labor walkout.

> *Martin*: I don't know what she said, but as soon as she stepped in, everyone went back to work. It was a mess. Everyone was mad about overtime. We had been working seven-day weeks and they walked out. Then we put Gloria in and suddenly it was like there was no problem.... I never asked her how she did it.
>
> *Gloria*: Well, it was a big problem with the other manager. So as soon as she left, I called together the supervisors and said, we need to get this place working again. We can figure out the problems after we get to work.
>
> *Emi*: We told our people that if they came back to work that we would take care of the overtime. We would be more lenient. The Americans don't understand how it works. They just said, "No, you have to work overtime." They don't know how to be reasonable.... As soon as she [the former U.S. manager] left, then we [the Mexicans] took charge. It's different

now with Gloria. She knows how to treat people because she knows what it's like to work here.

MW: Why did you want to help Gloria work this out?

Emi: I wanted her to go all the way to the top. She's the best worker here. She is Tres Reyes.

According to all accounts—managerial and supervisory, "American" and "Mexican"—Tres Reyes production did get back on track after Gloria assumed the superintendent position.

Martin: Actually, things are working well under Gloria. Things have calmed down. Quality is back up.

Nonetheless, Gloria's stint in this position did not reflect skilled experience in the managers' eyes. They could not see how production was organized into networks of *confianza* and around Gloria's mapping of social space. Yet even when the managers could see that production was back on an even keel, they did not attribute the recovered stability to Gloria. She continued to represent the typical Mexican woman in their eyes. And so they decided to hire Mauricio, another supervisor, to be the new production manager.

The managers took almost six months to decide that Mauricio was to be the next production manager of Tres Reyes. Meanwhile, Gloria continued to perform the job of interim superintendent and in effect carry the load for the manager's position. Their decision and the ensuing protests revolved around a discussion of who Gloria really was—a typical Mexican woman or a skilled Tres Reyes employee? For the managers, the two together posed an impossibility. For Gloria and her supporters in production, her skills emerged precisely from her experience as a typical woman worker in the city's maquiladoras.

Tres Reyes versus Three Kings

Mauricio had worked at Tres Reyes for five years when I met him. He had started as an operator even though he had a master's degree in agricultural engineering.

Mauricio: I needed a job. We had a baby.... It was hard at 100 pesos a week.

Unable to support his family on the income, he worked two jobs for eighteen hours a day until he was promoted to supervisor about four months later.

MW: You were promoted quickly.

Mauricio: Yes, I think they realized that I was not your average operator here.... It is hard for everyone, but I have my degree.

Over several conversations with Mauricio, he explained his skills in terms of his being stricter and more authoritative than Mexican women, on average, and more than Gloria, in particular.

MW: How would you describe your own skills?

Mauricio: I understand computer systems and am a tough manager. I know how to handle people. I'm tougher than most here.

MW: Is being tough a skill?

Mauricio: Well I think so. It's something you have to figure out. I mean you need to be compassionate but also let them know who's boss. Some of the women, you know Mexican women, have a harder time with that.... Gloria is a good supervisor but she's not tough enough with the people to be a manager. That's what I've seen.

I asked Carmen to explain why she thought him to be well suited for the job, and she backed Mauricio's account that he was "tougher" that the average Mexican woman, of whom Gloria was one.

MW: How are his skills different from Gloria's?

Carmen: Well, he's a man, for one thing. I think Gloria is a good supervisor but she might have a hard time.

Georgina: Yes, you may not like it, but Mexicans really don't respect Mexican women. You've got to be a man for them to listen.... Mauricio definitely benefits from being a man.

Throughout these conversations, I heard that Mauricio was qualified for the position precisely because he did not present the image of the typical Mexican woman. These same conversations reified this historical representation of this sort of woman who is submissive to male authority and bound to a culture which forces her into traditional roles and to a life with minimal economic power. Another example for this discourse of her and Mauricio's difference from this historical image occurred when managers spoke of Mauricio's ability to Americanize, or to escape the cultural traditions that bind him to the national domain of least skill and power in the Tres Reyes schema.

Georgina: Mauricio is the kind of person who can work in both worlds.

MW: How does he demonstrate this ability to work in both worlds?

Georgina: He makes an effort to speak English, and he works well with us over here. He fits in more than most Mexicans.

Martin: Mauricio comes over to [administration] and talks, has a cup of coffee. Sometimes he goes out for drinks with the American staff in El Paso.

His ability "to fit in" with the American managers was a reflection of his professionality according to Carmen. "He presents a professional, American, image.... He speaks English, always wears a tie, and has a real sense of the company, of the business."

Martin: I think everyone wants Mauricio in the position because, well, it's embarrassing to say, but I think that the group is leaning towards Mauricio because he's more like they are. You know, it's a big step to put a Mexican national in this job, and they want someone who seems more American than most Mexicans.

MW: Who do you want?

Martin: Well it's tough call. Gloria is probably the most knowledgeable one here, but Mauricio does have some things working in his favor.

MW: Like what? Could you give me an example?

Martin: It's image, I guess. He just seems right for the job here. And I think the managers would have an easier time working with him.

MW: Does his engineering degree have anything to do with his image?

Martin: Oh sure, he's very smart. I think the degree has a lot to do with it, but also his demeanor.... Like his clothes.

Ironically, Gloria had almost completed her master's degree in the seemingly more relevant field of business administration from the same university. When she started working at Tres Reyes, she had only finished the seventh grade, but after years of night courses, she finally attained her goal of a college degree. Yet, her education and years of work experience at Tres Reyes did not lay the foundation of skilled experience according to the managers.

The invisibility of her education contrasted to the visibility of his provides further evidence for Bourdieu's (1984) argument that recognition of social capital, such as skill, operates through an interpretation of material tastes and styles as the markers of this capital. To present the appearance of masculinity by wearing suits and talking more "toughly" to the workers marked Mauricio as a man of skill, whereas Gloria's continual negotiation with workers was interpreted to be "soft" or "womanly," and her personal appearance certainly did not evoke the markers of professionalism that her managers understood.

After some time, I realized that Gloria's clothing presented some real obstacles to the managers. She simply looked out of place to them.

> *Martin*: Now this is tacky but Gloria really should tone it down. Did you see her today?
>
> *MW*: No, not yet.
>
> *Martin*: She is in this bright orange, tangerine almost, outfit. Tight and lace. Carmen just about passed out.
>
> *MW*: What did she say?
>
> *Martin*: She hoped we didn't have any clients today. I have to agree that it's not a very professional look.
>
> *Georgina*: It's one thing in production but not over here.... I've tried to talk to Gloria about how she dresses but she looks at me like I'm crazy. You can't have a manager who looks like she's heading out to the disco with the operators after four. That's how Gloria looks sometimes.
>
> *Carmen*: Well it's a delicate issue but Gloria, I don't think, will change. She's a Mexican woman. That's how they dress and it's a problem for her career. It's a problem for us. But you can't change her. It's her culture. It's who she is, I guess.

Gloria's self-presentation fed directly into the managerial interpretation of her as unprofessional and unskilled after all the years she had worked there.

> *Georgina*: I know you've been talking with Gloria, and she's been here for twenty-one years, but she doesn't understand what it takes to run a business. The hard hours. Always having to learn how to overcome problems.
>
> *MW*: She hasn't learned....
>
> *Georgina*: No, she hasn't picked up the skills that I think she should.

Carmen: Gloria is a good supervisor. She's good with people, but I don't think she should be in charge of production.

MW: Why? She's been here for a long time.

Carmen: Yeah, and I guess that's part of the problem. You would think after being here for so long that she would have developed more…. You know, gotten a better sense of the computer system and finances. I just don't think she has.

Martin disagreed with their assessment that Gloria did not understand the computer or financial systems, but he did believe that her persona struck everyone in management as nonprofessional.

MW: Do you think Gloria knows how to work the computer system? Do whatever you need to do as a manager?

Martin: Oh sure. I think Gloria could go toe-to-toe with anyone here. I know she knows how to diagnose and program the system, and the finances she could pick up, if she hasn't done it already. Gloria has her ways.

MW: Why do some others think she doesn't have the computer skills?

Martin: It's who she is, I think. Gloria refuses to compromise and be more appealing to people like Georgina, Berta [the vice president in El Paso], and probably Carmen.

MW: What do you mean?

Martin: She won't learn English, for example. That's just not good form here. There's this sense that we're an American company.

MW: Does she need English in that job?

Martin: Not really. But she doesn't seem the right type.

MW: What's that?

Martin: I guess Mauricio.

That Gloria not only did not speak English but also actually refused to take classes was considered to be proof-positive that she would not make a good manager.

Martin: You know she would start to take classes and then just quit. I think that really bothered everyone. It was like she didn't really try or want to learn the language.

MW: Do you think her monolingual Spanish made her seem too Mexican?

Martin: Certainly. She just seemed like every other maquila worker, not a manager.

Georgina: Gloria is an older generation of maquila worker. She came in when we were hiring like crazy and she found a good deal. It's not easy for someone like her to get a promotion. Most of these girls who come in, like she did, just stay at the ground level. *We gave her a break* [my emphasis].

Carmen: She's a good production worker, a good supervisor, but not managerial material.

Unsurprisingly, when Martin and the managers decided to hire Mauricio, Gloria and her *gente de confianza* were not pleased.

Emi: They are trying to get rid of Gloria but it won't work. She knows how to run this place with her eyes closed, and they will soon see that.

MW: What do you mean?

Emi: Just wait. Gloria will get the job.

Two days later, she did. On that morning, everyone came to work and sat quietly at their desks and work stations. The coupons were not moving.

Martin described the scene: "It was eerie. Everyone there but nothing happening. I got about as far as the scanning area when Emi motioned for me to come over and said that we better offer the job to Gloria or the supervisors would not make it work for a while. And then Lulu came over and said the same thing. In no uncertain terms, they were threatening to walk out.... The whole plant."

By the time he had walked off the floor, all of the supervisors, except for Mauricio and the other male supervisor, Fernando, had told him that they would protest any decision other than to make Gloria the production manager. After consulting with the other managers, he made the executive decision to give the job to Gloria and promised Mauricio that he would probably be promoted and transferred to another facility in the next year.

Martin: I didn't think the company would endure a strike. So I made what I thought was the only decision.

Gloria did not want to talk to me about the show of force. I saw her evasion of this topic to be evidence of her lack of *confianza* with me. I am an "American" in this schema, after all. Nonetheless, Emi told me, "We were prepared to do what was necessary because without Gloria, this place would fall apart. They're too dumb to know it. Bur she runs this place and they can't expect to make her work for Mauricio. She trained him. She trained all of us. It's humiliating and they don't know how this place really works."

I talked to several section leaders and operators who said that they would have done what the supervisors told them to do in that situation because they needed to stay on their good side. If the supervisors said, "Don't show up for work," then they wouldn't.

Ezequiel, one operator, explained his interpretation of events: "I've worked here for two years and Gloria is demanding but she also listens. In these maquilas when you have someone who listens to you, you want to work for them, even if they ask for a favor sometimes."

Another operator, Celí, said, "I couldn't afford to miss the work really, but I think they were wrong. They should have picked Gloria."

MW: Were you willing to protest?

Celí: It wasn't a protest. I was doing what my supervisor told me. Isn't that what I'm supposed to do?

As it turned out, a walkout did not take place and Gloria was officially offered the job. The other three managers—Carmen and Georgina in Ciudad Juárez, and Berta in El Paso—were furious with Martin and with the entire production staff. They called a meeting and Georgina, speaking for the group, announced that he had just sold the "future of the company" for nothing. Afterwards I asked her to explain why she was so upset: "This place is going down the drain. Now we have an operator in charge, someone who doesn't know anything about the business, and it's a disgrace."

Carmen: Things have been going downhill for a while. But this is really a mistake. Gloria does not belong in management. It will be chaos.

Two weeks later, Martin was fired by his boss in Tennessee, who had received complaints from the other managers that Martin was mismanaging Tres Reyes; one even accused him of embezzling, a charge that was subsequently dropped. I was informed that I was a persona non grata, but Gloria insisted that I keep visiting the plant. My access to managers, except for Martin who was no longer a Tres Reyes employee, was cut off, but from production I could see a tug-of-war over the reins of Tres Reyes. Gloria remained tight-lipped regarding the whole situation, and I relied on Emi to tell me the goings-on.

Emi: Berta [the vice president] quit.

MW: Why?

Emi: She didn't say but I know it's because she can't get rid of Gloria. She and Gloria don't get along.

Within one month, Georgina, who had worked with Tres Reyes for eighteen years, quit without explanation. Again, Emi translated the events for me and said it was over Gloria having access to the El Paso office. Although this facility was diminished in comparison to the company's salad years, managers still had office space in El Paso. Gloria was the first Mexican employee to have an office in the El Paso building. Then Carmen left, and then Mauricio, until Gloria oversaw the searches for all of these positions. A new general manager finally arrived, and Gloria was the only production manager he knew. She bought some new clothes, most of them bright, some with rhinestones, and all with matching pumps. I continued research for another month until one day when Gloria explained that she was too busy now to have me tag along and ask questions.

Conclusion

Gloria's struggle to make herself visible as a valuable employee at Tres Reyes takes aim at the discourses that correlate Mexican femininity with disposability, more broadly. To move up the Tres Reyes corporate ladder, she confronts not only the prejudices of her own managers but also the arsenal of discourses, radiating beyond this factory, that are readily available for identifying female Mexican maquiladora workers as emblematic of permanently unskilled, unprofessional, and untrainable workers who will never amount to anything in the business. This battle is waged at numerous scales: at the scale of her body, where her sartorial style is dissected as an indicator of her intrinsic worth; at the scale of the production floor, where her knowledge of social relationships is pitted against the U.S. managers'; and at the scale of the multinational corporation, where corporate executives from other locations weigh in on the dispute over Gloria's significance to the company. And as Gloria (with her supporters) and her managers quarrel over the question of her worth, we see how negotiations over local identities are actually the processes through which global capital takes shape as a spatialized set of relationships organized around a division of labor and the embodiment of value in people and in the things they make.

Gloria is undoubtedly resisting a form of power that has been used in an effort to subjugate her in a variety of ways. This power consists of the discourses that label her as unworthy and in the practices that, based upon them, deny her opportunities for more status and better pay within the company. She is, in other words, fighting against the myth of her disposability, and she succeeds in her struggle as a result of her own ability to control the production process, to extract value from laborers, and to build consensus across a diverse labor force. Her resistance, therefore, is not against the exploitation of labor or against capitalism as a system of material production and distribution. Indeed, she is quite clear that she is largely motivated by her loyalty to Tres Reyes, which she believes is being "mismanaged" by the current team. And, again, she uses her comprehensive knowledge of the significance of local identities for creating and managing the spaces of capitalist operations to demonstrate her superior capabilities. Through such efforts, she demonstrates that she is better than the U.S. managers at exploiting the value of workers. In the process, she emerges as a subject whose very existence challenges entrenched beliefs regarding the disposability of Mexican female workers and the third world women they represent. She is a skilled and valuable Mexican woman who knows how to use her power to grease the gears of global capital.

As such, Gloria's trajectory within Tres Reyes raises some of the questions addressed in chapter 5 regarding the conceptual separation between notions of power and resistance. Her acts of resistance are simultaneously power moves designed to solidify her grip over workers and the production process. These internal dynamics also demonstrate the complexities similar, again, to those discussed in the previous chapter behind the negotiation of identity and social difference as questions over the meaning of "mexicana" overlap with those regarding the divisions between "Mexicans" and "U.S.-Americans," "women" and "men," "professional" and "unprofessional," "valuable" and "disposable," and so on. When Gloria resignifies the identity of "mexicana" to represent a "valuable" Tres Reyes employee, she destabilizes the chain of binaries that have depended upon its oppositional connotation, and, unsurprisingly, the company experiences upheavals. But the resignification of her identity, as radical as that might be, is not a resignification of capitalist processes. Exploitation of labor continues to be her primary goal.

In the years since I conducted this research, much has changed. Gloria continued to manage coupon processing at Tres Reyes until the company was sold in the late 1990s to another multinational corporation and its coupon facilities closed. I lost contact with Gloria and do not know if she found another job. Martin told me in 2002 that the coupon processing formerly done in Tres Reyes had moved to a U.S. prison operation, and news reports from Chihuahua indicate that the Mexican maquiladoras are also looking to move operations into local prisons (Frontera Norte Sur 2005). All of this shows that the myth of third world disposability can change with the times. Its central protagonist may take on different traits—transforming from single and female to incarcerated and male—but the intrinsic quality of disposability remains intact, along with the capitalist value that emerges from it.

7

Paradoxes and Protests

I believe that a grave danger for women exists in each point of
the city. I believe that the simple fact of being a woman here is
a grave danger.

**Guillermina González, human rights activist in Ciudad Juárez,
Frontera Norte Sur, 3 March 2001**

In this chapter, I examine a social movement that has arisen in northern
Mexico, primarily in the urban centers of Ciudad Juárez and Chihuahua
City, along with international support to protest the violence that has
claimed the lives of hundreds of women and girls in the region. Many of
the victims have been workers in the Ciudad Juárez maquiladora industry. This movement consists of numerous organizations and individuals
who, in one way or another, are confronting also the discourse of female
disposability. They are fighting against the logic I illustrated in chapter
4 that describes female workers as disposable in a region where female
bodies have been dumped like trash in the desert. In this chapter, I focus
on one group in particular, the Mujeres de Negro (Women in Black),
to illustrate some of the difficult paradoxes that activists encounter as
they attempt to topple the myth of third world female disposability and
replace it with another discourse that declares all women and girls to
be always, a priori, valuable. In examining some of the fits and starts of
this movement, and of this organization's efforts to move it forward, I
hope to show that the fight against female disposability must be waged
on several fronts. And while we see in this case that there is no perfect

or single strategy for doing so, we also see that the fight against the myth is also a fight for civil rights, for workers' rights, and for, even, the rights of women to exist at all.

On November 25, 2002, thousands of people marched through the streets of Mexico City and demanded, in the name of social justice, an end to the violence against women in northern Mexico. "Ni Una Más" (not one more) was their chant and the name of their social justice campaign. Their words referred to the hundreds of women and girls who have died violent and brutal deaths in northern Mexico and to the several hundreds more who have disappeared over the last ten years. Many of the victims reveal patterns of ritualistic torture and serial murders. Others appear to be victims of domestic violence, drug-related violence, random sexual violence, and the like.[1] The Ni Una Más marchers, many working with human rights and feminist organizations in Mexico, are protesting against the political disregard and lack of accountability, at all levels of government, in relation to this surging violence against women. And the symbolic leaders of their movement are the Mujeres de Negro, a group of women from the northern capital city of Chihuahua, where some of the murders have occurred and about 360 kilometers south of Ciudad Juárez, the border city where the vast majority have taken place.

Over the last decade, as international coverage of the violence has grown, various new organizations have emerged to lead the protests and to provide structure for people who want to express their outrage over the crimes and the lack of governmental response to them.[2] As is so often the case in social justice causes, the various organizations that constitute the Ni Una Más campaign stake out different areas of expertise and terrain, and tensions often run high among them over the controversial issues of religion, feminism, abortion, and definitions of family. Particularly in Ciudad Juárez, such tensions have contributed to the proliferation of distinct organizations, as opposed to the formation of a consolidated umbrella group, and disputes among them often play out publicly in the local newspapers.[3] While these organizations do sometimes work together in the border city on major events, their mutual antagonisms are widely known and often interfere with the coordination of activities. Yet, in contrast to the Ciudad Juárez organizations, the Mujeres de Negro have succeeded in pulling together a wide and diverse coalition of groups that are located primarily in Chihuahua City and that, despite internal political and other differences, have established an umbrella organization to serve as a base for their activities.

In order to understand how this group has succeeded in forming such alliances, I chose to focus on the Mujeres de Negro in my research into the new civic networks that have grown through the formation of the Ni Una Más campaign. From January 2003 through July 2004, I interviewed Mujeres de Negro members and other participants of the Ni Una Más campaign, I participated in coordinated events, and I followed the constantly changing dynamic of the social networks that constitute the campaign. This research on the Mujeres de Negro represents one piece of a larger ethnographic project on the Ni Una Más campaign, more generally, and its impact on changing notions of transnational citizenship. To do this work, I lived in Ciudad Juárez for over a year, traveled regularly to Chihuahua City, and became integrated with the participants of this movement. My research was an ethnography of this movement, not of any particular organization, but of the movement as it unfolded through the social networks of its participants, some of whom worked directly with specific organizations and others who merely attended the activist and academic events that keep this movement going. Like any social movement, the structure of this phenomenon lies in these networks that are constantly transforming via the formation and disappearance of organizations, the making and breaking of alliances, the shifts in strategies, and the other mundane activities that generate social ties. And this chapter on the Mujeres de Negro represents one attempt to present how some of these dynamics form, change, and contribute to a larger social movement.

In the course of this research, I relied heavily on Rosalba Robles, an instructor at the Universidad Autónoma de Ciudad Juárez, who helped me set up interviews and whose own work on domestic violence directly informs my analysis (Robles 2004). I conducted archival research that consisted primarily of searching all of the regional dailies (in northern Mexico and in El Paso) for coverage, since the mid-1990s, of the protests surrounding the violence against women and of the incipient formation of the Mujeres de Negro and the other organizations within the campaign. In addition, I conducted interviews with civic and business leaders in Ciudad Juárez, Chihuahua City, Mexico City, and El Paso for their perspectives on the movement and its impact on the economic development of the border region.

Early in this research, I realized that the Mujeres de Negro confronted a powerful paradox in their efforts to form a public coalition to advocate for the rights of women to be safe on the street and to demand government accountability in relation to these rights. The paradox is the following: in taking their protests to the public sphere and exercising their democratic rights as Mexican citizens, the Mujeres de Negro are publicly declaring the right of women to exist in the public sphere both as citizens and as people who deserve to be free from violence and fear. Yet, as they take to the streets, they are vulnerable to attacks that they are "public women" in a discursive context where that label continues to be used effectively to dismiss and devalue women for "prostituting" themselves by venturing beyond the domestic sphere, that traditional domain of female purity and obligation (see Castillo 1999; Wright 2004). Therefore, the Mujeres de Negro face the paradox that by exercising their democratic voices through public protest, they are dismissed, by their detractors, as "unfit" citizens, based on their contamination as "public women," whose causes are equally contaminated by their public presence. This gendering of space and of the democratic process, a process which by definition requires the active public participation of the citizenry, and the dismissal of women's democratic voices based on their exercise of democratic rights create a powerful conundrum that the Mujeres de Negro cannot ignore.

One of my aims in this chapter is to demonstrate that even as the Mujeres de Negro challenge the twisted logic that dismisses their public protest due to its public nature, they cannot fully escape its implications. For, as Michel Foucault (1995) well illustrated, there is no total escape from the discursive context in which this paradox makes sense. Like women activists through time and space, the Mujeres de Negro do not have the luxury of ignoring or escaping the contradictions of modern democracies that, while proclaiming equality and liberty, have been founded around the exclusion of women from the democratic process (see Scott 1997; Landes 1998). They must, as geographer Lynn Staeheli (1996) has shown, constantly reconfigure the boundary between public and private as they confront the tautological argument that women are not fit for the public sphere because their proper place is in the private sphere and, thereby, their trespass beyond the latter represents a degradation of the former. Consequently, women who dare to question such exclusions encounter the vexing tautology that their future exclusion from the public sphere—the domain of modern democracy—is justified by their past exclusion from this sphere.

Likewise, the Mujeres de Negro have to engage constantly with the discourses by which "public women" come to represent social and human contamination and, as a result, are not suitable citizens or democratic participants (see also Castillo 1998; Hershatter 1997). They do not have the option of broadly declaring that such assertions are "nonsense" or "ludicrous," in an environment where this discourse is commonly used to blame women for the violence they suffer, to deny them access to public protections, and to enforce a patriarchal concept of the domestic domain as the proper place for women. And as I endeavor to show here, while they take on the discourse that dismisses their public protests on the basis that they are "public women," they do indeed open up new spaces for women's civic activism in Mexico, even as they paradoxically reinforce many of the traditional prohibitions against women's access to politics and to the public sphere.

Public–Private Women

The leaders of the Mujeres de Negro are primarily middle-class women with experience in activist organizations and nongovernmental organizations (NGOs), and its members include anyone who is willing to put on a black tunic and pink hat and carry a sign as a Mujer de Negro in protest over the crimes against women and the political incompetence surrounding them.[4] Their public protests and events usually incorporate dramatic gestures. In addition to their own stark clothing, they often march with crosses, which they sometimes adorn with dismembered mannequin parts to evoke images of the suffering endured by the victims. They have walked hundreds of miles across Mexico and left crosses with victims' names throughout the Chihuahuan desert. They have led marches in numerous Mexican cities. They have orchestrated funerary processions into public offices. They have interrupted military parades, held up traffic at the international bridges spanning the Mexico–U.S. divide, held silent vigils in city plazas, yelled at government officials during public events, and lain down in front of cars on busy avenues. Through such activities, these women have directed international attention on the impunity of the criminals, on the political disregard for the crimes, and on the suffering of the victims and their families.

According to several of its members, the Mujeres de Negro drew their inspiration for their public image from the many other women, around the world, who have used the black clothing of mourning, domesticity, and female modesty to express their identities as social justice and human rights activists (see also Bejarano 2002). Particularly throughout the Americas of the twentieth century, the black-dressed woman activist has played a high-profile role in challenging repressive governments, neoliberal politics, and state-sanctioned violence (Bouvard 1994; Del Olmo 1986; Friedman 1998; Stephen 1995). Probably the most internationally famous of such activists are the Madres de la Plaza de Mayo, in Buenos Aires, whose question "Where is my child?" provoked a crisis of legitimacy for the brutal military dictatorship that terrorized Argentina from 1977 to 1982. The group's self-portrayal as mothers provided legitimacy for them as women who were on the street not as political subversives or as "women of the street," but rather as women doing what women are publicly sanctioned to do. They were looking for their children.

As Joan Scott (2002) has written, the woman-in-black activist is paradoxical since she "signifies powerlessness" while simultaneously posing a powerful challenge to governing elites in the name of social justice. For their rage is borne of sorrow, grief, and a mother's worry, and beneath their black capes and pink hats, we expect to find soft, feminine bodies—no weapons, no muscles, no phallus. Theirs is a politics of emasculation. In this way, the Mujeres de Negro of northern Mexico, like women activists in black around the world, take to the streets, neither as aggressive youth nor as politicians, but as women whose provenance from the private sphere legitimates their public activities. In other words, their legitimacy as public agents derives from their self-portrayal as women bound by the private domain.

This paradox is particularly salient in the case of the Mujeres de Negro because this group is composed principally of women who are well known for their participation in other activist and political organizations. The most prominent spokespeople of the Mujeres de Negro group have experience or make a living in legal aid, feminist, and political organizations; some have served in statewide political offices; and some have organized radical activist operations, particularly against the privatization of public utilities in the mid-1990s. Therefore, in order to portray themselves as women whose motivations derive from the domestic, rather than the public, sphere, many of these women have had to change from women known for their public convictions into women known for their private ones. This transformation takes place in public space since it is there—on the streets, in the plazas, and in public offices—that the Mujeres de Negro come to life as a group of women who stand in the public sphere in order to represent the private sphere. As such, the Mujeres de Negro illustrate, as many feminist geographies have shown, how women activists often resort to paradoxical spatial strategies for navigating the myth of the private-public divide and the gendered hierarchies its supports (see Rose 1993; Desbiens 1999; Mahtani 2001). The Mujeres de Negro deploy this spatial strategy for publicly reinventing themselves as private women as a way to neutralize accusations by regional elites that women on the street, no matter their purpose, represent the source of social trouble rather than its resolution. As "family-minded" women, the Mujeres de Negro are able to deflect such accusations and claim, as many black-dressed women activists before them have, that they have taken to the street in order to protect their families and cultural traditions. And they emerge as "public-private women," women whose domestic allegiances are publicly performed.

In addition to justifying their own presence on the street, this strategy of publicly defining themselves as family women also allows the activists to define the victims as fundamentally "family girls," or "daughters" (*hijas*). This strategy has arisen in direct response to the allegations of regional elites that the victims had, through their own illicit behaviors, invited the violence that ended their lives. This age-old "blame the victim" strategy is a transparent effort on the part of regional elites and the police to deflect criticism of their responsibility vis-à-vis the violence as they, instead, blame the women who attracted trouble by venturing into the street, by wearing short skirts, by dancing, and by not being at home.

This discourse for blaming the victim gains its footing in the story of the woman-on-the-street who signifies "the whore," who is, in turn, the woman whose embodiment of contamination extends to the cultural spaces she inhabits. As shown in chapter 4, this discourse validates the idea of "the whore" as the justifiably disposable woman—the one whose death and dumping represent a normal course of events. For if "whore" signifies "contaminant," then efforts to clean up and improve society require her removal from the public spaces she sullies. And any woman who behaves like a "whore" is thereby inviting her own, often violent, elimination.

The women of Ciudad Juárez have gained a particular prominence over the last half century as emblematic of this cultural contamination as they have made the city infamous as a place where they, in contrast to *traditional* Mexican women, are easily found on the street, either as women walking the street for a living or as women who walk the street en route to their factory jobs.[5] This presence of women on the streets of Juárez has contributed to the city's ignominy, throughout Mexico, as the place where Mexican culture has been corroded by the perverse influences of globalization and the cultural intrusions of its northern neighbor (see Tabuenca Córdoba 1995–1996). And as the Mujeres de Negro take to the street under the Ni Una Más campaign, they constantly encounter the accusation that they are violating the boundaries separating pure family women from those sullied by public ambitions, as they "prostitute" themselves and victims' families for personal political gain.

The Mujeres de Negro are thus in a difficult position of having to navigate this Janus-headed discourse of "the whore," which binds women's presence on the street to the concept of contamination and disposability, while they are actively taking on a multilevel system of government where corruption, torture, and lack of accountability are still common. These activists have taken on two different political parties, two different gubernatorial administrations, several mayors, and resistant police officers who have all tried, at one point or another, to downplay the significance of the murders and kidnappings and to dismiss the activists as "misplaced" women—as women who should be at home. They have, however, finally provoked a response from the current president, Vicente Fox, who at the International Women's Day celebration in Mexico City on 8 March 2004 declared that he would use all of the power of his office to punish the criminals while calling upon Chihuahua's governor to correct the incompetence of the state's juridical system (Vargas 2004). They are also taking on the systemic problem of violence against women, whose roots in domestic violence (which, according to domestic abuse facilities in Ciudad Juárez, afflicts 70 percent of women in the state of Chihuahua)[6] challenge the myth of the home as the sanctity of Mexico's daughters, sisters, wives, and mothers (see also Robles 2004).

While their activist strategy—based on their own reinvention as public-private women—has proven effective for galvanizing an international movement around the issues of political accountability, misogyny, and human rights abuses, this approach is not without its pitfalls. In recreating the dichotomy that distinguishes the "public" woman from the "private" one, and by basing their own authenticity as activists upon this difference, they reproduce the very prohibitions that so often limit women's access to the public sphere. As they justify their public movement on the strength of their private convictions, the Mujeres de Negro are vulnerable to their exposure as women with political careers and public professions. Such exposure takes direct aim at their authenticity as traditional Mexican women who represent the honest convictions of the traditional Mexican family since any evidence of their public lives links them to the notion of the "public woman," who is always suspected of some form of "prostitution." Consequently, the Mujeres de Negro must navigate the paradox that their presence in public space undermines their legitimacy as public agents in an environment where a woman's legitimacy in the public sphere depends upon the strength of her domesticity.

In the following, I begin with a brief discussion of how the Mujeres de Negro have effectively deployed their contradictory positioning as public-private women as a means for inspiring an international human rights campaign. I then examine how this strategy coincides with that used by the movement's antagonists, who seek to expose the public source of the Mujeres de Negro activism and, in the process, discredit the Ni Una Más campaign.

Public–Private Women

The group of women now officially known as "Las Mujeres de Negro" originated in November 2001, in Chihuahua City, when a handful of civic organizations rallied in response to the discovery of eight young women's corpses in Ciudad Juárez. The bodies, showing signs of prolonged torture and sexual assault, had been found in an empty lot that sits at a highly trafficked intersection in southeastern Ciudad Juárez, across the street from the Maquiladora Association (AMAC) offices, about two kilometers from Wal-Mart, and down the street from a prestigious country club. This shocking discovery exposed the impunity of the murderers and the undeniable danger that young women face in Ciudad Juárez on a daily basis. On 15 November, Alma Gómez, a former state legislator and schoolteacher and the current director of Las Mujeres Barzonistas, a rural legal aid organization, announced to the press that there would be a protest in Chihuahua City during the 20 November celebration of the Mexican Revolution. Other participants in the protest included women who had worked with the following organizations: Mujeres por México (Women for Mexico), an organization that works for women's civil rights; La Comisión de Solidaridad y Defensa de los Derechos Humanos (the Commission for the Solidarity and Defense of Human Rights); the el Círculo de Estudios de Género (Gender Studies Reading Group), an organization of women who read feminist scholarship; El 8 de Marzo (the 8th of March), an organization formed in the early 1990s to support women's reproductive rights and to make domestic violence a crime under Mexican law; Red Nacional de Abogadas Feministas (the National Network of Feminist Lawyers); and el Fondo National de Mujeres (Mexico's National Organization of Women); among others. And on 20 November, the Mujeres de Negro made their debut when some three hundred women dressed in black interrupted the parade in Chihuahua City, declared a moment of silence in what is usually a festive event, and publicly admonished the governor for his negligence concerning the murders. Journalists referred to this diverse assemblage of women as "Mujeres de Negro." As one member of the *mujeres* told me, "They called us Mujeres de Negro out of laziness [*por flojera*]. So now it's our name."

A few months later, their identity as Mujeres de Negro was firmly established when some 100 women walked the 360 kilometers across the desert, from Chihuahua City to Ciudad Juárez, to join with the hundreds who protested the violence against women as part of the International Women's Day celebration on 8 March. The Chihuahua group called their march "Éxodo por la Vida" (Exodus for Life). For this event, they had coordinated their uniforms of a black tunic and pink hat, which they handed out to anyone who would join the event. They designed a large black cloth that could be worn simultaneously by some twenty women, as if they were wearing the same dress, with their pink-covered heads poking through holes in the fabric, which they wore as they marched down the 16 de Septiembre, a principal avenue in Ciudad Juárez. The use of crosses and black clothing by the Mujeres de Negro had antecedents in the victims' family organization, Voces Sin Eco (Voices without a Sound), established in 1998, which had organized the painting of pink crosses on black telephone poles throughout Ciudad Juárez. The symbol of the cross, along with the wearing of black mourning clothing, was calculated, as one of the Mujeres de Negro leaders told me, to let the public know that "our movement is about family." The march's culminating moment occurred when, flanked by the other protestors, the Mujeres de Negro erected a large wooden cross at the international bridge (Santa Fé) in downtown Ciudad Juárez. The cross was decorated with torn clothing, photographs, and 268 nails to represent each woman murdered in Ciudad Juárez since 1993. Since that time, the Mujeres de Negro have participated in marches and events throughout northern Mexico and in Mexico City.

The Mujeres de Negro do not represent an official organization. They are not a registered civil association; they have neither an organizational charter nor office space. In other words, the Mujeres de Negro exist only when these women get together, put on their tunics and pink hats, and stand in the street. Some of the Mujeres de Negro do not like each other; some even are publicly known to have deep political differences. For instance, one Mujer de Negro explained, "We are not all friends. Some of us fight politically with each other. Serious fights. I mean *hasta la muerte* [to the death]. But we come together when it is important. And this is important." As another Mujer de Negro, Alma Gómez, explained, "The Mujeres de Negro are a strategy for political activism. It doesn't exist for any other reason." In short, the women who constitute the Mujeres de Negro are creating a public identity that does not exist privately. And the space of this identity is on the street. As Irma Campos, one of the leaders of the Mujeres de Negro, put it, "If we didn't put on black clothing and stand in the street, then there would not be the Mujeres de Negro."

Yet, ironically, this public identity of the Mujer de Negro hinges directly on the public performance of the private woman, which the women who constitute the Mujeres de Negro achieve by subsuming their public identities as politicians and activists to private identities as family women. As Alma explained, "People know who I am. I was a state legislator. I have been active in politics with the Barzón. But when I am part of the Mujeres de Negro, I am not acting on behalf of any political party. I am a woman concerned about what is happening." And, as Irma explained, "When we dress in black, we are identifying ourselves as women who want a response. We are women concerned about our city and our community." Isabel, another of the Mujeres de Negro who works with a political party, explained this combination of symbols: "We are not about political campaigns. We are women who want this violence to stop." Or, as another Mujer de Negro explained to me at a protest in Ciudad Juárez (February 2003), "Some of us have political experience. But right now we are here as women, as mothers, and we are concerned for our daughters and the young women of Juárez and Chihuahua."

This strategy for reinventing themselves as a public group organized by private, rather than politically seasoned, women ties directly into the discourse, used by numerous activist groups, to portray the victims as innocent daughters. This discourse of victims as daughters speaks directly to the accusation, launched by political and corporate elites since the mid-1990s, that the victims provoke this violence by being on the street, by dancing in cantinas, and by being sexually provocative (Tabuenca Córdoba 2003). As shown in chapter 4, this accusation effectively declares that the victim, by virtue of her own contamination and disposability, is not worth worrying over, investigating, or even protecting. She is a lost cause. According to this logic, a prostitute, or anyone suspected of being one, is still a woman who is understandably violated and murdered in public space. As author Debbie Nathan has noted, "Between a rock and a hard place, families are thus loathe to deal with the fact that many beloved daughters *do* go to cantinas, and many *do* communicate sexuality through their clothing. Yet to acknowledge this is to imply that one's child is a slut undeserving of redress. It's a cruel conundrum that has forced activists in Juárez to use a public rhetoric in which victims are all church-going, girlish innocents" (2002, 6). But first, before declaring the innocence of the daughter, the victim has to be recognized as a "daughter" above other possible identifiers, such as "woman," "girl," "friend," "worker," "lover," and so forth. And the Mujeres de Negro as well as several other activist organizations, such as Nuestras Hijas de Regreso a Casa (May Our Daughters Return Home) and Justicia Para Nuestras Hijas (Justice for Our Daughters), constantly reiterate the familial condition of the victim as daughter. In this way, they have a response to the question repeated by two governors and by corporate leaders when they ask, why wasn't she at home in the first place? The answer from these organizations is that this daughter was on the street, just like the Mujeres de Negro, for a legitimate family reason, and this reason makes her a legitimate and worthy victim. She is not disposable.

This strategy for legitimating the public presence of women, as both activists and victims, around their private identities has succeeded in intensifying international pressure on the Mexican government to take action. International human rights organizations, representatives of the United Nations, and legislators from the United States, Brazil, and Spain, among others, have criticized the Chihuahua state government for incompetence and for harassment of activists. Heated attention has also turned to the responsibility of the maquiladora industry, which continues to rely on low-waged women workers who live in impoverished neighborhoods that lack many basic services, such as drainage, potable water, and electricity. Visual artists, filmmakers, playwrights, and poets, among others, have turned a critical eye to the role of international companies, Mexican politicians, and corrupt police forces in the perpetuation of the violence and the lack of convictions.

As a result of their efficacy in generating international pressure on state and federal officials, the Mujeres de Negro have increasingly been the targets of public hostility. The governor's office, particularly under the former Patricio Martínez administration, has been particularly aggressive in its efforts to diffuse the group's impact, and it has organized counterprotests which sometimes resort to violence in order to intimidate the activists. For instance, in June 2002, after the cross was stolen from the plaza in front of the governor's office, the Mujeres de Negro marched to the governor's office while carrying a banner that declared, "Se Busca Una Cruz" (A Cross at Large). They were met in front of the governor's office by women wearing white who were flanked by men holding baseball bats. When the men started pounding the pavement with their bats, the Mujeres de Negro sat on the street, and some made phone calls to the press to alert them to the events. Despite the fact that they were sitting directly in front of the governor's office, no police officers could be found. As one of the Mujeres de Negro explained, "I'm sure if the press hadn't arrived, there would have been violence." When, a few months later, the new cross that the Mujeres de Negro had commissioned from a local blacksmith shop was stolen at gunpoint by eight heavily armed men who tied up the workers and threatened to kill them, the Mujeres de Negro commissioned yet another cross. The second cross is also still at large.

Like many participants in the Ni Una Más movement, the Mujeres de Negro have reported anonymous threats, phone taps, unknown vehicles parked outside their homes, intimidating men following them on foot or in cars, in addition to physical abuse. "There are a lot of people who are scared, but we can't let that stop us," said Alma. "This is a bad time in Chihuahua."

While these forms of intimidation do frighten many of the activists, they have not been largely effective in stopping their activities. However, one strategy used by the governor's office has proven somewhat successful in, at least, causing the Mujeres de Negro to pause and regroup. The governor's office has forced the Mujeres de Negro into a defensive position by extending the "prostitution" and "bad mother" accusation to include the allegation that the Mujeres de Negro are prostituting themselves by benefiting financially and politically from the "pain of the mothers." This accusation revolves around the concept that the Mujeres de Negro are accepting "dirty money," or "filthy lucre," which represents how the activists contaminate motherhood, defile Mexican culture, and display their own whorishness when they take to the streets.

Filthy Lucre

This allegation made the headlines in Chihuahua City on 23 February 2003, when the state's attorney general announced that the Mujeres de Negro were taking money from the families of the victims in order to launch a political campaign against the governor's Partido Revolucionario Institucional (PRI) party. The headline of the *Heraldo de Chihuahua* declared, "Lucran ONGs Con Muertas" ("NGOs Profiting from Deaths"; see Piñon Balderrama 2003) based on the state's attorney general's allegation that the Mujeres de Negro, and other activist groups, were embezzling money from victims' families. The allegation also implied that many of the Mujeres de Negro were personally fortifying their own coffers and political futures by peddling the sorrow and pain of families to international organizations, who provided donations, and to sensationalist reporters who made them famous. The charge carried extra weight given that many of the Mujeres de Negro live in middle-class circumstances while the victims' families are usually economically impoverished. This accusation pointed to a most terrible distortion of motherhood as the Mujeres de Negro were accused of feigning grief and making a mockery of the victims' mothers for their own political ambition and greed.

On 24 February, the Mujeres de Negro met in the office of the women of the Barzón to discuss their response. "This accusation is very serious," explained Alma, "because many people are ready to believe it. Mainly because we are women, and women who are not in the home, taking care of their families, are suspicious." She added that the class differences between the middle-class Mujeres de Negro and the economically poor families made the accusation even worse. As Irma put it, "These families don't have any money to steal. How can we steal what they don't have?"

In the ensuing days, the governor declared that the activists, such as the Mujeres de Negro, were, through their public rabble-rousing, impeding the judicial process and presenting obstacles to the investigations. He reproached the Mujeres de Negro for contributing to the social decomposition of northern Mexico which the Mujeres de Negro were fostering by forsaking their private duties in the interest of their public ambitions. He declared that the crimes did not originate with government negligence but rather with a "series of social problems, of a weakening of the family" (Barrientos Marquez 2003, 3–9). Irma responded in the press by stating that the governor and his attorney general had "declared war" on civil organizations instead of declaring war against the criminals (Perea Quintanilla 2003). Graciela, another of the Mujeres de Negro, elaborated, "All of us here [in the room where they were discussing their response] work with organizations. We are women who work outside of the home. This makes us an easy target." "It is easy for him to blame us," she said. "That's what he is good at."

"The problem," explained Alma, "is that we need to discuss what we mean by this word 'lucrar.' If 'lucrar' means that some of us work with organizations that have budgets, well, yes, then we are lucrando. We have to support our activities. But if it means that we are getting personally rich, no, that is not happening. There is just a general ignorance over the meaning of 'lucrar.'"

"One of the problems," said Irma, "is that this kind of accusation can create tensions between us and the victims' families. Most of the families are poor. They live in very humble circumstances. When they hear that we are making money, even though this is a lie, it creates problems." Another of the Mujeres de Negro elaborated, "The families sometimes feel used by the Mujeres de Negro. And the idea that people are earning a living from this movement, when they are poor and suffering a terrible trauma, is very difficult for them. It is difficult for everyone."

A Mexican researcher, Julia Monárrez, who has studied the violence against women in Ciudad Juárez, explained that this government strategy for dismissing the Mujeres de Negro had a corrosive effect on the relationship between victims' families and nonfamily activist organizations. She said, "A lot of families feel that they are being used by political organizations and by individuals for their own reasons. It creates an impossible situation." Alma summarized the problem this way: "We have to have a political strategy. You cannot organize for social justice without a political strategy. And we have to support ourselves. This takes time and resources. The government uses this fact against us."

This government campaign has also fostered divisions among the many women-run organizations who participate in the Ni Una Más campaign, who want to distance themselves from the groups charged with prostituting themselves in order to remain in good public standing as organizations motivated by "clean" intentions. For instance, Astrid González of Lucha Contra La Violencia (The Fight Against Violence) announced in an article that appeared in the *Heraldo de Chihuahua* on 25 February (two days after the lucre accusation) that, in an echo of the governor's words, the "social decomposition of Ciudad Juárez" had penetrated the nongovernmental organizations. She said, "There are pseudo-organizations and pseudo-leaders who benefit [*lucran*] not only politically, but also with the donations that they receive in bank accounts in the name of women assassinated in Ciudad Juárez" (Meza Rivera 2003, 2–25). She continued, "The time has come to identify a difference, in order to clean up the image of the NGOs." Meanwhile, more articles appeared in which the Mujeres de Negro were linked with delinquency, graffiti, familial distress, and the general destruction of society (see Lurueña Caballero 2003, 3–4).

Another issue used to "out" the Mujeres de Negro as inherently public rather than private women has been the affiliation of some of its members with political organizations, particularly the Partido Revolucionario Democrático (PRD). The PRD is a political party with a traditionally stronger presence in the central part of the country, while in the North it represents an alternative to the other two major parties, the Partido Revolucionario Institucional (PRI) and the Partido Acción Nacional (PAN), which have dominated local and state office. The PRD represents "the Left" in contrast to the PRI, which formerly governed the entire country under an autocratic system, and the socially conservative and pro-business PAN. Several of the Mujeres de Negro have been active in the PRD, with some running and serving in public office, and with some having familial relation to PRD members. Because their activism has politicized the issue of violence against women, the governor's office, which is under the PRI banner, has accused the Mujeres de Negro of using the murders as a means to gain ground in statewide elections. The previous governor, Martínez, who at one point was considered to be a possible favorite for the PRI's presidential nomination, is now under attack for his failure to live up to his campaign promise to resolve the murders. The response from his office has thus been to charge that the Mujeres de Negro are hiding their PRD affiliations and bald political ambition behind a cloak of domesticity and mourning. The women have also been accused of being "feminists," "lesbians," and women who cater to the lust of an American audience always hungry for a tasty story of sex and violence.

This strategy for "outing" the Mujeres de Negro as *public* women has fed into another strategy for dismissing victims who do not have a *real* mother to protest on their behalf. While, of course, all women are "daughters," even if they do not have living parents, the discourse that narrows the legitimacy of daughter status to only those victims who have mothers actively searching for them represents one more tactic for ignoring the severity of the violence against women in general, for those victims who do not emerge as *daughters* disappear from public discourse concerning the crimes. These victims include women and girls who could be identified as workers, neighbors, friends, mothers, prostitutes, or simply people in general whose lives were brutally ended. And these women represent the large majority of those murdered in northern Mexico over the last decade. For instance, even though domestic violence is widely recognized as a serious problem throughout the region (Robles 2004), the connections between this crime and the murders are rarely broached. Instead, the discourse of victim-daughters recreates the myth that the family is the haven of women's honor and safety, even though recent studies reveal that most victims are murdered and/or raped by their current or former husbands or lovers. As a result, this discourse that stakes the authenticity of the victim on her filial status contributes to the trivialization of the gendered violence that is pandemic in northern Mexico.

Moreover, when the Mujeres de Negro and other activists try to include the murders of other, nondaughter women in the discussion, they are accused of "inflating" the numbers and flaming the sensationalist fires of an international press that is damaging northern Mexico's reputation among businesses and tourists (Guerrero and Minjáres 2004). This accusation, again, leads to another, in which the governor's office has maintained that the Mujeres de Negro and other activist groups are the reason why northern Mexico's economy is faltering. This charge holds a great deal of weight at this time, particularly in Ciudad Juárez, which has lost a quarter of its manufacturing jobs in the maquiladora sector since 2000. Unemployment rates are rising, and regional elites are visibly panicked over the possibility that more maquiladoras will shut their doors and move to China. Several business organizations and the governor's office have claimed that part of the problem is Ciudad Juárez's negative reputation that is being perpetuated by the activists who generate international attention to the crimes against women. As one business leader exclaimed during a 2003 public forum in Ciudad Juárez organized around the economic crisis, "The news media just covers the women who talk about murders. They just cover trash. That's all it is is trash. And that's what everyone thinks of now when they think of Juárez. They don't know that this is a good place for families. Where traditional families are strong. All they know is that we've got murders, and dead girls and all the trouble." Similar statements have surfaced from the governor's office, which has reiterated that the Mujeres de Negro contribute to the "social disintegration" of Ciudad Juárez and Chihuahua by "manipulating information" and creating the idea that Ciudad Juárez is the "murder capital of the world," which scares off business and tourist dollars (Prado Calahorra 2003a, 5A). As a result, according to the governor's office, it is this social disintegration and the bad reputation generated by these public women that are destroying both Mexican tradition and the Mexican economy (Prado Calahorra 2003b; Martínez Coronado 2003).

Shortly after these statements, the Mujeres de Negro vowed to renew their Ni Una Más campaign. Irma Campos put it this way: "It scares them to see women taking charge, being political. And it is easy to criticize us for not being at home. It makes things hard for us. We have to create a certain image. But we don't have a choice. We have to do something. We can't just sit at home while women are being murdered and kidnapped all around us."

The paradoxes that the Mujeres de Negro both confront and perpetuate with their activist strategy again surfaced when they dramatically interrupted the International Conference of Forensic Sciences, which was being held in Chihuahua City in August 2003. As a result of their disruptions to the otherwise orderly meetings, they succeeded in extracting a public promise from the federal attorney general to pay attention to the crimes. Yet his carefully worded statement revealed the caveat surrounding his promise. He said, "We want to strengthen families, to strengthen people, and I am not going to hide [in the face of activists' accusations over incompetence], and all of the public officials have to respond to those people who *legitimately demand attention, because of the pain they have suffered*. You have to attend to them." Of course, the attorney general and much of the public realize that the Mujeres de Negro have not suffered the pain of the mothers who have lost their daughters to the violence. His statement therefore leaves open the possibility that these activists are not the legitimate ones. And without legitimacy, neither they nor their concerns are worthy of attention.

Conclusion

The Mujeres de Negro, like activists around the world, do not have the luxury of choosing the circumstances for their battles. They do not create the discourse that aligns public women with public trouble. Nor do they author the story that women in the home are the keepers of tradition and cultural authenticity. Especially in Ciudad Juárez, a city plagued with social problems, the meaning of the public woman has been bantered about as political incumbents try to evade culpability over the city's ills and turn the blame, instead, on the young women who commute at all hours of the day and who go dancing at all hours of the night. The old story of the whore—as the consummate public woman—who contaminates the cultural space she inhabits is having new applications in Ciudad Juárez today as the Mujeres de Negro must navigate its spatial implications.

Their own success in organizing an international human rights movement speaks to their determination not to be defined by this discourse of the public woman as whore and as cultural contaminant. They have, through their activism, rebuffed the claims that the victims of the murders are disposable third world women and girls who are not worthy of concern. And as people around the world hear them, they turn a critical eye to the governing and corporate elites who argue that the violence stems from the inherent disposability found within the victims.

All of this attention to the violence is undoubtedly disrupting business as usual in northern Mexico. To be sure, this is a central complaint of the political and corporate elites who grumble that the activists are scaring away business with their protests. But what, if this were to be the case, could be the source of this fright? Could it be that political and business elites fear not the violence against women but instead *the public image of third world women protesting the idea of their disposability*? Indeed, the political and corporate elites who blame the activists for tarnishing the border's reputation as a good place for investment do not point to the murderers as the problems, but instead to the women who bring attention to them. For, in taking to the streets and organizing an international movement, these activists shatter the notion that Mexican women are by nature docile, submissive, and patient. And their campaign condemns the political and corporate practices that treat women as if they were disposable members of society. They thereby defy the myth and spoil its capacity to present "third world female disposability" as a cultural and natural fact. And if they, as some specific versions of third world women, refuse this myth's characterization of them, then what does that mean for the capitalist processes that depend upon the constant materialization of this very characterization?

The Mujeres de Negro activists, just as the other women I high-light in previous chapters who tackle this myth, do not strictly repre-sent resistors to power. They also reinforce certain hierarchies, based upon very familiar modes of exploitation. Again, to invoke Joan Scott, the Mujeres de Negro illustrate how feminist politics has only paradoxes to offer since the productive effects of their contradictory positioning are not contained within a single dialectical continuity. For, by binding their legitimacy as social activists to their private concerns as women and as mothers, rather than as politicians, femi-nists, or human rights activists, they recreate the dialectic by which a private woman has more legitimacy in the public sphere than a self-avowed public one. Consequently, they demonstrate the follow-ing contradiction. While they are asserting their rights as citizens and their concerns as people who care about family, politics, community, and their country, their location on the street threatens the very basis upon which they can make such claims, since public women repre-sent, according to the familiar refrain of the story of the disposable whore, threats to all of the above. They find themselves defending their policies and an economic model of development that relies upon ready acceptance of this tale.

What they also certainly show is that as long as the story of a dis-posable third world woman is told—whether that story be articulated through one of disposable workers or of disposable whores, or how-ever it might come together—then women activists around the world will continually face the sorts of paradoxes confronting the Mujeres de Negro in northern Mexico. This old story, whose roots extend far beyond the here and now of northern Mexico, is a most versatile and contemporary technology for justifying the many forms that violence against women takes in factories, on the street, and in the home. And, as such, this story has directly contributed to what Amnesty International has labeled an "intolerable negligence" on the part of Mexican political officials and of corporate leaders who have acted as if these "intolerable murders" were not significant at all (Amnesty International 2003, 65). At the root of this disregard is an identifiable logic stating that if the victims are disposable, then their murders are unremarkable.

Because the Mujeres de Negro expose the political and corpo-rate investment in this logic, they do represent a threat to northern Mexico's reputation as a "good place for business" in a climate that seeks disposable third world women workers. For this reason, their activities contribute to the making of a politics against the myth of the disposable third world woman and against the discursive-material dialectic at its core. It is a politics that takes root in public skepticism, including among academic researchers, regarding managerial justifications for why their companies treat workers as if they were not worth training or rehabilitating, or as if they had no future potential. It is a politics that requires strategies for working across local and international scales and for building alliances among people who do not necessarily claim shared experience in life and who do not share even the same social and physical spaces (see also Sandoval 2000; Laclau and Mouffe 1985). It is a politics for sabotaging the stories that explain how some people are simply, eventually, worthless.

Notes

Chapter 1

1. Pratt is referring here to the geographic scholarship that has extended Michel Foucault's (1995) elaboration of the discursive production of subjectivity to include how this production involves not only the materialization of embodied subjects but also the materialization of the spaces they inhabit, shape, and signify.
2. A significant body of geographic research has employed such tools for investigations into the geographies of subject formation (Keith and Pile 1993; McDowell 1995; Pile and Thrift 1995). For further discursive analyses of political economy, see Gibson-Graham (1996); and for untangling the discursive regimes of power that guide interpretations and uses of diverse landscapes, see Braun (2002). Henri Lefebvre's (1991) *The Production of Space* has been extremely influential in this discussion.
3. Or, as Roland Barthes says, "Myth is a type of speech."
4. My discussion here is informed by the elaboration of myth in *Mythology: The Illustrated Anthology of World Myth and Storytelling* (Littleton 2002).
5. For an insightful discussion into the problematic of this regional reference, see Dipesh Chakrabarty (2000).
6. A wealth of feminist scholarship has critiqued the idea of an essential female nature that forms the basis of common experience. For an astute examination of this issue, see Linda Alcoff (1994).
7. Pierre Bourdieu's (1977) theorization of habitus has also informed my understanding of this disciplining as a practice for determining the spatial contours of normativity.
8. My use of Althusser here draws directly from Judith Butler's (1997b) discussion in "Conscience Doth Make Subjects of Us All."
9. In compliance with human subjects review requirements, I use pseudonyms for all of my informants and for all companies.

10. Within the firms I studied, the 1997 minimum paid to factory workers in China was about one fifth that paid to their Mexican counterparts.
11. The population figure fluctuates depending upon the migrant labor population (Yeung 2001).
12. Several researchers have written about the varying degrees of access offered them in their investigations of factories located in China. See, for instance, Ngai Pun (2005) and Ching Kwan Lee (1998).
13. My understanding of Marx's exegesis on labor and value owes much to David Harvey's (1982) *Limits to Capital* and to Diane Elson's (1979) article "The Value Theory of Labour."
14. My thinking on the production of the body and its social meaning draws most directly from Elizabeth Grosz's (1994) *Volatile Bodies*, Judith Butler's (1993) *Bodies That Matter*, and Teresa de Lauretis (1987) *Technologies of Gender*.
15. Miranda Joseph (1998 and 2002) has an excellent discussion of the compatibility of Marxian with poststructuralist theorizations of material production.
16. Lefebvre (1991) helps here also with his theories in *The Production of Space*.
17. For instance, campaigns called "Sweat-Free Communities" and "No More Sweatshops" bring together organizations in the United States with worker groups around the world to protest against poor labor conditions. The antiglobalization and antineoliberal protests against the World Trade Organization and the World Bank have also focused attention on sweatshop conditions and on particular companies that engage in unhealthy labor practices.
18. Sherry Ortner's (1997) *Making Gender: The Politics and Erotics of Culture* has helped me clarify the ethnographer's dilemma when dealing with actions that resemble both power and resistance.

Chapter 2

1. Within the company, and always in my presence, the AOTW managers and engineers referred to themselves by a combination of an English first name with their family surname. The general manager, whom I call "Howard Li," explained that his American (U.S.) colleagues were not comfortable with the Chinese names, so it was standard practice for all Chinese employees to choose an English first name to be used as their corporate identity. Indeed, their counterparts in Mexico knew the AOTW team only by these invented names. Since these names are the ones they used when talking with me, I have created pseudonyms similar to them here.
2. My discussion of the relationship linking conceptions of a "modern China" and "modern Chinese subjects" with the gendered configurations of kinship owes a great deal to Lisa Rofel's (1998) *Other Modernities: Gendered Yearnings in China after Socialism*, and also

to a number of the chapters in Christina Gilmartin et al.'s (1994) edited collection, *Engendering China: Women, Culture, and the State*. See also Carolyn Cartier's (2001) *Globalizing South China* for further illustration of the importance of studying discourses of social subjects and female worker embodiment for understanding the industrialization of southern China.

3. In this analysis, I do not treat any descriptions of a "Chinese-ness" or "American-ness," or any other social identity, as evidence of a particularly "Chinese" or "American" (or "East/"West") viewpoint but instead as part of the discursive continuum by which claims to essential identities are constantly recreated around conceptions of "others."

4. In her book *Made in China*, Pun (2005) also finds that companies count on a constant turnover rate to ensure a transient labor supply. The turnover in the company she studies was closer to four or five years. The figure will change depending upon technology, labor supply, and other related factors, but the crucial point is that these companies rely on the transience as a way to replenish their labor processes with "fresh" workers.

5. My references to skill mimic the managers' classification of "unskilled" and "skilled" tasks and people. For an in-depth discussion into the political and social complexities of skill classifications, and their implications, see Elson and Pearson (1989).

6. I am referring here to his words, in the *Economic and Philosophic Manuscripts of 1844* (Marx 1988), that "the worker becomes all the poorer the more wealth he produces" (71).

7. Shin (2001) documents changes in factory women's attitudes regarding pregnancy as a result of their work experiences and hopes for employability.

8. Of course, such associations between women's reproductive cycles and organs and the concept of "social trouble" are not isolated to China or to the industrial sector. These views have certainly proliferated throughout the West in numerous contexts. See, for instance, Tuana (1993), Laquer (1997), Grosz (1996), and Bashford (1998). Indeed, according to Gail Hershatter (1997), Chinese views of women and women's sexuality shifted from positive to negative connotations through the intensification of Western forms of modernity in China's urban areas.

9. For a fuller explanation of how the one-child policy represents the Chinese government's strategy to address population pressures by focusing on the biology of women and girls, see White (1994).

10. I would like to thank Gail Hershatter for pointing out this discrepancy in the usual enforcement of the policy and in the AOTW managers' description of it.

11. My findings also corroborate what Hsing (1998) found regarding pregnancy in his investigations into the hiring, retention, and

dismissal policies of companies doing business in China's export-processing zones.

Chapter 3

1. Sor Juana de la Cruz wrote in sixteenth-century New Spain, where she lived as a nun for most of her adult life in what is now Mexico. Her writings were highly acclaimed by the literati in both the colony and colonizing countries. But the church fathers eventually prohibited her access to reading and writing materials on the basis that her works were "unnatural" for the "feminine sex." I have translated the poem, but I was influenced also by Trueblood's (1988, 103) version.

2. Many of the supervisors in COSMO had begun their maquila careers as operators and had been promoted within a five-year period. They earned salaries ranging from US$700 to US$1,500 a year (depending upon the exchange rate between 1994 and 2001), while the hourly waged operators earned about 84 cents an hour, down to about 50 cents in 2001. The supervisor job is usually as high as any Mexican man, who begins as an operator, will rise in the corporate hierarchy. Nonetheless, it is far above any position that most Mexican women could ever hope to reach.

3. In 2003, two years after I completed this study, COSMO closed all of its Ciudad Juárez factories and moved many of them to China.

Chapter 4

1. Much of my discussion of Benjamin's theory of dialectics draws on Susan Buck-Morss's (1989) account.

2. Numerous scholars, artists, and journalists have examined the crimes and linked them to various methods for devaluing women and making them disappear, both figuratively and literally. See, for instance, Nathan (1999), Monárrez Fragoso (2001), and Tabuenca-Córdoba (2003). Filmmaker Lourdes Portillo addressed these issues in her film *Señorita Extraviada*, and performance artist Coco Fusco also picks up such themes in her one-woman play entitled *The Incredible Disappearing Woman*.

3. My discussion of the woman as waste-in-the-making is informed by the conceptualization of waste as a continual negotiation elaborated by Sarah Hill (2003).

4. All translations are provided by the author.

5. John Quinones interviewed Roberto Urrea, the then-president of AMAC, on *20/20* on 20 January 1999.

Chapter 5

1. Gloria Anzaldúa (1942–2004) was a Chicana lesbian-feminist, poet, writer, and cultural theorist. Her 1987 collection of prose and poems in *Borderlands/La Frontera: The New Mestiza* is a classic in Chicano border studies, feminist theory, gay and lesbian studies, and cultural studies.
2. This quote is from Qiu Jin's public appeal for the founding of a Chinese women's newspaper and can be found at www.suppressedhistories.net/articles/qiujin.html (Suppressed Histories Archives n.d.). I have corrected the spelling of "earth's" from "earths."
3. Bourdieu's (1984) discussion, in his book *Distinction*, of the significance of reading taste and behavior for establishing social hierarchies through space helped me sort through the various efforts to define "Mexican" versus "American" space, behavior, and attitudes in MOTW.

Chapter 6

1. Distinctions among Mexican, Mexican–American, white, Anglo, *Juarense* (someone from Ciudad Juárez), *Paseño* (someone from El Paso), and so forth are constantly shifting and vary across the social landscape. The ethnic and national labels also refer to complex racial distinctions. For an insightful discussion of these categories and their implications, see Vila (2000). In this instance, I am referring to how these individuals identified themselves to me in terms of national identity with a cultural and ethnic marker, in part to distinguish themselves from me, an Anglo-American. Again, references to "American" reflect local vernacular within the Ciudad Juárez–El Paso area in which "America" refers to the United States. I use "American" when evoking this common usage within the maquiladoras even though the term is problematic since it excludes most of the areas within the Americas.
2. At the time of my research (1993–1994), the average wage in Tres Reyes was 130 pesos per week (approximately US$40 per forty-eight-hour week in 1993 figures) and about 30 pesos above the average minimum wage per week. Supervisors in Tres Reyes earned about US$800.00, which was almost one third less than that made by Mexican supervisors in the electronics firms I studied and less than half the earnings of U.S. supervisors.
3. Alvarez and Collier (1994) have an analysis of *confianza* as a social system of "insiders/outsiders" critical for coordinating work among Mexican truckers. Ironically, within the maquilas, people will generally say that *gente de confianza* ("people of *confianza*") are those who are in with the management and should not be trusted by operators on the floor. Yet in Tres Reyes, Gloria had no *confianza* with management or anyone who was "in" with the people in that

domain. Her *gente de confianza* stretched in the other direction and covered the workers in production, from operator to supervisor.

Chapter 7

1. The actual numbers for the murders and kidnappings are not known. Official government figures are much lower than researchers' figures, which are also often lower than activists' figures (Monárrez Fragoso 2001; Nathan 2002). Official statistics do reveal, however, that the homicide rate for women in Chihuahua quadrupled during the 1990s.
2. For a discussion of the coverage of the V-Day events in February 2004, please refer to Rojas Blanco (2005).
3. For an example of how the local press presents antagonisms among organizations and participants in the Ni Una Más campaign, see Guerrero and Minjáres (2004).
4. Women and men participate as part of the activities, but men do not wear the black tunics and pink hats. They appear in supportive rather than in leading roles in the protests.
5. In Mexico, this intimacy binding the whore—as a contaminated woman—to the cultural contamination of the nation is most famously captured in the myth of La Malinche, the *Azteca* who gave herself to Hernán Cortez and, so goes the myth, betrayed her own people.
6. This figure is that used by Esther Chávez, the director of Casa Amiga, a sexual assault and rape crisis center in Ciudad Juárez that treats victims of domestic violence. She is referring to a study conducted since 2000 that estimates that at least 70 percent of adult women in the state of Chihuahua have experienced domestic violence. I was unable to obtain a copy of this study.

Bibliography

Alcoff, Linda. 1994. "Cultural Feminism versus Post-structuralism: The Identity Crisis in Feminist Theory." In *Culture/Power/History*, edited by N. Dirks, G. Eley, and S. Ortner, 96–122. Princeton, NJ: Princeton University Press.

Althusser, Louis. 1971. *Lenin and Philosophy and Other Essays*. New York: Monthly Review.

Alvarez, R., and G. Collier. 1994. "The Long Haul in Mexican Trucking: Traversing the Borderlands of the Morthern and the South." *American Ethnologist* 21: 606–27.

Amnesty International. 2003. *Muertes Intolerables—México: 10 años de desapariciones y asesinatos de mujeres en Ciudad Juárez y Chihuahua*. London: Amnesty International.

Anaya, Rodolfo, and Francisco Lomelí, eds. 1989. *Aztlán: Essays on the Chicano Home-land*. Albuquerque: University of New Mexico Press.

Anzaldúa, Gloria. 1987. *Borderlands/La Frontera: The New Mestiza*. San Francisco: Spinsters/Aunt Lute Press.

Anzaldúa, Gloria, and E. Hernández. 1995–1996. "Re-thinking Margins and Borders: An Interview." *Discourse*, 18 (1–2): 7–15.

Arjona, Arminé. 2005. *Delincuentos: Historias del narcotráfico*. Ciudad Juárez, Mexico: Al Límite Editores.

Asad, Talal. 2003. *Formations of the Secular: Christianity, Islam, Modernity*. Stanford, CA: Stanford University Press.

Bales, Kevin. 2004. *Disposable People: New Slavery in the Global Economy*. Berkeley: University of California Press.

Barrientos Marquez, Heriberto. 2003. "En 10 años la PGR No Ha Detenido Ni Un Homcida: Patricio." *El Heraldo de Chihuahua*, 13 March, 3A.

Barthes, Roland. 1972. *Mythologies*. New York: Hill & Wang.

Bashford, Alison. 1998. *Purity & Pollution: Gender, Embodiment & Victorian Medicine*. New York: St. Martin's Press.

Bejarano, Cynthia. 2002. "Las Super Madres de Latino America: Transforming Motherhood by Challenging Violence in Mexico, Argentina and El Salvador." *Frontiers: A Journal of Woman Studies* 23: 126–40.

Benjamin, Walter. 1969. *Reflections: Essays, Aphorisms, Autobiographical Writings*, edited by Peter Demetz and translated by Edmund Jephcott. New York: Harcourt Brace Jovanovich.

Beruvides, M. G., J. R. Villalobos, and S. T. Hutchinson. 1997. "High Turnover: Reduce the Impact." *Twin Plant News* 13 (3): 3740.

Bourdieu, Pierre. 1977. *Outline of a Theory of Practice*. Cambridge: Cambridge University Press.

_____. 1984. *Distinction: A Social Critique of the Judgement of Taste*. Cambridge, MA: Harvard University Press.

Bouvard, Marguerite. 1994. *Revolutionizing Motherhood: The Mothers of the Plaza de Mayo*. Wilmington, DE: Scholarly Resources.

Braun, Bruce. 2002. *The Intemperate Rainforest: Nature, Culture, and Power on Canada's West Coast*. Minneapolis: Minnesota University Press.

Braverman, Harry. 1974. *Labor and Monopoly Capital: The Degradation of Work in the Twentieth Century*. New York: Monthly Review Press.

Buck-Morss, Susan. 1989. *The Dialectics of Seeing: Walter Benjamin and the Arcades Project*. Cambridge, MA: MIT Press.

Butler, Judith. 1993. *Bodies That Matter: On the Discursive Limits of "Sex."* New York: Routledge.

_____. 1997a. "Merely Cultural," *Social Text* 52–53: 265–78.

_____. 1997b. *The Psychic Life of Power: Theories in Subjection*. Stanford, CA: Stanford University Press.

Carrillo, Jorge. 1990. *La Nueva Era de la Industria Automotriz en México*. Tijuana, Mexico: COLEF.

Cartier, Carolyn. 2001. *Globalizing South China*. Oxford: Basil Blackwell.

Castañon, A. 1998. "Buscan igualdad laboral." *El Diario de Ciudad Juárez*, 10 October, 3C.

Castillo, Debra. 1998. *Easy Women: Sex and Gender in Modern Mexican Fiction*. Minneapolis: University of Minnesota Press.

_____, M. Rangel, and B. Delgado. 1999. "Border Lives: Prostitute Women in Tijuana." *Signs* 24: 387–422.

Chakrabarty, Dipesh. 2000. *Provincializing Europe*. Princeton, NJ: Princeton University Press.

Chan, Anita. 1997. "China's Troubled Workers." *Foreign Affairs* 76 (2): 104–17.

_____. 2001. *China's Workers under Assault: The Exploitation of Labor in a Globalizing Economy*. New York: Sharpe.

Chang, Grace. 2000. *Disposable Domestics: Immigrant Women Workers in the Global Economy*. Boston: South End Press.

Chao, J. 2002. "Made in China." *Austin American Statesman*, 7 July, H1–H4.

Cockburn, Cynthia. 1983. *Brothers: Male Dominance and Technological Change*. London: Pluto Press.

_____. 1985. *Machinery of Dominance*. London: Pluto Press.

"The Comeback Kid." 2000. *Business China* 26 (12): 3.

Cravey, Altha. 1998. *Women and Work in Mexico's Maquiladoras.* New York: Rowman & Littlefield.

de Lauretis, Teresa. 1987. *Technologies of Gender: Essays on Theory, Film, and Fiction.* Bloomington: Indiana University Press.

Del Olmo, Rosa. 1986. "Women and the Search for the Detained/Disappeared Persons of Latin America." *Resources for Feminist Research* 15: 42–43.

Desbiens, Carolyn. 1999. "Feminism 'in' Geography: Elsewhere, Beyond and the Politics of Paradoxical Space." *Gender Place and Culture* 6: 179–85.

Douglas, Carol Anne, Priya Verma, Katherine Goktepe, Laura Nixon, and Jen Chapin Harris. 2005. "China: Women Wal-Mart Workers Demand Union." *Off Our Backs* 35 (1–2): 6. *Women's Interest Module,* ProQuest, www.proquest.com.

Dunn, Tim. 1996. *The Militarization of the U.S.–Mexico Border.* Austin: University of Texas Press.

Eckholm, E. 2001. "Workers' Rights Are Suffering in China as Manufacturing Goes Capitalist." *New York Times,* 22 August, A8.

Elson, Diane. 1979. "The Value Theory of Labour." In her *Value: The Representation of Labour in Capitalism.* London: CSE.

Elson, Diane, and Ruth Pearson. 1981. "Nimble Fingers Make Cheap Workers: An Analysis of Women's Employment in Third World Export Manufacturing." *Feminist Review* 8: 87–107.

_____, eds. 1989. *Women's Employment and Multinationals in Europe.* Basingstoke, UK: Macmillan.

Escobar, Arturo. 1994. *Encountering Development.* Princeton, NJ: Princeton University Press.

Farley, M. 1998. "Hard Labor: Women at Work in China's Economy." First of two parts, *Los Angeles Times,* 22 November 1998, Sunday, Home Edition.

Fernández-Kelly, María Patricia. 1983. *For We Are Sold, I and My People.* Albany: State University of New York Press.

Foucault, Michel. 1995. *Discipline and Punish: The Birth of the Prison.* New York: Vintage.

Fox, Claire E. 1995–1996. "The Fence and the River: Representations of the US-Mexico Border in Art and Video." *Discourse* 18 (1–2): 54–83.

Fraser, N., and L. J. Nicholson. 1990. "Social Criticism without Philosophy: An Encounter between Feminism and Postmodernism." In *Feminism/Postmodernism,* edited by L. Nicholson, 19–38. New York: Routledge.

Friedman, Emil. 1998. "Paradoxes of Gendered Political Opportunity in the Venezuelan Transition to Democracy." *Latin American Research Review* 33: 87–135.

Frobel, Folker. 1980. *The New International Division of Labor.* New York: Cambridge University Press.

Frontera Norte Sur. 2005. "Mexican Cross-Border Industries in Prisons." November 14. http://frontera.nmsu.edu/)

Furth, Charlotte. 2002. "Blood, Body, and Gender: Medical Images of the Female Condition in China, 1600–1850." In *Chinese Feminities, Chinese Masculinities*, edited by S. Brownwell and J. Waserstrom. Berkeley: University of California Press.

Gallagher, Mary E. 2005. *Contagious Capitalism: Globalization and the Politics of Labor in China*. Princeton, NJ: Princeton University Press.

Gereffi, Gary. 1991. "The 'Old' and 'New' Maquiladora Industries in Mexico: What Is Their Contribution to National Development and North American Integration?" *Nuestra Economía* 2: 39–64.

Gibson-Graham, Julie-Kathy. 1996. *The End of Capitalism as We Knew It*. Oxford: Basil Blackwell.

Gilmartin, Christina, Gail Hershatter, Lisa Rofel, and Tyrene White. 1994. *Engendering China: Women, Culture, and the State*. Cambridge, MA: Harvard University Press.

Gopwani, Jewel. 2002. "Survey Finds High Rate of Workplace Injuries to Garment Workers." *Knight-Ridder Tribune Business News*, 7 February, 1.

Grewal, Inderpal and Caren Kaplan, eds. 1994. *Scattered Hegemonies: Postmodernity and Transitional Feminist Practice*. Minneapolis: University of Minnesota Press.

Grosz, Elizabeth. 1994. *Volatile Bodies: Toward a Corporeal Feminism*. Bloomington: Indiana University Press.

_____. 1996. *Space, Time & Perversion Essays on the Politics of Bodies*. New York: Routledge.

Guerrero, Cecilia, and Gabriela Minjáres. 2004. "Hacen Mito y Lucro de Los Femincidios." *El Diario de Ciudad Juárez*, 22 July, 1A.

Guzmán, R. 1998. "Empresas maquiladoras buscan mano de obra en colonias." *El Diario de Ciudad Juárez*, 24 July, 5.

Hannah, Matthew. 2000. *Governmentality and the Mastery of Territory in Nineteenth-Century America*. Cambridge: Cambridge University Press.

Haraway, Donna. 1985. "A Manifesto for Cyborges: Science, Technology, and Socialist Feminism in the 1980s." *Socialist Review* 15: 65–107.

_____. 1988 "Situated Knowledges: The Science Wuestion in Feminism and the Privilege of Partial Perspective." *Feminist Studies* 14: 575–99.

Harvey, David. 1982. *Limits to Capital*. Oxford: Basil Blackwell.

_____. 1989. *The Condition of Post-modernity*. Oxford: Basil Blackwell.

_____. 1996. *Justice, Nature and the Geography of Difference*. Oxford: Basil Blackwell.

Hershatter, Gail. 1997. *Dangerous Pleasures: Prostitution and Modernity in Twentieth-Century Shanghai*. Berkeley: University of California Press.

Hill, Sarah. 2003. "The Wasted Resources of Mexicanidad: Consumption and Disposal on Mexico's Northern Frontier." In *The Social Relations of Mexican Commodities: Power, Production, and Place.* Casey Walsh, edited by Elizabeth Emma Ferry, Gabriela Soto Laveaga, Paolo Sesia and Sarah Hill, 157–85. La Jolla: Center for U.S.-Mexican Studies, University of California, San Diego.

Holmes, John. 1989. "New Production Technologies, Labor and the North American Auto Industry." In *Labor, Environment and Industrial Change*, edited by G. Linge and G. A. van der Knaap, 87–106. London: Routledge.

Hsing, Y. 1998. *Making Capitalism in China.* Oxford: Oxford University Press.

Hutzler, Charles. 2002. "Beijing Steps in to Curtail Labor Protests in 3 Cities—but Government's Inability to Enact Needed Reform May Mean More Unrest." *Wall Street Journal*, 25 March 2002, Eastern edition, A14. *ABI/INFORM Global*, ProQuest, www.proquest.com.

Joseph, Miranda. 1998. "The Performance of Production and Consumption." *Social Text* 16 (1): 25–62.

_____. 2002. *Against the Romance of Community.* Minneapolis: University of Minnesota Press.

Jackson, Cecile and Ruther Pearson, eds. 1998. *Feminist Visions of Development.* New York and London: Routledge.

Katz, Cindi. 1996. "The Expeditions of Conjurers: Ethnography, Power and Pretense." In *Feminist Dilemmas in Fieldwork*, edited by D. Wolf, 170–85. Boulder, CO: Westview Press.

Katz, Cindi, and Neil Smith. 1993. "Grounding Metaphor: Towards a Spatialized Politics." In *Place and the Politics of Identity*, edited by M. Keith and S. Pile. London: Routledge.

Keith, M., and S. Pile, eds. 1993. *Place and the Politics of Identity.* London: Routledge.

Kern, Suzan, and Tim Dunn. 1995. "Mexico's Economic Crisis Spawns Wildcat Strike in a Maquiladora Plant." *Labor Notes* 194: 16.

Laclau, Ernesto, and Chantal Mouffe. 1985. *Hegemony and Socialist Strategy: Towards a Radical Democratic Politics.* London: Verso.

Lamphere, Louise. 1987. *From Working Daughters to Working Mothers: Immigrant Women in a New England Industrial Community.* Ithaca, NY: Cornell University Press.

Landes, Joan. 1998. *Feminism, the Public and the Private.* Oxford: Oxford University Press.

Laquer, T. 1997. "Orgasm, Generation, and the Politics of Reproductive Biology." In *The Gender/Sexuality Reader*, edited by R. Lancaster and M. di Leonardo, 219–43. New York: Routledge.

Lee, Ching Kwan. 1998. *Gender and the South China Miracle: Two Worlds of Factory Women.* Berkeley: University of California Press.

Lefebvre, Henri. 1991. *The Production of Space.* Oxford: Basil Blackwell.

Limas Hernández, A. 1998. "Desproteción ciudadana." *El Diario de Ciudad Juárez*, 16 July, 11A.

Lin, V. 1991. *Health, Women's Work, and Industrialization: Semi-conductor Workers in Singapore and Malaysia.* New York: Garland.

Littleton, C. Scott. 2002. *Mythology: The Illustrated Anthology of World Myth and Storytelling.* San Diego, CA: Thunder Bay Press.

Lucker, G. William, and A. Alvarez. 1985. "Controlling Maquiladora Turnover through Personnel Selection." *Southwest Journal of Business and Economics* 2 (3): 1–10.

Lurueña Caballero, Manuel. 2003. "Mujeres de Negro." *El Heraldo de Chihuahua*, 4 March, editorial page.

Mahtani, Minelle. 2001. "Racial ReMappings: The Potential of Paradoxical Space." *Gender, Place and Culture* 8: 299–305.

Martin, Biddy, and Chandra Mohanty. 1986. "Feminist Politics: What's Home Got to Do with It?" In *Feminist Studies, Critical Studies,* edited by Teresa de Lauretis. Bloomington: Indiana Press University.

Martin, Emily. 1995. *Flexible Bodies: Tracking Immunity in American Culture from the Days of Polio to the Age of AIDS.* Boston: Beacon Press.

Martínez Coronado, Benjamin. 2003. "Desintegración sociofamiliar, germen de crímenes: Patricio." *El Heraldo de Chihuahua*, 20 February, 1A.

Marx, Karl. 1977. *Capital: A Critique of Political Economy,* vol. 2. New York: Vintage.

_____. 1988. *Economic and Philosophic Manuscripts of 1844.* Buffalo, NY: Prometheus Books.

_____. 1990. *Capital: Volume 1.* London: Penguin Books.

Massey, Doreen. 2004. "Geographies of Responsibility." *Geografiska Annaler* 86 (1): 5–18.

McDowell, Linda. 1995. "Body Work: Heterosexual Gender Performances in City Workplaces." In *Mapping Desire*, edited by D. Bell, 75–95. London: Routledge.

_____. 1997. *Capital Culture: Gender at Work in the City.* Oxford: Basil Blackwell.

_____. 1999. *Gender, Identity and Place: Understanding Feminist Geographies.* Minneapolis: University of Minnesota Press.

McGaw, Judith. 1992. *Most Wonderful Machine: Mechanization and Social Change in Berkshire Paper Making, 1801–1885.* Princeton, NJ: Princeton University Press.

Meredith, Robyn. 1996. "New Blood for the Big Three's Plans." *New York Times*, 21 April, business section.

Meza Rivera, Froilan. 2003. "Sí Reciben Donativos las ONGs." *El Heraldo de Chihuahua*, 25 February, 2, 25.

Mohanty, Chandra T. 1991. "Under Western Eyes: Feminist Scholarship and Colonial Discourses." In *Third World Women and the Politics of Feminism*, edited by Chandra T. Mohanty, Ann Russo, and Lourdes Torres, 51–80. Bloomington: Indiana University Press.

Monárrez Fragoso, Juliana. 2001. "Femincidio Sexual Serial en Ciudad Juárez: 1993–2001." *Debate Feminista* 25: 279–308. Also available as "Serial Sexual Femicide in Ciudad Juárez: 1993–2001," www.womenontheborder.org/articles.

Mouffe, Chantal. 1992. "Democratic Citizenship and the Political Community." In *Dimensions of Radical Democracy: Pluralism, Citizenship, and Community*, edited by Chantal Mouffe. London: Verso.

Mufson, Steven. 1997. "Communist China's Dilemma: Labor Strife; Worker Protests Grow as Leaders Try to Cut Losses at State Enterprises." *Washington Post*, 11 September 1997, A01. National Newspapers (27), ProQuest, www.proquest.com.

Narayan, Uma. 1997. *Dis-locating Cultures: Identities, Traditions and Third World Feminism*. New York: Routledge.

Nathan, Debbie. 1999. "Work, Sex and Danger in Ciudad Juárez." *NACLA Report on the Americas* 33 (November–December): 24–32.

_____. 2002. "The Missing Elements." *(Austin) Texas Observer*, 30 August, 1–9, www.womenontheborder.org/Articles/Senorita.

"New China, Old Vice." 2000. *Business China* 26 (7): 6–7.

Ong, Aihwa. 1987. *Spirits of Resistance and Capitalist Discipline*. Albany: State University of New York Press.

Orquiz, M. 1998. "Asesinatos de mujeres: Como dejar un dulce en un colegio." *El Diario de Ciudad Juárez*, 2 August, 3C.

Ortner, Sherry. 1997. *Making Gender: The Politics and Erotics of Culture*. Boston: Beacon Press.

Perea Quintanilla, Enrique. 2003. "Declaró PGJE la Guerra Sociedad Civil." *El Heraldo de Chihuahua*, 25 February, 1A.

Phillips, Anne, and B. Taylor. 1980. "Sex and Skill: Notes towards a Feminist Economics." *Feminist Review* 6: 79–88.

Pile, Steve, and Nigel Thrift, eds. 1995. *Mapping the Subject: Geographics of Cultural Transformation*. London: Routledge.

Piñon Balderrama, David. 2003. "Lucran ONGs con Muertas." *El Heraldo de Chihuahua*, 23 February, 1A.

Piore, Michael, and Charles Sabel. 1984. *The Second Industrial Divide*. New York: Basic Books.

Pomfret, John. 2002. "Thousands of Workers Protest in Chinese City: Rally Targets Corruption." *Washington Post*, 20 March, A20. National Newspapers (27), ProQuest, www.proquest.com.

Poovey, Mary. 1990. "Speaking of the Body: Mid-Victorian Constructions of Female Desire." In *Body/Politics: Women and the Discourses of Science*, edited by M. Jacobus, Evelyn Fox Keller, and Sally Shuttleworth, 29–46. New York: Routledge.

Powell, Bill, Richard Tomlinson, Eric Nee, Justin Fox, Cait Murphy, David Stipp, Julie Schlosser, Alex Taylor III, Janet Guyon, Andy Serwer, Jim Rohwer, Brian O'Reilly, Daniel Roth, and Patricia Sellers. 2001. "25 Rising Stars." *Fortune*, 14 May, 140–51.

Prado Calahorra, Edgar. 2003a. "Protestan Mujeres Ante Procurador." *El Norte de Ciudad Juárez*, 14 August, 5A.

———. 2003b. "Reiniciarán campaña Mujeres de Negro." *El Norte de Ciudad Juárez*, 9 July, 8A.

———. 2003c. "'Acachan' A Madres Desapariciones." *El Norte de Ciudad Juárez*, 3 June, 8A.

Pratt, Geraldine. 1999. "From Registered Nurse to Registered Nanny: Discursive Geographies of Filipina Domestic Workers in Vancouver, B.C." *Economic Geography* 75 (3): 215–36.

Pun, Ngai. 2005. *Made in China: Women Factory Workers in a Global Workplace*. Durham, NC: Duke University Press.

Rabinbach, Anson. 1990. *The Human Motor: Energy, Fatigue and the Origins of Modernity*. New York: Basic Books.

"Repetitive Motion: Mostly Blue-Collar." 1996. *Patient Care* 30 (11): 15–18.

Reygadas, Luís. 2003. *Ensamblando Culturas: Diversidad y Conflicto en la Globalizacion de la Industria*. Madrid: Gedisa Editorial.

Robles, Rosalba. 2004. "La Violencia Contra la Mujer: Una violencia que se expande." In *Violencia Contra la Mujer*, edited by Teresa Fernández de Juan, 57–174. Mexico City: Comisión Nacional de los Derechos Humanos. www.cndh.org.mx/Principal/document/libreria/ViolenciaMujer.pdf.

Rofel, Lisa. 1998. *Other Modernities: Gendered Yearnings in China after Socialism*. Berkeley: University of California Press.

Rojas Blanco, Clara E. 2005. "The V Day March in Mexico: Appropriation and (Mis)use of Local Women's Activism." *National Women's Studies Association Journal* 17: 217–228.

Rose, Gillian. 1993. *Feminism and Geography: The Limits of Geographical Knowledge*. Minneapolis: University of Minnesota Press.

Salzinger, Leslie. 1997. "From High Heels to Swathed Bodies: Gendered Meanings under Production in Mexico Export-Processing Industry." *Feminist Studies* 23 (3): 549–74.

———. 2003. *Genders in Production: Making Workers in Mexico's Global Factories*. Berkeley: University of California Press.

Sandoval, Chela. 2000. *Methodologies of the Oppressed*. Minneapolis: University of Minnesota Press.

Schoenberger, Erica. 1988. "From Fordism to Flexible Accumulation: Technology, Competitive Strategies and International Location." *Environment and Planning: Society and Space* 6: 245–62.

———. 1997. *The Cultural Crisis of the Firm*. Oxford: Basil Blackwell.

Scott, Joan W. 1997. *Only Paradoxes to Offer: French Feminists and the Rights of Man*. Cambridge, MA: Harvard University Press.

———. 1999. *Gender and the Politics of History*. New York: Columbia University Press.

———. 2002. "Feminist Reverberations." *Differences* 13: 1–23.

Shaiken, Harley. 1994. "Advanced Manufacturing and Mexico: A New International Division of Labor?" *Latin American Research Review* 29: 39–71.

Shin, Eung-Young. 2001. "The Effect of the Chinese Reform Policy on the Status of Rural Women." *Asian Journal of Women's Studies* 7 (3): 63.

Simison, R., and G. White. 1998. "Mexico's Growth May Explain GM Buildup There." *Wall Street Journal*, 13 July.

Sklair, Leslie. 1993. *Assembling for Development: The Maquila Industry in Mexico and the United States*. San Diego, CA: Center for U.S.–Mexico Studies.

Sparke, Matt. 1996. "Displacing the Field in Fieldwork." In *Body Space*, edited by N. Duncan, 212–33. New York: Routledge.

Stack, M., and D. W. Valdez. 1999. "Juárez Girl Accuses Driver in Attack." *El Paso Times*, 19 March.

Staeheli, Lynn. 1996. "Publicity, Privacy and Women's Political Action." *Environment and Planning D: Society and Space* 14: 601–19.

"Staff Report: Brain School." 1997. *Twin Plant News* 12 (8): 39–41.

Stephen, Lynn. 1995. "Women's Rights Are Human Rights: The Merging of Feminine and Feminist Interests among El Salvador's Mothers of the Disappeared (CO-MADRE)." *American Ethnologist* 22: 807–27.

Suppressed Histories Archive. n.d. "Qiu Jin (1879–1907)." www.suppressedhistories.net/articles/qiujin.html (accessed 1 March 2006).

Tabuenca Córdoba, María Socorro. 1995–1996. "Viewing the Border: Perspectives from the 'Open Wound.'" *Discourse*, 18 (1–2): 146–95.

———. 2003. "Día-V permanente en Ciudad Juárez." *El Diario de Ciudad Juárez*, 2 March, 21A.

Trueblood, Alan S. 1988. *A Sor Juana Anthology*. Cambridge, MA: Harvard University Press.

Tuana, Nancy. 1993. *The Less Noble Sex: Scientific, Religious and Philiosophical Conceptions of Women's Nature*. Bloomington: Indiana University Press.

U.S. Department of Labor. 1998. *Public Report of Review of NAO Submission no. 9701*. 12 January. Washington, DC: U.S. Department of Labor.

Vargas, Rosa E. 2004. "Toda la fuerza del Estado para aclarar los crímenes de Juárez." *La Jornada en Internet*, 9 March, www.jornada.unam.mx/2004/mar04/040309/017n1pol.php?origen=index.html&fly=1.

Vila, Pablo. 2000. *Crossing Borders, Reinforcing Borders: Social Categories, Metaphors, and Narrative Identities on the U.S.-Mexico Frontier*. Austin: University of Texas Press.

Villalobos, J. R., M. G. Beruvides, and S. T. Hutchinson. 1997. "High Turnover: What It Does to Production." *Twin Plant News* 3 (2): 41–44.

Whelan, C. 2000. "Emerging Markets That Live Up to the Name." *Fortune*, 18 December, 184.

White, T. 1994. "The Origins of China's Birth Planning Policy." In *Engendering China: Women, Culture and the State*, edited by C. Gilmartin, G. Hershatter, L. Rofel, and T. White, 250–78. Cambridge, MA: Harvard University Press.

Wilson, Pat. 1990. "The New Maquiladoras: Flexible Production in Low-Wage Regions." In *The Maquiladora Industry: Economic Solution or Problem?* edited by K. Fatemi. New York: Praeger.

Woo, M. 1994. "Chinese Women Workers: The Delicate Balance between Protection and Equality." In *Engendering China: Women, Culture and the State*, edited by C. Gilmartin, G. Hershatter, L. Rofel, and T. White, 279–95. Cambridge, MA: Harvard University Press.

Wright, Melissa W. 2001. "Global Firms, Masculine Heroes and the Reproduction of Ciudad Juárez." *Social Text* 69: 93–114.

_____. 2004. "From Protests to Politics: Sex Work, Women's Worth and Ciudad Juárez Modernity." *Annals of the Association of American Geographers* 94: 369–86.

Yeung, Godfrey. 2001. *Foreign Investment and Socio-economic Development in China: The Case of Dongguan*. New York: Palgrave.

Young, Iris. 1990. *Justice and the Politics of Difference*. Princeton, NJ: Princeton University Press.

Index

A

Accusations
    against Mujeres de Negro,
        163–168
Activism. *see* Social movements
Ambition
    gender and, 81
Americanization
    border politics, 94–97
    cultural division of labor, 129–132
    of men vs. women, 126
American values
    cultural influences and
        disposability, 75–76, 77
    significance in MOTW, 100–101
Anatomy, 49
Anti-Chinese sentiment
    in AOTW, 31–32
Anzaldúa, Gloria, 94–96, 120–121
AOTW. *see* Asia on the Water
Appearance
    cultural differences and, 110
    gender division and, 113–114
    managerial characterizations, 144
Asad, Talal, 3–4
Asia on the Water (AOTW)
    daughters and factory fathers,
        30–32
    managers in, 24–27
    modern Chinese managers, 42–44

B

Barrio, Francisco, 74
Barthus, Roland, 3–4
Benjamin, Walter, 72–73, 88

Binary opposites
    in manufacturing bodies, 45–46
Blame the victim strategy, 157
Bourdieu, Pierre, 131
Butler, Judith
    bodies and production, 104
    cross-border politics, 96
    epistemological approaches, 13–14
    variable capital of female workers,
        74

C

Cano, Esther Chávez, 77
Capital
    of female disposability, 27–30,
        68–69, 87–89
    variable. *see* Variable capital
Capitalism
    fear of activism, 168–169
    flexible production. *see* Flexible
        production
    global. *see* Global capitalism
    uneven development and, 126
Chan, Stephen
    OTW managers, 24
Chen, Harry
    OTW managers, 24
China
    AOTW in, 30–32
    author's research in, 8–12
    daughters and factory fathers in,
        42–44
Citizenship
    in MOTW, 100–101
Ciudad Juárez

organizations against violence,
    151–153
overview, 7–8
social disintegration in, 167
Class differences
    Mujeres de Negro, 163–164
Communication
    supervising flexible production
        and, 52–54
Confianza, 138–140
    power and, 138–140
Consumers
    political implications, 15
Contamination
    of male product, 115–119
    "whore" and activism, 157–158
Contracts
    female workers and, 36
    reinforcing disposability, 41
Control
    cultural ideas in China. *see*
        Daughters and factory
        fathers
    in production monitoring, 64–65
    significance in MOTW, 100–101
    social strength as source of,
        137–141
Corporate death, 78–87
Corporate fear
    of activism, 168–169
Corporate hierarchy
    Americans in MOTW, 100–101
    in production monitoring, 64–65
Corporate policy
    for manufacturing bodies, 46–48
    training women, 115–119
Corporate turnover, 27–28. *see also*
        Turnover rates
Corporeal anatomy
    in manufacturing bodies, 49
COSMO
    day in, 62–68
    manufacturing bodies. *see*
        Manufacturing bodies
Crime. *see* Violence and disposability
Cross-border politics, 94–97

Cultural death, 87–89
Cultural differences
    Americanizing MOTW, 100–101
    division of labor, 47–48, 129–132
    female contamination, 115–119
    feminist border politics, 94–97
    global capitalism effects, 49–50
    limited flexibility, 54–55
    manufacturing bodies, 46
Cultural values
    disposability morality, 74–78
    female ambition, 81–82
    feminist politics, 124–125
    justifying violence, 161
    political activism problems,
        153–155
    turnover rates and, 85–87

D

Daughters
    and activism, 157
Daughters and factory fathers, 23–44
    in AOTW, 30–32
    Chinese managers, 42–44
    daughters and defects, 36–42
    female disposability, 27–30
    managing feminine waste, 33–36
    overview, 23–27
Death. *see also* Violence and
        disposability
    corporate, 78–87
    by culture, 87–89
Defects
    disposable daughters and, 36–42
    female contamination, 115–119
Dehumanizing process, 73
Democratic process
    and political activism, 153–155
Deskilling of work
    vs. training, 128–129
Destiny
    in myth, 5–6
Development. *see also* Production
    flexible production, 50–52
    idea of vision in, 58–59

Dirty money
Mujeres de Negro and, 163–168
Disposable humanity. *see* Violence
and disposability
Disposable women, myth of
in book, 12–16
in chapters of book, 16–19
defined, 3–6
epistemological approaches, 12–16
overview of, 1–3, 6–12
Disposable workers
female. *see also* Disposable
women, myth of; Female
workers
male. *see* Male workers
necessity of, 127
production limitations and, 65–68
Division of labor
cultural justifications for, 129–132
manufacturing bodies and, 46–48
networks of *confianza* and,
137–141
production and disposability,
65–68
social geography of Tres Reyes,
133–137
Docility
activism and, 168–169
as feminine value, 84–85
Dongguan, AOTW in, 30
Double lives of women, 74–75
Dress. *see also* Appearance
Mujeres de Negro, 155, 159–160

E

Eaton, Robert, 50
Education. *see* Training
Elson, Diane, 99
Emasculation
as politics, 156
Epistemological approaches
book overview, 12–16
feminist. *see* Feminism
Marxist. *see* Marxism

Ergonomic design
of workers' bodies, 56–57
European supervision
division of labor and, 47–48
monitoring hierarchy, 64–65
Expendable workers. *see* Disposable
workers
Exploitation of labor, 148–150

F

Factories
and disposable women, 1–3
fathers and daughters. *see*
Daughters and factory
fathers
Female disposability, as capital
in cultural death, 87–89
disposable daughters, 27–30
in supervisory dynamic, 68–69
Female workers
desirable qualities, 82–83
flexible masculinity, 59–62
limited flexibility, 54–59
production and disposability,
65–68
in production line, 51–52
untrainability of, 80–82
value and waste, 72–74
Feminine waste, 33–36
Feminism
activism. *see* Social movements
along border, 94–97
identification and representation,
124–125
maquiladora mestizas and,
120–121
role in book, 12–16
social construction of value in
labor, 99
training vs. turnover, 79
Fernández-Kelly, María Patricia, 6–7
Filthy lucre (dirty money)
Mujeres de Negro and, 163–168
First world superiority. *see also*
Americanization

division of labor and, 47–48
third world inferiority vs., 46
Flexible production
disposability in, 50–52
economics of, 68–69
flexible masculinity and, 59–62
prosthetics of supervision in, 52–54
workflow at COSMO, 62–68
Foucault, Michel, 64

G

Gender division
flexible production line and, 51–52
management and, 105–109
segregation in AOTW, 33–35
spatial arrangements and, 102–103
training vs. turnover, 80–82
turnover rates, 72–74
General Motors Delphi Center, 80
Geographics
and feminist border politics, 94–97
Global capitalism. see also Capitalism
disposable women and, 1–6
female disposability. see Female disposability, as capital
overview of, 6–12
Good girls, 74–75
Government campaign
against Mujeres de Negro, 163–168
Grosz, Elizabeth, 49

H

Harrassment
of pregnant women, 85
violent. see Violence and disposability
Harraway, Donna, 58
Harvey, David, 12–13

Historical meaning
cultural. see Cultural values
maquiladora mestizas and, 96–97
Human bodies
approaches to, 12–14
Human bodies, as manufacturing bodies, 45–69
COSMO day, 62–68
flexible disposability and, 50–52
flexible masculinity and, 59–62
introduction, 45–49
limited flexibility and, 54–59
prosthetics of supervision and, 52–54, 68–69
sites of accumulation, 49–50
Human rights organizations, in Mexico, 162

I

Identity
of Mujeres de Negro, 160–163
representation and. see Representation
transforming to gain value, 124–127
Illness
justifiable dismissal, 36
menstrual cycles and, 40
repetitive stress syndrome, 40–41
Image. see Appearance
Imaginary anatomy, 49
Incentives
loyalty, 138–139
turnover rates and, 116
Injuries
ergonomic design and, 56–57
repetitive stress syndrome, 40–41
International humans rights organizations, 162
Intimidation
of Mujeres de Negro, 162–163
Invasive procedures, 39
Invisible MOTW women, 102–105

J

Joseph, Miranda, 7
*Justice, Nature and the Geography
    of Difference* (Harvey),
    12–13
Justifiable dismissal, 36

K

Katz, Cindi, 127

L

Labor
    epistemological approaches, 12–14
    female workers. *see* Female
        workers
    line workers. *see* Line workers
    male workers. *see* Male workers
    social construction of value in,
        98–99
    strikes, 146–148
    turnover. *see* Turnover rates
    workflow. *see* Workflow
Language
    professionalism, 130–131
    significance in MOTW, 100
Lee, Ching Kwan, 6
Legitimacy
    importance in activism, 169
Li, Howard
    OTW managers, 24
Limited flexibility
    and manufacturing bodies, 54–59
Line workers
    labor turnover, 27–29
    managers relationship to, 25–26
    product quality and, 31–32

M

Machismo culture
    limited flexibility and, 54–55
Madres de la Plaza de Mayo,
    155–156

Male workers
    dismissal policies, 37–38
    vs. female in flexible production,
        58–59
    flexible masculinity, 59–62
    in flexible production line, 51–52
    supervision, 33–35
    variable capital of, 73–74
Managers
    American, 100–101
    female disposability and, 24–27
    flexible production and, 58
    manufacturing bodies and, 46–47
    modern Chinese, 42–44
    paternal. *see* Daughters and
        factory fathers
    production monitoring hierarchy
        and, 64–65
    Rosalía's transformation as an
        American, 105–109
    vision and, 58–59
Manufacturing bodies, 45–69
    COSMO day, 62–68
    flexible disposability, 50–52
    flexible masculinity, 59–62
    introduction, 45–49
    limited flexibility, 54–59
    prosthetics of supervision, 52–54
    sites of accumulation, 49–50
    supervisory dynamic and, 68–69
Maquiladora industry
    defined, 7
    disposability and morality, 76–78
    flexible production in, 50–52
    turnover and corporate death,
        78–87
Maquiladora mestizas, 93–121
    along border, 94–97
    Americanizing management,
        105–109
    Americanizing MOTW, 100–101
    cross-border politics, 109–112
    female contamination, 115–119
    feminist politics and, 120–121
    invisible MOTW women, 102–105
    Mary, 112–115

in MOTW, 97–99
overview, 93–94
Marketability
    gender division in MOTW,
        103–104
    national identity and, 101
Married women, 39–40
Martin, Emily, 7
Marxism
    labor turnover and, 28
    role in book, 12–15
    social construction of value,
        98–99
    training vs. turnover, 78–79
    worker's bodies, 50
Mass production, 50, 54–55
McDowell, Linda, 7
Menstrual cycles. see also
        Reproductive cycles
    monitoring of, 85
    regulation of, 39–40
Mexico. see also Maquiladora
        mestizas
    author's research in, 7–9
    author's research in China vs.,
        11–12
    flexible production in, 50–52
    Mexican employees, 47–48,
        129–132
Mexico on the Water (MOTW)
    defined, 24
    maquiladora mestizas in. see
        Maquiladora mestizas
Mexico-U.S. border, 94–97
Modern development
    flexible production, 50–52
    idea of vision in, 58–59
Monárrez, Julia, 164–165
Monitoring, corporate hierarchy and,
        64–65
Morality
    disposability and, 74–78
    "the whore" and activism,
        157–158
Mothers
    legitimacy of activism, 155–157

Mujeres de Negro and, 166–168
MOTW. see Mexico on the Water
Mujeres de Negro (Women in Black)
    conclusion, 168–170
    filthy lucre and, 163–168
    overview of movement, 151–155
    public vs. private women, 155–163
Murder stories, 74–78
Myth. see Disposable women, myth
        of

N

Narayan, Uma, 76
National identity
    cultural differences. see Cultural
        differences
    cultural values. see Cultural values
    in MOTW, 100–101
Ni Una Más (not one more)
        campaign, 152–153

O

On the Water (OTW), 24, 42–44
One child policy, 39–40
Ong, Aiwha, 6
OTW. see On the Water

P

Partido Revolucionario Democrático
        (PRD), 165–166
Partido Revolucionario Institucional
        (PRI), 165–166
Paternal managers. see Daughters and
        factory fathers
Perception. see also Representation
    female contamination and,
        115–119
    value determination, 79
Personality
    and myth, 4–5
Physical exams, 39–40

Physical violence and disposability.
see Violence and
disposability
Pigeonholing of women, 82
Policy
one child, 39–40
training women, 115–119
Politics
activism. *see* Social movements
Americanization, 105–109
cross-border ideas, 109–112
of disposable third-world women,
169–170
disruption and, 14–15
on Mexico-U.S. border, 94–97
Postcolonial theory, 12–16
Poststructuralist feminism. *see also*
Feminism
in production monitoring, 64–65
role in book, 12–16
training vs. turnover, 79
Power
of social strength, 137–141
Pratt, Geraldine, 3
PRD. *see* Partido Revolucionario
Democrático
Pregnancy
justifiable dismissal and, 36–37
required testing in China, 39–40
required testing in Mexico, 85–86
PRI. *see* Partido Revolucionario
Institucional
Private domain
activist validation and, 155–158
cultural problem of political
activism, 153–155
Production
Americanizing MOTW, 100–101
female contamination, 115–119
flexible disposability, 50–52
manufacturing bodies, 49
representation issues, 103–105
turnover rates and quality, 31–32
workflow of COSMO day, 62–68
Professionalism
language and, 130–131

managerial characterizations,
141–148
Profit
supervisory dynamic and, 68–69
training vs. turnover, 78–79
Promotions
flexible masculinity and, 59–60
in flexible production, 58
skilled vs. unskilled labor,
125–126
Prosthetics of supervision. *see*
Supervisory dynamic
Prostitution, 34–35, 157–158
Protests. *see* Mujeres de Negro
(Women in Black)
Public domain
Mujeres de Negro and, 160–163
political activism and culture,
153–155

Q

Quality
female contamination and,
115–119

R

Racism
in AOTW, 31–32
Recruitment
of female workers, 82–83
Representation
cross-border politics, 109–112
invisible MOTW women and,
102–105
managerial characterizations,
141–148
marketability and, 100–101
skilled vs. unskilled labor, 126
Reproductive cycles
daughters and defects, 36–37
daughters and factory fathers,
29–30
monitoring of, 85–86
required testing, 39–40

worker productivity, 32
Resignification
cross-border politics, 109–112
feminist border politics, 96–97
feminist politics, 120–121
social construction of value in
labor, 99
through Americanization,
105–109
Responsibility
and myth, 5–6
Robles, Rosalba, 153

S

Salaries, reducing turnover, 86–87
Salzinger, Leslie, 7, 62–68
Schoenberger, Erica, 7
Scott, Joan, 156, 169
Segregation, sexual, 33–35
Sexual behavior
daughters and factory fathers,
29–30
disposability and morality, 74–78
justifiable dismissal, 36–37
worker productivity, 32
Sexual segregation, 33–35
Sites of accumulation, bodies as,
49–50
Skilled workers
deskilling of work and, 128–129
in flexible production line, 57–58
manufacturing bodies and, 46
training vs. turnover, 78–79
Social disintegration
Mujeres de Negro and, 167
Social geography, 133–141
Social identity, 100–101
Social movements, 151–170
conclusion, 168–170
filthy lucre and, 163–168
Mujeres de Negro, 155–163
overview, 151–155
Socially useful lies, 3–6

Spatial arrangements
gender division in MOTW,
102–103
implications of disruption, 106
Staeheli, Lynn, 154
Standing
as masculine trait, 60–61
Supervisors
deskilling of work and, 128–129
in flexible production, 58
production and disposability,
65–68
production monitoring, 64–65
Supervisory dynamic
economics of, 68–69
flexible masculinity and, 59–62
in manufacturing bodies, 46–47
prosthetics of, 52–54

T

Taylor, Frederick Winslow, 56
Technical work
and flexible masculinity, 60–61
Theoretical approaches, 12–16
Third world inferiority
division of labor and, 47–48
vs. first world superiority, 46
production monitoring hierarchy,
64–65
Tradition. see also Cultural values
death by culture, 75–76
problems of political activism,
153–155
Training
deskilling of work vs., 128–129
female contamination, 115–119
flexible masculinity, 59–62
production and disposability,
65–66
resignification of female workers,
114–115
supervision, 53–54
vs. turnover, 78–79
Tres Reyes
division of labor, 137–141

Gloria's struggle within, 125–127
managing tour of, 127–133
social geography of, 133–137
Three Kings vs., 141–148
Turnover rates
in AOTW, 31–32
corporate death, 78–87
corporate and labor, 27–29
in flexible production line, 57
in male vs. female workers, 37–38
production and disposability,
65–66
two-year contracts and, 41–42
violence and disposability, 72–73

U

United States (U.S.)
division of labor and, 47–48
Mexico border, 94–97
monitoring hierarchy, 64–65
Unskilled labor
deskilling of work, 128–129
flexible masculinity and, 61–62
production and disposability,
65–66
training vs. turnover, 78–79
U.S. *see* United States (U.S.)

V

Value
death by culture and, 87–89
disposability and morality, 74–78
resignification of, 148–150
social construction of, 98–99
training vs. turnover and, 78–79
as turnover rate determinant,
84–86
violence and disposability, 72–73
workforce representation and,
103–105
Values
cultural. *see* Cultural values

Variable capital
training vs. turnover, 78–79
violence and disposability, 72–73
workers as, 28–29
Victims
blame of, 157
dismissal of, 166–168
Violence and disposability, 71–89
blame the victim strategy, 157
cultural death, 87–89
murder stories, 74–78
overview, 71–74
political activism against, 152
turnover and corporate death,
78–87
victim dismissal, 163–168
Vision
flexible masculinity and, 59–62
male vs. female, 58–59
Visual monitoring
corporate hierarchy and, 64–65

W

Wages
reducing turnover, 86–87
Waste
in cultural death, 87–89
disposability and morality,
74–78
violence and disposability, 72–73
Whore, 157
Women in Black (Mujeres de Negro).
see Mujeres de Negro
(Women in Black)
Workers. *see also* Labor
manufacturing bodies. *see*
Manufacturing bodies
organizations in Mexico, 84–85
resistance of, 11
Workflow
COSMO day, 62–68
of flexible production, 51–52
social geography and, 133–137